Beyond The Information Systems Outsourcing Bandwagon

Wiley Series in Information Systems

Editors

RICHARD BOLAND   Department of Management and
Information Systems, Weatherhead School of
Management, Case Western Reserve University,
699 New Management Building, Cleveland,
Ohio 44106-7235, USA
RUDY HIRSCHHEIM   Department of Decision and
Information Systems, College of Business Administration,
University of Houston, Houston, Texas 77204-6283,
USA

Advisory Board

NIELS BJORN-ANDERSEN   Copenhagen Business School,
Denmark
D. ROSS JEFFERY   University of New South Wales,
Australia
HEINZ K. KLEIN   State University of New York, USA
ROB KLING   University of California, USA
TIM J. LINCOLN   IBM UK Limited, UK
BENN R. KONSYNSKI   Emory University, Atlanta, USA
FRANK F. LAND   London School of Economics, UK
ENID MUMFORD   Manchester Business School, UK
MIKE NEWMAN   University of Manchester, UK
DANIEL ROBEY   Florida International University, USA
E. BURTON SWANSON   University of California, USA
ROBERT TRICKER   Hong Kong University, Hong Kong
ROBERT W. ZMUD   Florida State University, USA

Beyond The Information Systems Outsourcing Bandwagon

The Insourcing Response

MARY CECELIA LACITY
University of Missouri, St Louis
RUDY HIRSCHHEIM
University of Houston

JOHN WILEY & SONS
Chichester · New York · Brisbane · Toronto · Singapore

Copyright © 1995 by M. C. Lacity and R. Hirschheim

Published 1995 by John Wiley & Sons Ltd,
                   Baffins Lane, Chichester,
                   West Sussex PO19 1UD, England
                   National   01243 779777
                   International (+44) 1243 779777

Other Wiley Editorial Offices

John Wiley & Sons, Inc., 605 Third Avenue,
New York, NY 10158-0012, USA

Jacaranda Wiley Ltd, 33 Park Road, Milton,
Queensland 4064, Australia

John Wiley & Sons (Canada) Ltd, 22 Worcester Road,
Rexdale, Ontario M9W 1L1, Canada

John Wiley & Sons (SEA) Pte Ltd, 37 Jalan Pemimpin #05-04,
Block B, Union Industrial Building, Singapore 2057

Library of Congress Cataloging-in-Publication Data

Lacity, Mary Cecelia.
    Beyond the information systems outsourcing bandwagon : the
insourcing response. / Mary Cecelia Lacity, Rudy
Hirschheim.
        p.   cm. — (Wiley information systems series)
    Includes bibliographical references and index.
    ISBN 0-471-95822-0
    1. Electronic data processing departments—Contracting out.
2. Information resources management.   I. Hirschheim, R. A. (Rudy
A.)   II. Title.   III. Series: John Wiley Information systems series.
HF5548.2.L225   1995
658'.049—dc20   95–12057
                                                        CIP

British Library Cataloguing in Publication Data

A catalogue record for this book is available from the British Library

ISBN 0-471-95822-0

Typeset in 10/12pt Palatino from authors' disks by Dorwyn Ltd, Rowlands Castle, Hants
Printed and bound in Great Britain by Biddles Ltd, Guildford, Surrey

This book is printed on acid-free paper responsibly manufactured from sustainable
forestation, for which at least two trees are planted for each one used for paper
production.

Contents

Series Preface

The information systems community has grown considerably since 1984, when we first started the Wiley Series in Information Systems. We are pleased to be part of the growth of the field, and believe that the series books have played an important role in the intellectual development of the discipline. The primary objective of the series is to publish scholarly works which reflect the best of research in the information systems community.

PREVIOUS VOLUMES IN THE SERIES

Watkins & Eliot: *Expert Systems in Business and Finance—Issues and Applications*
Lacity & Hirschheim: *Information Systems Outsourcing—Myths, Metaphors and Realities*
Österle, Brenner & Hilbers: *Total Information Systems Management—A European Approach*
Ciborra & Jelassi: *Strategic Information Systems*
Knights: *Managers Divided*
Krcmar: *EDI in Europe*

THE PRESENT VOLUME

As the information systems field matures, there is an increased need to carry the results of its growing body of research into practice. The series desires to publish research results that speak to important needs in the development and management of information systems, and our editorial mission recognizes explicitly the need for research to inform the practice and management of information systems. The present volume, *Beyond the Information Systems Outsourcing Bandwagon*, by Mary Cecelia Lacity and Rudy Hirschheim, is the second of their books reporting on an extensive and careful series of field studies into the reality of the information services outsourcing experience.

In *Beyond the Information Systems Outsourcing Bandwagon*, Mary Cecelia Lacity and Rudy Hirschheim first review the lessons learned from their studies of information system outsourcing and then present the other face of this important management decision, insourcing. They do so through six case studies of companies who chose their internal bid for information system services and succeeded in achieving significant savings. There are important lessons to be learned from these successful insourcing decisions, not the least of which is the need to consider the information system sourcing decision from a broader organizational perspective of selective sourcing.

Selective sourcing is a process of considering multiple stakeholders, strategies and competencies that combine to make for the successful sourcing of information services. Lacity and Hirschheim present a phased methodology for selective sourcing that encompasses the entire process and locates it in ongoing management practice. This book will prove invaluable to managers responsible for information services as well as those responsible for and concerned about the future of their firm more generally. It provides lessons from today's practice and guidelines for tomorrow's that are important to students and managers alike.

RUDY HIRSCHHEIM
University of Houston,
Texas

DICK BOLAND
Case Western Reserve University
Ohio

Preface

Ever since Eastman Kodak announced that it was outsourcing its information systems (IS) function in 1988 to IBM, DEC, and Businessland, large companies have found it acceptable (some might say fashionable) to transfer their IS assets, leases, and staff to third party vendors. Senior executives of *Fortune* 500 companies such as Continental Bank, Enron, Freeport-McMoRan, National Car Rental, and Continental Airlines, have followed Kodak's example and signed long-term contracts worth hundreds of millions of dollars with outsourcing "partners." Recently, a number of high-profile multibillion dollar "mega-deals" have been signed by Xerox, General Dynamics, and McDonnell Douglas. Nor is this trend only fashionable in the United States. Lufthansa in Germany, KF Group in Sweden, Inland Revenue and British Aerospace in the UK, and Canada Post in Canada have all signed significant contracts with outsourcing vendors such as IBM, EDS, CSC, and SHL Systemhouse. Such deals signal an important change is taking place in the sourcing of IS activity. CIOs and other prominent members of the IS community have responded with warnings of the dangers of surrendering management control of a "strategic asset." In many cases, these predictions have proved valid, with "partnerships" experiencing severe problems. Some companies have paid out significant sums of money to extricate themselves from outsourcing contracts and rebuilt their in-house IS capability. On the other hand, CIOs who have adamantly refused to deal with outsourcing vendors have met personal misfortune when their own organizations have failed to demonstrate value for money. These high profile events have tended to obscure the real phenomenon, a significant and irreversible move to what we call the selective sourcing of IS activity. They key question is not "should we outsource IS?", but rather *"where* and *how* can we take advantage of the rapidly developing market of IS services providers?" This book seeks to provide answers to this question.

EXECUTIVE SUMMARY

Chapter 1 describes the rationale and motivation for this book. In 1993, we published the results of a two-year research project looking at IS outsourcing in the book *Information Systems Outsourcing: Myths, Metaphors and Realities.* We discovered many myths about total outsourcing—the practice of turning over the entire IS department to a vendor for a period of 7–10 years. In particular, the economies of scale stated by vendors were largely oversold. Instead, vendors submitted bids based on efficient managerial tactics rather than on economies of size. In theory, we believed that internal IS departments should be able to implement these managerial tactics without outsourcing to a third party vendor. To investigate this hypothesis, we conducted six case studies of organizations that undertook an outsourcing evaluation, gathered external vendor bids, but selected the internal IS department's bid. We questioned participants:

- If IS was equipped to reduce costs, why have they not done so in the past, in other words, what is different now?
- Does the IS department actually reduce costs after winning an internal bid?
- If so, how did IS achieve cost savings?

Chapter 2 summarizes the lessons learned from the outsourcing study. In particular, we discovered the following seven lessons.

Lesson 1: The Published Literature Portrays an Overly Optimistic View of IS Outsourcing

The overall lesson learned from the published literature is that these sources often portray an overly optimistic view of outsourcing. Three reasons can be identified to explain the optimism. First, reports are made during the honeymoon period when clients first sign an outsourcing contract. Second, the literature only reports projected savings instead of actual savings. Third, public reports underrepresent outsourcing failures because few companies wish to advertise a mistake.

Lesson 2: Outsourcing Appears to Be a Symptom of the Problem of Demonstrating the Value of IS

In the participating companies, an overwhelming majority of senior managers viewed their IS functions as cost burdens. As such, IS managers could not appeal to effectiveness or strategic significance to justify their existence. Instead, they must somehow demonstrate efficiency.

Lesson 3: Organizational Members may Initiate Outsourcing Evaluations for a Variety of Reasons, Cost Efficiency being Only One

Although industry watchers imply that the primary reason why organizations initiate outsourcing is to reduce costs, the results of our research suggest that such a belief is too simplistic. Participants identified four broad categories of reasons: *financial*—cut costs, improve cost controls, and restructuring the IS budget; *business*—return to core competencies, facilitate mergers and acquisitions, start-up companies, and devolution of organizational and management structures; *technical*—improve technical services, gain access to new technical talent, provide access to new technologies, and focus the internal IS staff on core technical activities; and *political*—react to the efficiency imperative; acquire or justify additional resources; react to the positive outsourcing media reports; reduce uncertainty; eliminate a burdensome function; and enhance personal credibility.

Lesson 4: An Outsourcing Vendor may Not Be Inherently More Efficient than an Internal IS Department

Many practitioners assume that outsourcing vendors are inherently more efficient due to economies of scale. In the outsourcing arena, however, the applicability of the economies of scale model may be questioned. First, small shops may have lower costs per MIP (Million Instructions Per Second) than large shops by employing older technology, offering below market wages, and maintaining tight controls and procedures. Second, a vendor's hardware discounts are negligible in many instances. Third, changes in software licensing agreements diminish a vendor's advantage. Fourth, labor expertise is largely a myth since clients are usually supported by the same staff that transitioned to the vendor.

Lesson 5: The Internal IS Department may be Able to Achieve Similar Results without Vendor Assistance

If the vendor is not inherently more efficient than internal IS shops, then perhaps the company can reduce its own IS expenses through data center consolidation, resource optimization, chargeback implementation, and other sundry methods.

Lesson 6: If a Company Decides to Outsource, the Contract is the Only Mechanism to Ensure that Expectations are Realized

When some companies decide that outsourcing is the preferred mechanism for achieving IS objectives, they often like to view their vendors as partners. Vendors are not partners because profit motives are not shared: a dollar out of the client's wallet is a dollar in the vendor's wallet. An outsourcing contract is the only way to ensure an equitable balance of power. Service level measures, arrangements for growth, penalties for non-performance and other contract provisions must be stipulated prior to outsourcing commencement.

Lesson 7: The Metaphor that IS is Merely a Utility is Misguided

These metaphors are based on the assumption that IS services are homogeneous—one unit of IS service is equal to any other. The problem with this metaphor is it ignores the idiosyncratic nature of an organization's information needs.

Lesson 8: Outsourcing Often Constrains Organizational Flexibility

Outsourcing will likely significantly constrain any flexibility of how IS is delivered. It might also inhibit how an organization responds or adapts to a changing business environment.

Chapter 3 contains the detailed descriptions of the six successful insourcing cases. For each case, we describe the financial and political environment of the company, senior management's perceptions of IS before insourcing, the outsourcing evaluation process which led to the selection of the internal bid, the subsequent insourcing project, and senior management's resulting change in the perceptions of IS. These cases highlight the savings that internal IS departments can achieve:

- FIRM15: reduced IS costs by 54%
- FIRM16: reduced IS costs by 20%
- FIRM17: reduced IS costs by 40%
- FIRM18: reduced IS costs by 43%
- FIRM19: reduced IS costs by 46%
- FIRM20: reduced IS headcount by 25% while increasing workload by 30%

Chapter 4 discusses the IS manager's role in insourcing. The chapter highlights the specific cost reduction tactics identified and implemented by IS managers. These tactics focus on reducing the cost drivers of IS: people, hardware, and software. In our cases, IS managers reduced costs through:

- *Data center automation* to reduce headcount
- *Chargeback systems* to curtail user demand
- *Data center consolidation* to reduce headcount, and hardware and facility costs
- *Departmental reorganization* to reduce headcount
- *Employee empowerment* to reduce headcount and respond better to user needs
- *Hardware negotiations* to reduce hardware costs and maintenance costs
- *Just-in-time resources* to reduce inventory carrying costs
- *More efficient resource usage*
- *Service elimination* to reduce headcount and support costs
- *Software negotiations* to reduce software license costs
- *Software standards* to reduce the number of software packages

Chapter 5 discusses the role of benchmarking in insourcing decisions. Benchmarking allegedly provides a rational assessment of current IS performance by comparing cost and service levels to other IS shops of comparable size. As such, benchmarks are critical inputs to outsourcing evaluations. This chapter highlights that case participants sometimes use benchmarking for political reasons to "obtain an alibi" rather than to assess performance. The chapter includes a prescription for minimizing the political uses of benchmarks. To ensure valid benchmarks are achieved, IS managers must:

- Benchmark what is important to management, whether it be service excellence or cost efficiency
- Secure senior management's participation and buy-in of the benchmarks

- Select the stiffest competition to benchmark against
- Benchmark during peak periods rather than average periods
- Validate data before benchmark calculations to minimize political sabotage
- Repeat benchmarks to determine trends rather than rely on one-time snapshots of performance

Chapter 6 summarizes the lessons learned from the insourcing cases. Based on participants' experiences, we identified five lessons.

Lesson 1: Conflicting Stakeholders' Expectations Place IS Managers in the Precarious Position of Providing a Rolls Royce Service at a Chevrolet Price

The first lesson captures the cost/service dilemma which prompted outsourcing evaluations. In general, there is a direct relationship between IS cost and IS service. Thus, IS can either provide a premium service at a premium cost *or* IS can provide a minimal service at a minimal cost. In our cases, senior management wanted a minimal cost but business units and end-users wanted a premium service. As a result, organizations expected that IS perform a premium service at a minimal cost—an unrealistic expectation for most IS departments. These two stakeholder groups set a conflicting agenda for IS because IS managers cannot provide a Rolls Royce service at a Chevrolet price. As a result of the dilemma, IS satisfied neither requirement, resulting in senior management's perception that IS cost too much and users' perceptions that service was poor. We depict the IS cost/service dilemma in Table P.1.

Lesson 2: Senior Management must Empower IS to Implement Change

Implementing cost saving measures requires IS to adopt policies which may not be readily agreed to by the business units in the organization.

Table P.1

	Minimal cost	Premium cost
Premium service	Senior management's and users' expectations of IS performance	Realistic IS performance
Minimal service	Realistic IS performance	Senior management's and users' perceptions of IS performance

Internal politics often drives what can and cannot be implemented. It is only when senior management empowers the IS department does it actually have the authority, i.e. the political muscle, to implement changes. To put it differently, IS needs a "big stick" to hammer resistance with in order to implement cost saving policies. This big stick can only come from senior management.

Lesson 3: Successful Sourcing Depends on Comparing Vendor Bids against a Newly Submitted Internal Bid, *not* against Current IS Performance

As noted above, IS is often unable to implement the necessary cost reduction strategies until senior management empowers them to do so. But how is this done? Only after senior management threatened the organization with outsourcing, were IS managers able to overcome resistance. The outsourcing evaluation permitted IS to submit a bid which incorporated cost reduction strategies.

Lesson 4: Cost Efficiency Largely Depends on Adoption of Efficient Management Practices and to a Lesser Extent, Economies of Scale

One of the lessons generated from the outsourcing studies is that internal IS departments may be able to achieve similar results without vendor assistance. We noted that vendor bids are often based on efficient management practices, such as data center consolidation, that could allegedly be replicated by in-house IS. This would explain why many companies in our studies found that insourcing was a more cost efficient alternative—cost efficiency has more to do with these efficient practices than just economies of scale. Just because vendors are bigger, does not mean they are better.

Lesson 5: Internal IS Departments Often Possess Equivalent or Superior Economies of Scale to Vendors for Many IS Functions

In general, we have concluded that vendors are inherently more efficient at providing technical expertise and serve to minimize a customer's opportunity costs by providing commodity IS services while internal IS departments focus on more strategic IS issues. In general, internal IS departments are inherently more efficient at providing business expertise, minimizing transaction costs (cost to coordinate, monitor, and manage an IS function), minimizing shareholder costs

Table P.2

Sources of IS costs	Internal IS departments	Outsourcing vendors
Data center operating costs	Comparable to a vendor for 150–200 MIP range	Comparable to large IS departments. Inherent advantage over small IS departments
Hardware purchase costs	Large companies: volume discounts comparable to a vendor	Volume discounts comparable to large IS departments. Inherent advantage over small companies
Software licensing costs	Comparable due to group licenses	Comparable
Cost of business expertise	Inherent advantage	
Cost of technical expertise		Inherent advantage
Cost to shareholders (the need to generate a profit)	Inherent advantage	
R&D costs		Inherent advantage
Marketing costs	Inherent advantage	
Opportunity costs		Inherent advantage
Transaction costs	Inherent advantage	

(internal IS departments do not need to generate a profit), and minimizing marketing costs (internal IS departments do not have to advertise or solicit customers). In addition, large IS departments have comparable economies of scale as vendors in the area of data processing costs, hardware purchase costs, and software licensing costs. Table P.2 depicts the inherent advantages.

Lesson 6: Selective Sourcing—which Treats IS as a Portfolio is the Key to Rightsourcing

Taken as a whole, the previous lessons generated all support the conclusion that selective sourcing is the key to rightsourcing. This is based on our belief that:

1   Total outsourcing is a poor strategy for most companies because it fails to capitalize on the inherent cost advantages possessed by internal IS departments for certain IS functions.

2 Total insourcing is a poor strategy because it fails to capitalize on the inherent cost advantages possessed by vendors for certain IS functions.

3 Selective sourcing, which capitalizes on the inherent advantage of both, is the key to rightsourcing.

We note that several trends in the market place facilitate selective sourcing: a growing number of vendors that offer more market-focused products and services rather than only offer total outsourcing; shorter contracts enable customers to achieve efficiency without losing flexibility; tighter contracts enable customers to better define their service needs and minimize vendor opportunism.

Chapter 7 presents an IS sourcing methodology based on the lessons learned from the outsourcing and insourcing case studies. The methodology comprises six phases.

Phase 1: Stakeholder Assessment

Purpose: Understand why stakeholders possess different perceptions and expectations of IS performance.

1 Senior management's view: cut costs
2 Business units' and end-users' view: service excellence
3 IS managers' view: caught in the middle
4 Understanding stakeholder perspectives: the cost/service trade-off

Lesson: Conflicting stakeholders' expectations place IS managers in the precarious position of providing a Rolls Royce service at a Chevrolet price.

Phase 2: Create a Shared Agenda for IS

Purpose: Create a shared agenda by evaluating the business contribution for the portfolio of IS activities.

1 Align IS strategy with business strategy
2 Classify IS activities as "differentiators" or "commodities"

Lesson: Stakeholders must ignore generalizations about alleged IS commodities and differentiators and not let superfluous accounting mask IS's contribution.

Phase 3: Select Outsourcing Candidates from IS Portfolio

Purpose: Identify outsourcing candidates among the IS commodities by examining the economic efficiency.

1   Efficient IS management practices
2   Economies of scale

Lesson: Cost efficiency largely depends on adoption of efficient management practices and to a lesser extent, economies of scale.

Phase 4: Compare In-house Provision with Vendor Offerings

Purpose: Conduct an official outsourcing evaluation for the outsourcing candidates.

1   Inform IS staff of the evaluation
2   Create teams
3   Create a request-for-proposal (RFP)
4   Create evaluation criteria
5   Invite internal and external bids
6   Assess validity of submitted bids

Lesson: Successful sourcing depends on comparing vendor bids against a newly submitted internal bid, *not* against current IS performance.

Phase 5: Negotiate Contract with External Vendor

Purpose: If an external bid is selected, stakeholders must attend to 15 rules of contract negotiations.
Lesson: Value talk of "partnership" is no substitute for a sound contract.

Phase 6: Post-decision Management

Purpose: Whether internal or external bids are selected, continued management of IS activities is vital to ensure success.

1   Insourcing: providing continued support for internal IS managers
2   Outsourcing: creating the role of the contract manager

Lessons: For insourcing, senior managers must support IS managers against user backlash and commit to IS investments to reduce costs.

For outsourcing, contract managers must learn four new skills: manage contract, manage demand, manage profit and loss (P&L), and balance risks and costs of monitoring.

Chapter 8 offers our thoughts about the future of IS sourcing, in particular what lies beyond the outsourcing bandwagon. We begin by taking issue with the belief, apparently held by many senior managers, that IS is no different from any other outsourcing candidate. Based on our research we conclude that IS is not like other organizational resources which have been successfully outsourced in the past. This is because of six distinctive features associated with IS:

1   Information technology (IT) evolves rapidly.
2   The underlying economics of IT changes rapidly.
3   The penetration of IS to all business functions is ubiquitous.
4   The switching costs to alternative ITs and IS suppliers are high.
5   Customers' inexperience with IS outsourcing.
6   IS management practices rather than economies of scale lead to economic efficiency.

Lastly, we conclude by noting that *selective sourcing*, which capitalizes on the inherent advantage of both internal IS departments' and external vendors' inherent cost advantages, is the recommended IS sourcing strategy. We recognize several trends in the outsourcing market that will facilitate selective sourcing in the future. In particular: an increase number of vendors and vendor offerings; shorter contracts; and tighter contracts. We will also likely see the growth of performance-based arrangements involving the sharing of risks and rewards between the client and vendor. These trends are in response to more intelligent customers who demand more equity in their outsourcing relationships.

Acknowledgements

In undertaking the outsourcing and insourcing projects, which are the basis of this book, many individuals contributed in one way or another. We would like to offer our sincere thanks to all of them. First, are the 61 study participants. Since they were guaranteed confidentiality, we cannot thank them by name, but nonetheless wish to express our gratitude to each and every one of them for devoting their time and efforts to this project. The research could not have been done without their generous sacrificing of their time. Second, there were a number of individuals who assisted us by providing contacts and comments on various aspects of outsourcing, insourcing, and benchmarking. They are Denny McGuire, Warren Gallant, Peter Beeman, Dick Hansen, and Tom Blitz. Third, Leslie Willcocks offered excellent advice on the content and structure of the book. Fourth, the Information Systems Research Center (ISRC) at the University of Houston provided the financial backing for the projects. Fifth, Winnie White and Michael Weng of the ISRC assisted in the typing and editing of the various drafts of the book. Lastly, we would like to thank Diane Taylor and the staff at John Wiley & Sons for their technical assistance and support in the production of this book. To all of you, our deepest thanks.

Oxford and Houston   MARY CECELIA LACITY
December 1994   RUDY HIRSCHHEIM

1
The Outsourcing/Insourcing Phenomenon

INTRODUCTION

Increasingly, the key concerns of IS managers no longer center around technology, but rather managers today wrestle with difficult organizational issues. During the 1980s, while most academics were writing articles about harnessing information technology (IT) for competitive advantage, most managers were grappling with grim corporate realities: leveraged buyouts, tremendous corporate debts, downsizing, acquisitions, increased competition from abroad, and a stagnant economy. In this environment, most senior executives and prudent IS managers questioned whether information services could be delivered more efficiently. These queries started the tremendous interest in IS outsourcing and insourcing evaluations.

Some may argue that IS outsourcing, which we define as the use of a third party vendor to provide information products and services that were previously provided internally, does not warrant attention—after all, outsourcing options have existed since the dawn of data processing. Nor is insourcing particularly interesting as it is nothing more than keeping what was internally done internal. However, we would argue that both views miss the mark. It is true that as early as 1963, Perot's Electronic Data Systems (EDS) was handling data processing services for Frito-Lay and Blue Cross; and that other outsourcing options, such as the use of contract programmers, timesharing, and purchase of packaged software, have been widely used for over two decades. But what is of particular interest today is the dramatic change in scope of outsourcing and insourcing decisions. Early forms of IS outsourcing typically dealt with single-system contracts comprising a small portion of the IS budget. Today outsourcing has recently grown to span multiple systems and represents a significant transfer of assets, leases, and staff to a vendor that now assumes profit and loss responsibility.

Consider the case of Eastman Kodak. When Kodak turned over the bulk of its IS operations to three outsourcing "partners" in 1988, it signaled an important change had occurred in the "sourcing" of IS activity. Other companies are following Kodak's example and jumping on the outsourcing bandwagon. Senior executives of other *Fortune* 500 companies such as Continental Airlines, General Dynamics, Delta Airlines, Continental Bank, Enron, Xerox, and McDonnell Douglas have signed long-term contracts worth hundreds of millions of dollars with outsourcing partners such as IBM, EDS, CSC, SHL Systemhouse, Andersen Consulting, and AT&T. Nor is the trend likely to abate. Conservative estimates suggest that over 20% of *Fortune* 500 companies will have signed IS outsourcing contracts by the end of 1994, with more jumping on the bandwagon in the following years. Moreover, the trend is a worldwide phenomenon. Recent deals by Lufthansa in Germany, Inland Revenue and British Aerospace in Britain, KF Group in Sweden, Canada Post in Canada, and the city of Adelaide government in Australia signal the rise of outsourcing globally.

Companies contemplate IS outsourcing for a variety of reasons: financial, business, technical, and political. *Financial* issues typically relate to: desires for reduced costs, improvements in cost controls, and/or restructuring IS budgets. *Business* issues concern: returning to core competencies, facilitating mergers and acquisitions, dealing with start-up companies, and/or devolving organizational and management structures. *Technical* issues relate to: improving technical service, accessing hard to find technical talent, accessing new technologies, and/or focusing the internal IS staff on core technical activities. *Political* issues usually involve: proving the efficiency of IS, justifying new resources, duplicating success stories, exposing exaggerated claims, eliminating a troublesome function, and breaking the "glass ceiling" (Lacity, Hirschheim, and Willcocks, 1994). Although companies outsource IS for many reasons, industry watchers generally attribute the growth of the IS outsourcing market to two primary phenomena. First, interest in IS outsourcing is largely a consequence of a shift in business strategy. Many companies have recently abandoned their diversification strategies—once pursued to mediate risk—to focus on core competencies. Senior executives have come to believe that the most important sustainable competitive advantage is strategic focus by concentrating on what an organization does better than anyone else while outsourcing the rest. As a result of this focus strategy, IS came under scrutiny: is IS a competitive weapon or merely a utility? Senior executives frequently view the entire IS function as a non-core activity, and believe that IS vendors possess economies of scale and technical expertise to provide IS services more efficiently than internal IS departments. Second, the growth in outsourcing is a function of the unclear value delivered by IS. In many companies, senior executives perceive that IS failed to deliver the promise of competitive advantage promised in the 1980s. Consequently, many senior executives view IS as an overhead—an essential cost but one to be minimized.

These two phenomena—refocus to core competencies and the perception of IS as a cost burden—prompt many senior executives to sign outsourcing "mega-deals" for the provision of all IS services. But while such mega-deals afford these companies with much press, we have some concern about the long-term viability of these deals. We are not alone.

Some prominent IS professionals have cautioned against the wholesale transferal of the management and control of a "strategic asset" such as IS. In a number of cases, these concerns proved valid, with "outsourcing partnerships" experiencing grave problems. A few companies have paid out significant sums of money to extricate themselves from outsourcing contracts and then rebuilt their internal IS capability. On the other hand, some IS managers who have refused to deal with outsourcing vendors or ignored them, have either been fired or had their jobs marginalized when their IS shops have failed to demonstrate value for money. So clearly outsourcing must be taken seriously.

Moreover, all indicants suggest that IS outsourcing will touch many more lives during this decade. Outsourcing will affect senior managers as they are courted by outsourcing vendors, IS managers as they struggle to reduce costs on their own, IS personnel as they contemplate working for an outsourcing vendor, and users as they adjust to new faces and procedures. The alternative to outsourcing—insourcing—also poses new challenges for: senior management (should they or should they not believe that cost reductions equivalent to external vendors can be achieved internally), IS personnel (can they effectively implement the cost reduction strategies which are an inevitable part of insourcing), and users (who might well see a reduction in services due to the cost saving measures adopted by IS). These challenges are explored in this book.

In particular, we summarize the findings of a research project started in January 1991 looking at 14 organizations which evaluated outsourcing (see Lacity and Hirschheim, 1993). We then report on our latest research project started in June 1993 where we specifically focused on insourcing. In particular, we analyzed: the reasons why organizations considered outsourcing their IS functions and then chose insourcing over outsourcing; how they went about their evaluation process: and what overall lessons can be learned from the successes and failures of practitioners who have implemented the insourcing option. Based on the results of these two projects, we also offer some thoughts about how organizations might fruitfully approach the broad issue of IS sourcing. It is our belief that the key question facing companies is not "whether to outsource IS or not", but rather *"where and how* to take advantage of the rapidly developing market of IS services providers." Fundamentally, companies need to consider how best to obtain the needed IS services—this is the "sourcing dilemma."

When one speaks of "sourcing," three variations appear valid. *IS outsourcing* refers to the third party management of IS assets, people, and/or activities required to meet prespecified performance levels. We use the term *outsourcing* to refer to those organizations that decided to outsource at least 80% of their IS budgets to third party providers. *Insourcing,* on the other hand, refers to organizations that formally evaluated outsourcing but selected their internal IS departments' bid over external vendor bids, thus keeping over 80% of the IS budget provided by the internal IS department. *Selective sourcing* refers to organizations that opted to use third party vendors for certain IS functions which represents between 20 and 60% of the IS budget (typically around 40%) while still retaining a substantial internal IS department. This is consistent with the studies done by Fitzgerald and Willcocks (1993) which show that selective sourcing usually takes up between 30 and 40% of the formal IS budget.

OUTSOURCING OPTIONS

Although outsourcing is often portrayed as an all or nothing proposition, or more specifically that outsourcing constitutes the taking of a significant portion of the IS budget (e.g. in excess of 80%), in actuality, there are a variety of outsourcing options. According to Millar (1994) there are four basic types of outsourcing arrangements: (1) *general outsourcing;* (2) *transitional outsourcing;* (3) *business process outsourcing;* and (4) *business benefit contracting.* In the first option (*general outsourcing*) there are three alternatives: (a) selective outsourcing—where one particular area of IS activity is chosen to be turned over to a third party, such as data center operations; (b) value added outsourcing—where some area of IS activity is turned over to a third party who is thought to be able to provide a level of support or service which adds value to the activity that could not be cost-effectively provided by the internal

IS group; and (c) cooperative outsourcing—where some targeted IS activity(ies) is (are) jointly performed by a third party provider and the internal IS department.

The second option (*transitional outsourcing*) typically involves the migration from one technological platform to another. Such transitional outsourcing has three phases: (i) management of the legacy systems; (ii) transition to the new technology/system; and (iii) stabilization and management of the new platform. Any one or all of these three phases could be turned over to a third party provider. Sun Microsystems deal with CSC to handle the maintenance of Sun's legacy systems for a three-year period is a good example of such transitional outsourcing (*I/S Analyzer*, 1993).

The third option (*business process outsourcing*) is a relatively new outsourcing arrangement. It refers to an outsourcing relationship where a third party provider is responsible for performing an entire business function for the client organization. According to Millar, a number of industries are considering business process outsourcing; in particular, government, financial services (banks and insurance companies), health care, transportation, and logistics. Targeted services include hotlines, help desks, call centers, claims management, and document processing.

The last option (*business benefit contracting*) is also a relatively recent phenomenon. It refers to a "contractual agreement that defines the vendor's contribution to the client in terms of specific benefits to the business and defines the payment the customer will make based upon the vendor's ability to deliver those benefits. The goal is to match actual costs with actual benefits and to share the risks." Given the risks associated with traditional outsourcing, there is considerable interest in this form of outsourcing. Millar notes, however, that while business benefit contracting is frequently used in the marketing of outsourcing services by third party providers, it typically is not actually adopted because of the difficulty associated with measuring benefits. Benchmarking in this area is particularly problematic (see Chapter 5). Since vendor revenue and margin potential are directly tied to the benchmarks, it is not surprising that getting agreement by both parties on the benchmarks proves especially thorny.

Outsourcing options have also been discussed by Wibbelsman and Maiero (1994) but under the context of the sourcing of IS activities. According to Wibbelsman and Maiero, the key issue facing organizations is not "should we outsource" but "how should we source." They refer to the sourcing question in terms of "multisourcing," i.e. the multiple sourcing of IS services. More specifically, they see multisourcing as a continuum running from insourcing through cosourcing to outsourcing. The end points of their continuum span from "OK as is" to "divest completely." The "OK as is" point on the continuum relates to the belief that the status quo is the best sourcing strategy; IS activities are insourced. Another insourcing strategy which moves along the continuum is termed "fix and keep in-house." This strategy believes that insourcing is the best strategy but the internal IS department needs to adopt better practices to become more efficient and effective. Moving to the "cosourcing" arrangement, Wibbelsman and Maiero talk about a "rehabilitation and return" strategy whereby the IS organization is reformed through the assistance of a third party and then kept in-house. Another cosourcing strategy is the "transition assistance" strategy where a third party takes on certain IS activities while the internal IS group transitions itself to a new set of skills. The next arrangement is termed "capability development" where a third party takes on either permanently or temporarily IS activities while the IS organization develops new capabilities. This option allows the IS organization to focus on certain core capabilities. Moving to the outsourcing end of the continuum, Wibbelsman and Maiero speak of "option to reverse" whereby IS is outsourced to a third party but there is a specific plan which would allow the function to return in-house without undue hardship at a later time if the management of the company deems this desirable. Lastly, there is the "divest completely" strategy where the IS function is outsourced permanently. In such cases, IS is perceived to be a non-core business function best handled by an outsourcer.

Wibbelsman and Maiero note that a multisourcing strategy may vary depending on what IS activity one looks at. For example, data center operations might best be handled via a "fix and keep in-house" strategy, while applications development might adopt an "OK as is" arrangement, while applications maintenance might best be dealt with using a "divest completely" strategy. Whatever multisourcing strategy is adopted, it must optimize three critical objectives. The first is the strategic objective. Here, the multisourcing strategy must ensure that mission critical IS capabilities and services are in place to support the strategic business needs of the company. The second is the tactical objective. Here, the multisourcing strategy must ensure that the appropriate IS capabilities and services are available to support the day-to-day business operations in a effective and efficient manner. Lastly, there is the financial objective which translates into the need to optimize the overall IS cost/service/value relationship.

We shall return to the issue of outsourcing options and explore what we think are the future directions of IS sourcing in the concluding chapter of the book.

BACKGROUND TO OUR WORK

In early 1993, we concluded a project on IS outsourcing which led to the publication *Information Systems Outsourcing: Myths, Metaphors and Realities* (Lacity and Hirschheim, 1993). We discovered several myths about outsourcing which suggested that most internal IS departments should be able to reduce costs without the assistance of an outsourcing vendor. The question remained, however, whether internal IS departments could overcome political and organizational obstacles to reduce costs on their own. To investigate this question, we researched companies that decided to *insource*, where insourcing is defined as an outsourcing evaluation outcome which results in the selection of the internal IS department's bid over external vendor bids. Note how this requires a formal outsourcing evaluation process and necessitates that the internal IS department formally bids against outside vendors.

Our research findings support the general hypothesis that most internal IS departments can reduce costs on their own. Through inventive cost reduction tactics identified by IS managers and benchmarking firms, the participating companies were able to reduce IS costs by 20–54%. Severe cost reductions, however, are often accompanied by service degradation—a consequence senior managers are willing to accept in exchange for lower IS costs.

Despite some of the negative consequences of insourcing, participating firms feel that insourcing is preferred over outsourcing as a way to reduce IS costs. Rather than committing to an often inflexible outsourcing arrangement for 5–10 years, insourcing provides flexibility to alter IS plans as new challenges, such as client/server technology, emerge.

This book presents the findings of our combined two studies. The first part of the book describes the results of our most recent study— the insourcing project—while the second part synthesizes what has been learned from both the outsourcing and insourcing projects into an IS sourcing methodology. More specifically, the first part contains five chapters. These follow from this first chapter where we present the motivation for undertaking the insourcing project as well as the research methodology used in our study. Chapter 2 summarizes the lessons learned in our outsourcing study. Chapter 3 presents six insourcing cases in detail. Chapter 4 articulates 11 generic tactics for reducing IS costs. Chapter 5 describes the role of benchmarking in insourcing decisions. Chapter 6 summarizes the primary lessons learned from the insourcing cases. The second part of the book then follows; it is concerned with how to evaluate the various IS sourcing options: outsourcing, insourcing, and selective sourcing. To accomplish this task, Chapter 7 presents a methodology for IS sourcing decision-making. Finally, Chapter 8 looks at what makes IS different from other candidate functions for outsourcing as well as what the possible future of IS sourcing is likely to be.

QUESTIONS ARISING FROM OUR OUTSOURCING STUDY

After conducting 14 in-depth case studies of *Fortune* 500 companies that evaluated IS outsourcing, several outsourcing lessons emerged which subsequently led to a number of questions about the sourcing of IS activities. Perhaps the most important lesson generated from the outsourcing research is that senior management's perceptions of IS in general and outsourcing in specific are largely influenced by an overly optimistic trade press. Senior managers rely on practitioner information sources to formulate IS strategies—such as outsourcing. These information sources, however, portray an overly optimistic view of outsourcing because they underrepresent failures and only report expected savings rather than actual savings. For example, every company that outsourced in our study published positive outsourcing expectations in the trade journals at the time their contracts commenced, although many subsequently experienced higher IS costs and service degradation. Outsourcing disappointments are rarely reported to nullify previously optimistic reports.

Thus, one important function of academic research is to provide a balanced investigation of IS practices to counter the large bandwagon effect generated by the trade press. For example, research conducted by MIT's Loh and Venkatraman (1992a, b) and corroborated by our study suggests that outsourcing is largely attributed to senior management's desire to duplicate the Kodak success story. Unfortunately, few organizations have enjoyed the "strategic partnership" Kodak shares with IBM, which leads to the next outsourcing lesson.

The term "strategic partner" is unsuitable to characterize the relationship between an outsourcing vendor and their customer because the profit motive is not shared. Account managers at outsourcing providers are rewarded for maximizing profits, primarily by charging customers additional fees for services that extend beyond the contract (in the outsourcing parlance, these are called "excess fees"). When a customer's costs increase, so do the vendor's profits. How, then, can an outsourcing vendor be conceived of as a partner? Claiming that vendors are partners is like claiming that Chrysler is a partner just because you purchase a LeBaron. The term "customer" is more appropriate.

Another lesson is that outsourcing is often used to refinance the IS department. Outsourcing vendors offer financial packages whose net present value is extremely attractive to the prospective customer. Cash infusions for information assets, postponing payments until the end of the contract, and even purchases of the customer's stock may render outsourcing desirable. Furthermore, outsourcing finances IS as an expense rather than carrying IS assets on the company books. These outsourcing arrangements are not based on sound IS management decisions, but rather are solely a financial arrangement.

The First City and EDS outsourcing arrangement provides an example of the cash an outsourcer can bring to a faltering organization. EDS provided a much needed cash infusion by purchasing First City's IS assets. EDS also hired their IS staff. In addition, EDS purchased $20 million in First City's preferred stock. "Both companies insist the transactions are unrelated, but the facts are that EDS landed a $550 million dollar account, and the bank completed a badly needed recapitalization" (Mason, 1990, p. 287). An interview with an EDS manager on the First City account stated, "Currently, the whole banking industry is scaling back and systems falls low on the list of the bank's priorities."

In essence, outsourcing is being used to salvage a losing enterprise. Is it sound business practice to liquidate the IS department to rescue a firm? Many shareholders believe so—stock prices systematically rise just after an outsourcing announcement (Loh and Venkatraman, 1992c).

A final lesson which emerged was that outsourcing vendors are not necessarily more efficient than internal IS departments. The theory of economies of scale suggests that outsourcing vendors have lower average costs through mass production, volume discounts, and labor specialization. In practice, however, large corporations often receive volume discounts comparable to an outsourcing vendor; changes in software license agreements from site licenses to group licenses greatly reduce a vendor's advantage; labor expertise is often a myth because vendors hire the previous IS staff; access to new technology is often expensive because it constitutes a "change of character" and is subject to excess fees; finally, the availability of bargains on used hardware allows even smaller companies to achieve low average costs. Thus—at least theoretically—internal IS departments should be able to achieve IS costs comparable to an outsourcing vendor. Still the following questions remained:

1 If IS is really equipped to reduce costs without vendor assistance, why have they not done so?
2 Does the IS department actually reduce costs after winning an internal bid?

3   If so, how does an internal IS department reduce costs?

In other words: How does insourcing work in practice? This then provided the motivation for undertaking our study of IS insourcing.

RESEARCH METHODOLOGY

Participant Details of the Outsourcing Study

The 14 case participants of the outsourcing study represent a wide variety of industries. Using *Fortune* magazine's industry classification taxonomy, 10 companies are classified as members of the manufacturing sector and 4 as members of service sector. Of the 10 manufacturing companies, 2 belong to the chemical industry, 3 to the petroleum refining industry, 2 to the mining industry, and 1 to the aerospace industry. The two remaining companies belong to large holding companies. All but 2 of the 10 manufacturing companies appeared on *Fortune* magazine's 1990 *Fortune* 500 list, which ranks companies in terms of revenues. One of these exceptions is expected to enter the *Fortune* 500 this year after a series of significant acquisitions. The other exception, although not in the *Fortune* 500 in terms of revenues, made *Fortune*'s top 50 list of the most profitable US firms (McManus, 1991a).

The remaining 4 of the 14 companies are classified by *Fortune* magazine as members of service industries. Two case participants appeared on *Fortune*'s 1990 list of top 100 diversified services company (McManus, 1991b). The only financial company that participated in this study was listed in *Fortune*'s 1990 top 50 commercial banks list despite a $60 million dollar loss. Since *Fortune* compiles this list based on assets, it is interesting to note that 18 of the top 50 commercial banks posted negative earnings that year. Another of our case participants can be classified as a holding company and was listed in the *Fortune*'s 1990 top 50 transportation companies despite a major loss. This case participant may be more appropriately classified as an IS company since it serves as the IS department to its sister and parent companies. Given that 12 of the 14 companies appear somewhere in the *Fortune* 500 or *Fortune* Service 500, it is clear that case participants were large in terms of revenues or assets.

Thirty-seven individuals were interviewed in this research project. Of the 14 cases, 10 IS managers were interviewed. Of the remaining four cases, one company no longer had an IS manager since the outsourcing vendor reports to the controller, one IS manager had no information about the outsourcing decision, one IS manager was located at a site not easily accessible to us, and the last delegated his interview to his subordinate in charge of the outsourcing decision. We also interviewed seven people to whom the IS managers reported. Their titles included: treasurers, controllers, and chief financial officers (CFOs).

Fourteen IS staff people were interviewed. These participants were usually responsible for gathering the technical and financial details for the request for proposals (RFP). In some cases, these participants were placed in awkward positions—they assisted the outsourcing effort even though outsourcing would eliminate their positions.

Four outsourcing vendors were interviewed. After these initial interviews, it was realized that the vendors were reticent to talk about their outsourcing experiences because they felt the interviews breached their supplier–client confidentiality agreements. They advised us to direct all questions to the client.

Two consultants, both experts in outsourcing contracts, were interviewed. Rather than let their clients sign the vendor contracts, these consultants insisted that a custom contract be designed that included service level measures and penalties for non-performance. Interestingly enough, the companies that used a consultant considered the investment worthwhile.

The most important characteristic of the group interviewed in the outsourcing research is that all participants were privy to the details of the outsourcing decisions in their respective companies. Whether they initiated outsourcing, compiled information, analyzed bids, participants had strong opinions about the decisions their companies made about outsourcing. The disparity of views expressed by participants provided a rich picture of these outsourcing decisions.

Participant Details of the Insourcing Study

A similar approach was adopted in the insourcing study. To investigate the insourcing outcome of an outsourcing decision, the same research approach involving a series of in-depth interviews was used. This time we conducted interviews with 24 participants from seven companies. One of the seven companies also participated in the previous study. It was revisited because it had specifically documented what cost savings it expected and how the savings were to be obtained through insourcing. It was the only company which did so, and there was sufficient time between their IS sourcing decision (to insource in 1991) and the interview time (summer of 1993) to see if the proposed savings were in fact realized.

Of the seven participants, five were *Fortune* 500 companies. Three of the seven are classified, according to *Fortune* magazine's criteria, as manufacturing companies; while four are considered service companies. The manufacturing industries represented include: petroleum refining, apparel, and food. The service industries include: public university, telecommunications, energy, and retail. One of the two participants not classified as *Fortune* 500—the telecommunications company—felt that through mergers and acquisitions, it would likely become a *Fortune* 500 company by 1995. As in our outsourcing study, all participants were very large in terms of revenues or assets. Even the public university was large by university standards.

The seven participants all evaluated insourcing as a formal alternative to outsourcing. Each was willing to outsource its IS if there were demonstrable advantages in doing so, yet each chose the internal bid over going outside. The rationale for this choice and the criteria used in the evaluation process were a key focus of the interviews.

Of the seven cases, six chief information officers (CIOs) or IS directors were interviewed. The IS director was unavailable in the seventh case but a senior IS manager answered questions on his behalf. Fifteen IS staff personnel, including one lawyer attached to the evaluation team, participated in the study. They were generally involved in developing an internal bid to compete against vendor bids, and occasionally, helping with bid evaluation. We also interviewed three consultants who had been engaged in RFP development, bid evaluation, and benchmarking.

Only six of the companies' stories are written up as case studies because the seventh company was not far enough along in their insourcing project to provide any significant conclusions. This organization, a large retail company which we have termed FIRM21, was visited because of the supposed "best practices" implemented within their in-house IS department. We have used some of the information gathered from this company in the discussion on benchmarking in Chapter 5.

Research Technique

For both studies, the same research technique, i.e. data gathering approach, was used. All interviews were tape-recorded and transcribed into separate case write-ups. These transcribed interviews provided the basis of the findings presented below. In addition to the interviews, the following supporting documentation was gathered: outsourcing RFP, internal bids, external bids, bid evaluation criteria, annual reports, and organization charts.

The duration of the interviews, on average, lasted one and one half hours. Although some interviews were shorter or longer, all interviews followed the same protocol which proceeded from a very unstructured to a very structured format. During the unstructured portion, participants were merely asked to tell their insourcing or outsourcing story. This allowed the participant free reign to convey his or her interpretation of events. After they completed their stories, participants were asked semi-structured questions designed to solicit information on specific insourcing/outsourcing issues that may have been absent from their previous recollections. In addition, all participants were assured of anonymity.

An organization's "insourcing or outsourcing story" was "cross-checked" by interviewing multiple individuals at each organization (where possible). In cases where there were differences in opinion between participants at the same organization, follow-up telephone calls were conducted with participants to clarify their positions. In many instances, interesting differences of opinion persisted. These differences provided us new insight into how individuals variously perceived their organization's insourcing/outsourcing evaluation. It provided a richer interpretation than might have otherwise been possible.

The combined insourcing and outsourcing projects involved the interviewing of 61 individuals who were actively engaged in the IS sourcing decision-making process. These tape-recorded interviews were subsequently transcribed into a 637 page single-spaced document which formed the basis for our analysis. We have used actual quotes from the participants to highlight the salient details of their experiences. Table 1.1 summarizes the number of participants and their job positions of our combined projects.

Table 1.2 provides a composite of the 20 organizations participating in the two studies. It classifies the case studies by industry, sourcing decision(s), year of decision(s), whether there was a formal RFP or not, the number of bids received, duration of contract, anticipated cost savings, whether the cost savings had been achieved, and who initiated the insourcing/outsourcing evaluation. Because participants were guaranteed confidentiality, their companies are assigned generic company numbers.

Table 1.1 *Job positions of participants*

Participants' job positions	Number of participants
Senior Manager (CFO, Controller, Treasurer)	7
CIO or equivalent title	16
IS staff member involved in evaluation	29
Vendor Account Manager	4
Consultant	5
Total	61

Table 1.2 Case study profiles

Firm	Industry*	Sourcing decision(s)†	Year of decision(s)	Formal RFP	No. of bids	Length of contract	Expected cost of savings	Cost savings achieved?	Initiator of the decision(s)
1	Chemicals*	Insourcing	1991	Yes	3	N/A	No cost savings estimated	Yes	IS Manager and Senior Manager
2	Diversified services*	(a) Insourcing (b) Selective sourcing—applications development	(a) 1991 (b) 1992	(a) N/A (b) Yes	(a) N/A (b) 2	(a) N/A (b) 5 years	(a) No cost savings estimated (b) 20%	(a) No cost savings achieved (b) Too early	(a) IS Manager (b) Senior Manager
3	Petroleum refining*	Insourcing	1988	N/A	1 informal	N/A	No cost savings estimated	No cost savings achieved	Senior Manager
4‡	Petroleum refining*	Insourcing	1991	Yes	2 plus internal	5 years	43%	Yes, achieved within 5 years	Senior Manager
5	Petroleum refining*	Insourcing	1990	Yes	2	Open time limit	0%, remain as is	Yes, costs remained the same	IS Manager
6	Commercial bank*	Outsourcing	1990	No	1	10 years	15–18%	Yes, as of 1994	Senior Manager
7	Diversified services*	(a) Insourcing (b) Outsourcing	(a) 1988 (b) 1988	(a) No (b) No	(a) 0 (b) 1	(a) N/A (b) 10 years	(a) 0% (b) 20%	(a) None (b) No, customer threatened to sue vendor	(a) IS Manager (b) Senior Manager

#	Industry	Type	Year	Yes/No	Number	Duration	Estimated savings	Savings achieved	Respondent
8	Petroleum refining	Selective—data center	1991	Yes	2	5 years	16%	Unable to determine	IS Manager
9	Metals*	Outsourcing	1990	Yes	2	10 years	16%	Unable to determine	IS Manager
10	Transport-ation*	Outsourcing	1991	No	1	10 years	20%	Unable to determine	Senior Manager
11	Mining*	Outsourcing	1991	No	1	10 years	Savings anticipated but not quantified	Some savings achieved	Senior Manager
12	Chemicals*	(a) Outsourcing (b) Insourcing—return in-house	(a) 1984 (b) 1988	(a) No (b) No	(a) 1 (b) 0	(a) 7 years (b) indefinitely	(a, b) Savings anticipated but not quantified	(a) No, terminated contract early due to excessive costs	(a) Senior Manager (b) IS Manager
13	Rubber and plastics*	(a) Outsourcing (b) Insourcing—return in-house	(a) 1987 (b) 1991	(a) No (b) N/A	(a) 1 (b) N/A	(a) 7 years (b) N/A	(a, b) Savings anticipated but not quantified	(a) No, IS costs rose to 4% of sales; contract terminated early	(a) Senior Manager (b) IS Manager
14	Aerospace*	Outsourcing	1993	Yes	1	10 years	No savings estimated	Unable to determine	IS Manager
15	Apparel manu-facturer and retailer*	Insourcing	1988	No	1 informal	N/A	54%	Yes, achieved within 4 years	

Table 1.2 (cont.)

Firm	Industry*	Sourcing decision(s)†	Year of decision(s)	Formal RFP	No. of bids	Length of contract	Expected cost of savings	Cost savings achieved?	Initiator of the decision(s)
16	Public university	Insourcing	1992	No	1 + internal	N/A	20%	Yes, achieved within 1 year	IS Manager
17	Food manufacturer*‡	Insourcing	1988	No	1 + internal	N/A	45%	Yes, achieved within 3 years	Senior Manager
19	Telecom-munications	Insourcing	1991	Yes	2 + internal	5 years	46%	Yes, achieved within 2 years	Senior Manager
20	Energy*	Insourcing	1989	Yes	3	5 years	25%	Yes, achieved within 2 years	Senior Manager
21	Retail*	Insourcing	1993	No	N/A	N/A	Not specified	Too early	Senior Manager

* = *Fortune* 500.
† = Some companies evaluated outsourcing on multiple occasions.
‡ = FIRM4 in the outsourcing study is the same as FIRM18 in the insourcing study; we therefore list it only once.

PART 1

Results of the Outsourcing and
Insourcing Projects

2
Information Systems Outsourcing: Lessons from the Field

INTRODUCTION

While there is considerable literature trumpeting the benefits of IS outsourcing, citing examples of companies savings 10–50% of their IS budgets, the findings of the research project we began in January 1991 paint a different picture. Fourteen companies which had evaluated IS outsourcing were studied in some detail. We looked at: the reasons why organizations consider outsourcing their IS functions; how they go about evaluating outsourcing; and what overall lessons can be learned from the successes and failures of practitioners who have already evaluated the outsourcing alternative. The results of their experiences are summarized in this chapter. Further details can be found in Lacity and Hirschheim (1993).

SUMMARY OF FINDINGS/LESSONS LEARNED

Based on our interpretation of the interview data and an analysis of the published literature on IS outsourcing, a number of research findings become apparent. We summarize them in terms of eight lessons learned from the successes and failures of practitioners who have already evaluated the outsourcing alternative.

Lesson 1: The Published Literature Portrays an Overly Optimistic View of IS Outsourcing

The overall lesson learned from scrutinizing the published literature is that these sources often portray an overly optimistic view of outsourcing. Three reasons can be identified to explain the optimism. First, reports are made during the honeymoon period when clients first sign an outsourcing contract. At this point, the client and vendor possess high outsourcing expectations (cf. Hamilton, 1989; Kass, 1990; Gillin, 1990; Radding, 1990; Anthes, 1991; Rochester and Douglas, 1990). Second, the literature only reports projected savings instead of actual savings. American Standard, for example, expects their data center operations and network costs to be reduced by 40% through outsourcing (Rochester and Douglas, 1990). Southeast Corporation expects a 20% savings in IS costs over the 10-year life of their outsourcing contract (Kass, 1990). Hibernia National Bank projects a savings of between $25 and $100 million over their 10-year outsourcing deal (Kass, 1990). Therefore, the preponderance of literature that suggests that outsourcing can save 20–50% on IS costs is largely based on expectations. Public sources neglect to report that some outsourcing clients are charged exorbitant excess fees for above baseline measures. Third, public reports underrepresent outsourcing failures because few companies wish to advertise a mistake. Therefore, the literature misrepresents the spectrum of outsourcing experiences by focusing only on the success stories.

Our research reveals several findings that are absent from the published literature. First, outsourcing is not a panacea for IS problems. Several participants suffered severe service degradation and paid significant excess charges that negated expected savings (FIRMs 7, 12, and 13). These outsourcing failures warn others that outsourcing vendors are not partners because the profit motive is not shared. Second, outsourcing may be a viable alternative, but successful outsourcing relationships require substantial contract negotiations. The negotiation process may take six months or more to adequately measure services and to capture service expectations in an excruciatingly detailed contract (FIRM6).

As a final note on the published literature, optimistic IS trends are not limited to outsourcing—exaggerated claims are systemic to other practices. For example, the use of information technology (IT) for competitive advantage received ample press coverage in the past decade. However, when pressed to cite companies that truly strategically employ IT, the same examples surface: American Airlines, American Hospital Supply, Merrill Lynch. Therefore, practitioners should be wary that public information sources are not necessarily representative.

Lesson 2: Outsourcing Appears to be a Symptom of the Problem of Demonstrating the Value of IS

In the participating companies, an overwhelming majority of senior managers viewed their IS functions as cost burdens. As such, IS managers could not appeal to effectiveness or strategic significance to justify their existence. Instead, they must somehow demonstrate efficiency. However, IS managers have difficulty demonstrating efficiency because overhead accounts camouflage IS's contribution, meaningful measures elude the majority of IS services, increases in user demand burden the IS manager to request more and more resources, and IS professionals command high salaries that cannot be tied to profitability.

In the outsourcing context, we saw that the IS manager's inability to demonstrate value was tied to outsourcing evaluations in several ways. First, IS managers may use outsourcing evaluations to demonstrate efficiency by showing that outsiders cannot provide a cheaper service. An IS manager at FIRM2 explains why he initiated an outsourcing evaluation at his company:

> "Once we had those numbers in hand (from an IS efficiency audit), we were pretty comfortable with where we were. We were comfortable that a third party coming in with an outsourcing pitch would have a tough sell. But we also felt that it made an awful lot of sense to understand the outsourcing market and the kind of pitches people could hit us with."

He felt that the IS efficiency audit in combination with the outsourcing evaluation would prove to management that the IS department—or at least the data center—was efficient.

Second, IS managers may use outsourcing evaluations to justify resource requests. By bundling the resource request with an outsourcing evaluation, the IS manager "proves" that his request is cost-justified. FIRM1's Manager of Data Processing admitted that his outsourcing evaluation was partly motivated by the need to acquire a hardware upgrade. In particular, he wanted to upgrade to a more sophisticated operating system on his mainframe and move to relational databases. He notes:

> "At the same time I was kind of building a base I guess to upgrade to a CPU with a five year lease on it. That was my thought process at the time. While it was an outsourcing study, it was also designed to enhance my personal credibility when it came time to ask for bucks."

Acquiring additional resources for IS was particularly difficult in FIRM1 because senior management kept IS budget increases to a minimum.

Third, IS managers may use outsourcing to demonstrate their commitment to corporate objectives. By sacrificing part of their IS kingdom for the good of their company, IS managers demonstrate that they are good corporate citizens. A case in point is Barry, FIRM8's IS Manager. He needed to bolster his personal and departmental credibility and did so through outsourcing "his kingdom." As a consequence of outsourcing, Barry captured senior management's attention and respect:

> "Barry's first audience with the leaders of his company was when he presented the outsourcing decision to the Board of Directors.
>
> Barry's current boss, became Barry's most ardent fan, largely due to outsourcing; he now thinks Barry is the best IS manager he has ever met, and invites Barry to his lunches with the CEO.
>
> The by-line in a respected IS trade publication also enhanced Barry's credibility."

So in the case of FIRM8, Barry's outsourcing decision was successful at proving to management that he is corporate player, not a technician. From Barry's perspective, the IS manager's personal credibility is a prerequisite for effectively managing the department. In the future, perhaps senior management will be less likely to question Barry's recommendations and requests.

These are just a few examples of how IS managers struggle to overcome senior management's view of IS as a cost vortex. However, the larger problem of demonstrating efficiency must also be addressed. Several factors that seem correlated with demonstrated value are the IS accounting structure, reporting level of the IS manager, use of IS to support corporate strategies, top management support, and some measures (however pitiful) of effectiveness (particularly evaluations coming from benchmarking against other companies). The identification of these factors, however, provides few insights into *how* IS managers can politically and economically enact these policies. The problem is essentially one of the chicken and the egg: does demonstrated value come before or after top management support? Since the problem is ubiquitous, superficial platitudes are not offered. We do suggest, however, that benchmarking (especially if carried out by a benchmarking vendor with a large client database) may be one strategy that can help. But even benchmarking may not help if senior management simply perceive IS as a money vortex as evidenced by the following comment made by the Director of Corporate Planning for FIRM4:

> "All they (senior management) see is the amount of money that they have to write a check for every year. Year after year after year. Where is the benefit? IS says, 'Well we process data faster than we did last year.' They say, 'So

what?' IS says, 'Well, we can close the ledger faster.' And they say, 'So what? Where have you increased revenue? All you do is increase costs, year after year after year and I am sick of it. All I get are these esoteric benefits and a bunch of baloney on how much technology has advanced. Show me where you put one more dollar on the income statement.' "

Lesson 3: Organizational Members may Initiate Outsourcing Evaluations for a Variety of Reasons, Cost Efficiency being Only One

Although industry watchers imply that the primary reason why organizations initiate outsourcing is to reduce costs, the results of our research suggest that such a belief is too simplistic. Participants identified a variety of motives for initiating outsourcing decisions of which reducing costs is only one. We divide the reported reasons for initiating outsourcing evaluations into four broad categories: *financial*—cut costs (FIRMs 4, 6, 7, 9, 10, 11, 15, 16, 17, and 19), improve cost controls (FIRMs 6, 16) and restructuring the IS budget (FIRMs 3, 10, 14); *business*—return to core competencies (FIRMs 14, 19), facilitate mergers and acquisitions (FIRM9), start-up companies (FIRMs 1, 12), and devolution of organizational and management structures (FIRMs 18, 19, 20); *technical*—improve technical services (FIRMs 9, 13), gain access to new technical talent (FIRMs 9, 11, 13), provide access to new technologies (FIRMs 9,13), and focus the internal IS staff on core technical activities (FIRMs 14, 18, 20); and *political*—react to the efficiency imperative (FIRMs 1, 2, 4, 5, 6, 11, 12, 13); acquire or justify additional resources (FIRMs 1, 3, 5, 7, 9, 11, 13); react to the positive outsourcing media reports (FIRMs 1, 2, 4, 6, 8, 11); reduce uncertainty (FIRMs 8, 9); eliminate a burdensome function (FIRMs 1, 4, 11); and enhance personal credibility (FIRMs 3, 5, 8).

Financial Reasons

Many participants in our research, especially senior managers, cited financial reasons for outsourcing. In particular, participants viewed outsourcing as a way to cut costs, improve cost control, and restructure the IS budget.

Reduce Costs. Many participants expected that outsourcing would save them money. They perceived that vendors enjoy economies of scale which enable them to provide IS services at a lower cost than internal IS departments. In particular, participants believed that a vendor's unit costs are less expensive due to mass production efficiencies and labor specialization. One participant summarizes the perception of economies of scale:

> "One thing is the economies of scale of the processing. They leverage software by running a lot of customers from that utility. . . . And because of the depth of their organization, they are able to support us with a smaller staff."

Improve Cost Control. Another financial rationale for outsourcing described by participants was gaining control over IS costs. As any IS manager will attest, IS costs are directly related to IS user demands. In most organizations, however, IS costs are controlled through general allocation systems which motivate users to excessively demand and consume resources. General allocation systems are analogous to splitting a restaurant tab—each dinner companion is motivated to order an expensive dinner because the cost will be shared by the other parties. Participants saw outsourcing as a way to control costs because vendors implement cost controls that more directly tie usage to costs. In addition, users no longer call their favorite analysts to request frivolous changes, but instead must submit requests through a formal cost control process. This results in the curtailing of excessive user demands and thus reduces overall IS costs.

Restructure IS Budgets. Some participants described the reason for initiating outsourcing was for restructuring their IS budgets from cumbersome capital budgets to more flexible operating budgets. Through outsourcing, organizations could more efficiently purchase IS resources as needed rather than invest in capital. For example, rather than retain a $15 million mainframe on the books, participants could sell the asset to the vendor and merely buy the number of MIPs they need each year from the vendor. The sale of the asset also generates cash up front, which increases the participants' cash flow. In addition, some vendors will purchase stock and postpone the bulk of IS payments to the latter part of the contract, making the overall net present value extremely attractive to participants. In return for these financial incentives, vendors require long-term contracts, typically 10-years in duration.

Business Reasons

A number of participants expressed three business rationales for outsourcing: return to core competencies, facilitate mergers and acquisitions, and start up new companies.

Return to Core Competencies. During the 1990s, many large companies abandoned their diversification strategies—once pursued to mediate risk—to focus on core competencies. Succinctly put, many corporate executives now view that the most important sustainable competitive advantage is strategic focus, i.e. concentrating on what an organization does better than anyone else while subcontracting everything else to vendors. As a result of this core competencies focus, IS came under scrutiny: is IT a competitive weapon or merely a utility? Even within companies, perceptions over IS's contribution to core activities varied. In general, senior executives tended to view the entire IS function as a non-core activity whereas IS managers and some business unit managers contended that certain IS activities are core to the business.

Facilitate Mergers and Acquisitions. Because the participants were from large companies, as indicated by their presence in *Fortune* 500 list, many of the companies pursue a growth strategy through mergers and acquisitions. Mergers and acquisitions create many IS nightmares for IS managers because they are required to absorb acquired companies into existing systems. Participants expected outsourcing to solve the technical incompatibilities, absorb the excess IS assets, such as additional data centers, and absorb the additional IS employees generated by mergers and acquisitions.

Provide IS for Start-up Companies. Some participants explained that they outsourced IS when the company was first incorporated. At the time, participants expected that outsourcing was a quicker and cheaper way to provide IS services. As start-up companies, participants simply could not afford the capital investment required to erect internal IS departments.

Devolution of Organizational and Management Structures. Participants from a number of organizations initiated outsourcing evaluations in response to devolution of organizational and management structures occurring in a wider business context. Often termed "downsizing," participants intended to use outsourcing as a means to reduce headcount and thus the costs associated with salaries, pensions, and benefits. One participant explains how outsourcing was motivated by the downsizing of the centralized support functions:

> "Outsourcing fell out of the reorganization taking place in Head office . . . we slimmed it down. On IS, the central service organization has either been subsumed within the operating companies, outsourced, or just gone."

Technical Reasons

Technical issues associated with why participants considered outsourcing involve the technical difficulties associated with providing effective IS; more specifically, the desire to either improve technical services, gain access to technical talent not currently available in the organization, and/or provide access to new technologies.

Improve Technical Service. Some participants were dissatisfied with the technical services provided by their in-house IS departments. In particular, the IS departments delivered systems late and over budget and did not respond in a timely manner to user requests. Participants viewed outsourcing as a way to improve technical service, reasoning that outsourcing vendors possess a technical expertise lacking in internal IS departments.

Access to Technical Talent. Some participants thought outsourcing would provide access to technical talent. Many participants found it difficult to find and/or retain staff with the state-of-the-art technical skills. Vendors are felt to have core competencies in technology skills which allow them to bring these skills to the organization through outsourcing. Numerous companies consider outsourcing partly for the access to greater IS expertise it would bring as the following quote from one of our participants suggests:

> "We are a relatively small IS department and the spread of skills that's now required for the systems we've got to support and our customers are now asking us to support is growing. We are not able to keep pace with recruiting those people."

Access to New Technologies. Some participants felt outsourcing would provide a conduit to new, emerging technologies. They viewed outsourcing as a way to hedge bets on emerging technologies, providing them access to the products of the vendors' large research and development departments. Participants were particularly interested in client/server technology, expert systems, new development methodologies, and Computer Aided Software Engineering Tools (CASE) tools.

Focus the Internal IS Staff on Core Technical Activities. Participants from a number of companies initiated outsourcing evaluations to focus the internal IS staff on "core" technical activities, such as the development of new applications, while outsourcing "non-core" technical activities, such as the support of legacy systems. One of the participants explains:

"Our biggest use [of outsourcing] is in legacy systems . . . our own groups move on to more motivating, higher value work while we outsource work where our own business knowledge or skills cannot make the product better."

Political Reasons

Political reasons why organizations consider outsourcing revolve around the desire for more effectively dealing with the subjective nature of assessing the value of IS. In short, the political dimension of outsourcing involves the behavior of the various parties associated with the outsourcing decision-making process. In contrast to the rational description of outsourcing evaluation surrounding the above-mentioned financial, business and technical reasons, the political perspective interprets the behavior of the organizational actors in a subjective light, seeing outsourcing as one piece of a large puzzle involving the shaping of senior management's perception about IS. Political rationale for why organizations consider outsourcing include: proving efficiency (as a reaction to the efficiency imperative), justifying new resources, reacting to the positive media reports, reducing uncertainty, eliminating a troublesome function, and breaking the so-called "glass ceiling" (i.e. enhance credibility).

Reaction to the Efficiency Imperative. An oft cited reason for initiating outsourcing evaluations by participants was the reaction to the efficiency imperative. Since 12 of the 14 companies are accounted for as an overhead function, senior managers tend to evaluate the function solely on cost efficiency (Quinn, Doorley and Paquette, 1990). Since no concrete measures of *actual* efficiency exist, senior managers formulate only a *perception* of efficiency. When senior managers perceive that IS is inefficient, they initiated outsourcing evaluations to improve efficiency. In a similar vein, IS managers themselves initiated outsourcing evaluations. This way, IS managers "prove" that the IS department is already efficient or is making strides to become efficient.

The Need to Acquire New Resources. Participants initiated outsourcing decisions to acquire new resources, such as machine upgrades, additional personnel, or cash. Outsourcing evaluations helped participants acquire resources in two ways. First, if the participant showed that outsourcers could not provide the additional resources at a lower cost, the participant was usually granted the resource. Second, the participant may truly have used outsourcing to acquire new resources. This was particularly evident in cases where participants needed skilled labor or cash.

Reaction to the Bandwagon. Another reason identified was the reaction to the proverbial bandwagon. Favorable outsourcing reports triggered participants to initiate outsourcing for two reasons. First, participants—especially senior managers—wanted to duplicate the success stories they read in the literature. Since these senior managers did not truly value the IS function anyway, they hoped to at least reduce costs to the levels their competitors allegedly achieved through outsourcing. Second, participants—particularly IS managers—feared that the favorable reports would seduce their managers into outsourcing. By taking the initiative, participants used outsourcing evaluations to temper the many exaggerated claims made in public information sources.

Reduce Uncertainty. Participants initiated outsourcing evaluations to respond to their desire to reduce uncertainty. Because IS demand is erratic, IS managers have difficulty planning for IS services. Rather than react to demand fluctuations, IS managers outsourced. By including a clause that varies fees with volumes, IS managers effectively dispensed with the risks associated with uncertainty.

Eliminate a Troublesome Function. Another political reason identified was the desire of participants to eliminate a troublesome function. Since senior executives do not fully value IS, IS administrators receive few accolades for managing the function. When the function runs smoothly, senior executives do not notice. When the function experiences problems, senior management screams. Participants in the research felt, quite frankly, who needs the aggravation? Since no one cares about the function, why not outsource it and let the vendor worry about it?

Enhance Credibility. The final reason identified by the participants was the use of outsourcing evaluations to enhance personal or departmental credibility. Since senior managers do not fully value the services of the IS department, they may not value the contribution of the people who run the function. Studies have repeatedly shown that IS personnel

rarely break into the upper echelons of management. Several participants initiated outsourcing decisions to enhance their credibility. By
showing that they are willing to outsource their kingdom for the good
of the company, they prove to management that they are corporate
players.

A host of theories can be used to interpret these intentions. From a
rational perspective, participants responded to the efficiency imperative. However, since actual IS efficiency is ethereal, participants reacted to their perceptions of efficiency. From a political perspective,
members initiated outsourcing to promote their self-interests at the
expense of others. From a garbage-can perspective, members did not
proactively make outsourcing decisions but rather reacted to popular
IS management trends. From a bureaucratic stance, members wished
to avoid decision-making since risk-taking behavior is not rewarded.
In summary, the interpretation of the participants' outsourcing experiences extends far beyond the economic rationale purported in the published literature—costs are but one reason why participants considered
outsourcing.

Lesson 4: An Outsourcing Vendor may not be Inherently more Efficient than an Internal IS Department

Many practitioners assume that outsourcing vendors are inherently
more efficient due to economies of scale. The theory of economies of
scale states that large-sized companies achieve lower average costs
than small-sized companies due to mass production and labor specialization efficiencies. In the outsourcing arena, however, the applicability of the economies of scale model may be questioned. First, small
shops may have lower costs per MIP than large shops by employing
older technology, offering below market wages, and maintaining tight
controls and procedures. The IS Manager in FIRM8 obtained lower
costs by using older technology. He stated:

> "And I said as long as we stay on the trailing edge of technology—and I've
> been pushing this concept to senior management—we have an opportunity
> to capitalize on cheaper computing costs."

Second, a vendor's hardware discounts are negligible in many instances. This was concisely stated by one outsourcing consultant who
participated in our study. He said:

> "Can an outsourcing vendor buy a machine for less than, say, Enron? Sure
> they can. I'll give you numbers that aren't exactly accurate, but a large IBM
> 3090 probably is in the $15 million list range. An outsourcing vendor could

probably get it for $11 million. Enron could probably get it for about $11.5 million. Now over a 5–10 year period, there is not a whole lot of money being saved."

Third, changes in software licensing agreements diminish a vendor's advantage. The Account Manager in FIRM11 explained the impact of the new software licensing agreements on a vendor's costs:

"[Software vendor] is thinking 'All the time these deals are signed, the outsourcer can channel everything into one box, use one copy of the software. Therefore, we are going to lose money.' And from a business perspective, I suppose that makes sense. So what the software vendors have done is gone to group pricing. And of course, the outsourcer operates a larger box than my company, so they pay more fees. . . . This has dire consequences for outsourcing deals."

Fourth, labor expertise is largely a myth since clients are usually supported by the same staff that transitioned to the vendor. This was aptly put by the IS Manager of FIRM13 who said:

"They [the vendor] took over all the people as they usually do, so what happens in that environment is your unqualified IS people that you had become unqualified [vendor] people."

Of course you could purchase new technical expertise from the vendor, but this is costly. A Purchasing Manager in FIRM9 noted:

"None of it is cheap. I guess there is a perception that once you have [a vendor] locked in that you have a conduit to all this expertise, but you pay."

Lesson 5: The Internal IS Department may be Able to Achieve Similar Results without Vendor Assistance

When vendors submit bids that indicate savings, companies may question whether they can achieve similar results without vendor assistance. If the vendor is not inherently more efficient, perhaps the company can reduce their own IS expenses through data center consolidation, resource optimization, chargeback implementation, and other sundry methods. The case of Continental Bank (Huber, 1993) provides a good example. They outsourced to reduce the amount of overuse of their IS services. Outsourcing acted as a controlling mechanism. But could the same not be done without an outside vendor? Huber states:

"Perhaps half of Continental's problems with in-house services stemmed from overuse. For instance, the most routine documents were always sent to the legal department for review. 'Better safe than sorry' people would say, while thinking, 'and besides, it's just an internal cost, not real dollars.' " (pp. 122–123).

The implementation of a chargeback scheme can also dramatically reduce IS costs. An outsourcing consultant states:

"A chargeback system is typically the best run-time improvement there is. With a chargeback system you get a bill that shows you here's everything that you ran for that month. And if you were wasting resources, and the bill jumps as a result of that, you'd be amazed how much people reduce their costs the minute a chargeback system is implemented."

Lesson 6: If a Company Decides to Outsource, the Contract is the Only Mechanism to Ensure that Expectations are Realized

When some companies decide that outsourcing is the preferred mechanism for achieving IS objectives, they often like to view their vendors as partners. Vaughn Hovey of Kodak, for example, told an audience of practitioners: "We think of our strategic alliances as 'partnerships' because of their cooperative and long term qualities" (Hovey, 1991). Kodak sealed their partnerships with IBM, DEC, and Businessland with little more than a gentleman's agreement. Furthermore, according to Hovey, Kodak rarely refers to these "six or seven page contracts." While such an arrangement might work in the Kodak case, we feel the general assumption that the outsourcing vendor is a partner is dangerously flawed. Vendors are not partners because profit motives are not shared: a dollar out of the client's wallet is a dollar in the vendor's wallet. An outsourcing contract is the only way to ensure an equitable balance of power. Service level measures, arrangements for growth, penalties for non-performance and other contract provisions must be stipulated prior to outsourcing commencement. FIRM6 provides a good example where considerable effort went in to specifying the contract. The Financial Manager stated:

"And that's when Janet and I and the attorneys sat down every day for three solid months of drafting up the agreement, negotiating the terms, conditions and services."

Lesson 7: The Metaphor that IS is Merely a Utility is Misguided

It is possible to find in the published literature numerous examples of practitioner statements that compare the entire IS department to electricity, cafeterias, fruit stands, and laundry services. For example,

Henry Pfendt of Kodak claims that outsourcing comes down to one question: "Do you want to manage commodities?" (Kass and Caldwell, 1990, p.14). Similarly, Elliot McNeil of Southlands claims that IS is largely a utility—rather than pay for the entire plant, why not just pay for wattage used? "It's like the electricity company; you use less, you pay less" (Ambrosio, 1991). Ward (1991) states: "Like shoppers at a fruit stand, companies are picking an apple here or an orange there until they have selected a menu of outsourcing services" (p. 40). Gardner (1991) writes: "Outsourcing takes over all information systems functions, much the way an outside company would manage food service or laundry" (p. 35). These metaphors are based on the assumption that IS services are homogeneous—one unit of IS service is equal to any other. The problem with this metaphor is it ignores the idiosyncratic nature of an organization's information needs. Close communication between the organization and IS must occur to accurately relay requirements. As utility users, we do not have to call the power company to communicate our complicated changing business needs. We simply use more of the power when and as needed. As IS users, however, we do. So how is an IS department like electricity? In fact, the issue of the utility metaphor for IS will be expanded upon in the conclusions of the book when we question whether IS really is like other candidate outsourcing functions.

Lesson 8: Outsourcing Often Constrains Organizational Flexibility

While an "outsourcing" strategy might be appropriate in those cases where the organization wants to divest itself of IS (perhaps to focus on the business's core competency), this will likely remove (or at least significantly constrain) any flexibility of how IS is delivered. The outsourcing vendor will provide the level of IS services specified in the contract using the technological platform it deems appropriate. In such an environment, vendors typically run mainframes and mainframe software applications "into the ground" as they are sunk costs. Unless specifically spelled out in the contract, the flexibility of moving to new computing platforms is lost. Or if not lost, the vendor is likely to be the sole benefactor of any cost advantage of moving to new, more cost-effective technology, such as client/server computing. More worrying, however, is that outsourcing could constrain how an organization reacts or adapts to a changing business environment. Without the flexibility of having an internal IS capability, it might prove difficult (and/or expensive) to have the vendor provide a changed set of IS services.

CONCLUSION

One main conclusion derived from our study is that outsourcing vendors do not necessarily possess inherent cost advantages over internal IS departments. By examining how vendors actually cut costs—through benchmarking, chargeback, data center consolidation and other methods—internal IS departments could theoretically achieve service objectives without vendor assistance. But do they? Although a number of organizations have insourced IS, it is not clear to what extent these operations have been successful, i.e. have achieved the savings expected. To further investigate this idea, we examined organizations that pledged cost savings and improved service through insourcing. The results are explored next.

3
Insourcing Case Studies

INTRODUCTION

Based on our analysis of organizational experiences with outsourcing, it was clear that such an IS sourcing strategy was far from the panacea that had been hoped for. Indeed, if cost savings were the primary impetus behind outsourcing evaluation, could organizations which retain IS in-house not achieve cost efficiencies similar to those offered by outsourcers? This led us to formulate the following research questions which guided our study of companies who chose insourcing over outsourcing:

- Was there a formal decision process where insourcing was chosen over an outsourcing option? If so, on what grounds was insourcing chosen over outsourcing?
- Was there a legitimate commitment to insource or was insourcing primarily used as a defensive maneuver? What was the basis of this commitment?
- Did the organization actually achieve its objectives? Why or why not? How did organizations determine whether objectives were achieved?
- How do senior management's perceptions of the IS manager and IS department influence insourcing decisions?

In this chapter, we describe the insourcing decision-making process at six of the organizations who participated in our study. The material in this chapter provides the "raw data" which is used in subsequent chapters to analyze the nature of insourcing, and particularly senior management's and IS management's role in the insourcing decision-making process. We describe each case using the same basic structure: (1) overview of the case; (2) company background; (3) senior management's perception of IS prior to insourcing; (4) the outsourcing decision and/or insourcing project; (5) senior management's perception of IS after insourcing; and (6) conclusions and/or future of IS.

OVERVIEW OF INSOURCING DECISIONS

Table 3.1 provides an overview of the participating companies and their insourcing decisions. Because participants were guaranteed confidentiality, their companies are assigned generic company numbers, beginning with FIRM15. (The company numbering starts with 15 because the insourcing project builds upon the lessons learned from the 14 companies studied during the outsourcing project.)

FIRM15 is an apparel manufacturer and retailer in the United States. Due to increased competition from Italy, the Pacific Rim, and South America, FIRM15 was forced to cut costs across all business units. Although IS was able to contribute to the company's cost reduction efforts by reducing IS costs by 54%, senior management continues to perceive that IS is still too expensive. FIRM15's insourcing story reflects the frustration experienced by many IS managers: no matter what IS accomplishes, senior management still perceives IS as a cost burden.

FIRM16, although a public university, offers many lessons for IS managers in the private sector. A newly appointed CIO was able to thwart an imminent outsourcing contract and instead accomplish savings of over 20% without vendor assistance. He is also one of the few participants who changed senior management's perceptions of IS. In addition to the insourcing success, he created a unified IS vision and convinced the board of curators that IT can be used as a competitive weapon to attract new students.

FIRM17 is a human and pet foods manufacturer. On the eve of an outsourcing decision, the internal IS department convinced senior management—with the help of a reputable benchmarking service—they could reduce costs on their own. FIRM17's IS management subsequently reduced costs by 45%. Although service degraded somewhat, FIRM17's senior management willingly accepts this consequence.

FIRM18 originally participated in the outsourcing study of 1991. At the time, the internal IS department's bid had just been selected over two external bids. We revisited FIRM18 during the summer of 1993 to

Table 3.1 *Summary of insourcing decisions*

Case site	Industry classification	Functions insourced	Savings achieved	Year insource began	Initiator of the decision
FIRM15	Apparel manufacturer and retailer*	2 Data centers; 56 MIPS	Reduced costs by 54%; reduced headcount by 37%	1988	IS Manager
FIRM16	Public university	3 Data centers; 106 MIPS	Reduced costs by 20%; reduced headcount by 23%	1992	Senior Manager
FIRM17	Food manufacturer*	Data center; 180 MIPS	Reduced costs by 45%	1988	Senior Manager
FIRM18	Petroleum refining*	3 Data centers; 200 MIPS	Reduced costs by 43%; reduced headcount by 51%	1991	Senior Manager
FIRM19	Telecommunications	Data center; 32 MIPS	Reduced headcount by 46%	1991	Senior Manager
FIRM20	Energy*	Data center; 150 MIPS	Reduced headcount by 25%; increased workload by 25–30%	1989	Senior Manager

* = *Fortune* 500 company.

determine whether the IS department accomplished their aggressive insourcing objectives. Indeed, they had—IS costs were reduced by 45%. Other IS managers will find FIRM18's novel approaches to software licenses and chargeback systems insightful.

FIRM19, one of the largest diversified telecommunications companies in the United States, decided to outsource IS after learning of Kodak's success story. After FIRM19 employees convinced management to allow the internal IS department to compete with the outsourcing vendors, an internal response team prepared a bid that eventually won. A year and a half later, most insourcing objectives have been met, although changes in corporate strategy have altered IS plans. FIRM19 participants expressed relief that insourcing was selected over outsourcing because insourcing provided flexibility to adapt IS plans to changing corporate strategies.

FIRM20, one of the largest energy companies in the US, undertook an outsourcing evaluation in 1989. An internal bid was submitted and eventually chosen over two external bids. It offered the lowest costs (although there was little difference between the three on this criterion) and the greatest degree of flexibility. Four years into the insourcing arrangement, senior management has a positive impression. They very much like what they see. IS costs are down, workloads are up, and there is a general sense that IS has become a more integral part of the business. Evidence for this last belief comes from the hiring of a corporate CIO who is playing an active role in shaping the strategic direction of the business.

FIRM21, a large retail company, participated in the study, but their insourcing evaluation was still in progress. As a result, we included some of their benchmarking experiences in Chapter 5, but have not included a detailed case description. This firm was visited because of the supposed "best practices" implemented within their in-house IS department.

FIRM15

Introduction

FIRM15's insourcing project reflects the sentiments of many frustrated IS managers. Although FIRM15's IS manager reduced costs by 54% and reduced headcount by 37%, senior management continues to perceive that IS is non-responsive and expensive. Given senior management's disdain for IS, the IS managers continue to struggle to contribute to the strategic direction of the company.

Two IS managers were interviewed for this case, Randy, the vice president (VP) of IS and Cam, his direct subordinate, the director of IS administration. The documentation gathered for the case include the three benchmarking studies used to facilitate the insourcing project, annual reports, organization chart, and IS headcounts.

Company Background

FIRM15 purchases, manufactures, and retails apparel. As a major US apparel importer, FIRM15 annually purchases considerable apparel from Brazil, Italy, and the Far East. FIRM15 also manufactures its own brand of apparel in a number of manufacturing plants in the United States and Canada. FIRM15's retail outlets include enclosed malls, stand-alone stores in strip centers, and leased apparel departments in large department stores. In total, FIRM15 operates thousands of retail stores. FIRM15 employs 25 000 workers, of which approximately 60% are retail employees.

Corporate revenues for fiscal years 1989 to 1992 remained steady at almost $2 billion annually. Net profits were approximately 30 million in 1989 and 1990. Although profits dipped to 15 million in 1991, profits have recovered to 26 million in 1992. An article published in a leading investment magazine assessed that FIRM15 will enjoy continued prosperity as they adapt to the changing market.

In particular, FIRM15 has successfully responded to two significant changes in the industry over the past 10 years: (1) the lapse in government protection, and (2) changes in consumer behaviors.

Before the Reagan administration, the government enacted import quotas that protected domestic manufacturers. When Reagan took office, he let the import quotas expire with devastating consequences for domestic manufacturers because they could not compete with cheaper foreign labor costs. Two years after the import quota expired, 80% of the apparel sold in the United States was foreign made. Today, over 90% is manufactured outside the United States.

Changes in consumer buying patterns have also affected FIRM15. In the 1980s, FIRM15's retail outlets were primarily in enclosed malls. During the past five years, cost-conscious consumers increasingly patronize factory outlet malls or discount stores, such as Walmart or Target, to purchase apparel. The lower mall traffic combined with the high mall rents make enclosed malls a less lucrative retail outlet.

During the past decade, FIRM15 has responded to the lapse in government protection and changes in consumer behavior by downsizing its domestic manufacturing operations, increasing import trade, and moving retail outlets from enclosed malls to strip centers. Cam has witnessed 80% of FIRM15's manufacturing facilities close since he joined the company in 1979. The decreased mall business is attributed to a loss of its leased department accounts due to large department store bankruptcies as well as an abundance of retail competition. FIRM15's move to strip centers, where competition is less severe, has been prosperous. Profits in this line of business account for two-thirds of total profits. FIRM15 has also diversified by purchasing a successful specialty retail company that operates 380 stores. In total, the investments magazine concludes that FIRM15's financial outlook promises sound returns for investors.

Today FIRM15 is organized into five business units: three retail sales units, a manufacturing and wholesale unit, and an international unit that sources apparel from foreign countries such as China, Brazil, and Taiwan. Within each business unit, an IS manager reports to the financial officer. Each business unit's IS manager has a dotted line reporting relationship to the corporate VP of IS. The unit IS managers are responsible for applications development and support for that business unit. In addition, three of the business units run their own data center; two units use an AS400 platform and one unit uses PICK (an operating system).

The centralized IS function, headed by the VP of IS, Randy, reports to the corporate CFO. The centralized IS department is responsible for data center processing for two business units as well as corporate accounting and reporting functions. The platform is a 56 MIP rated mainframe running Multiple Virtual Storage (MVS). The centralized IS function also maintains a staff to develop and maintain applications such as electronic data interchange and financial systems, that cut across business units.

The centralized IS function, which is the focal point of the case study, currently employs 125 people. Seventeen employees work on corporate applications while the remaining employees are responsible for data communications, telecommunications, technical services, and two corporate data centers. Until recently, FIRM15 operated two data centers on the same property for contingency reasons; each center served as the hot site for the other. The IS manager who originally built the two data centers believed that maintaining two data centers was less expensive than subscribing to a disaster recovery service, which can cost several hundred thousand per year.

In total, FIRM15 spent $27 million on IS, with the corporate function accounting for 20 million. The large percentage of corporate IS spending is attributed to the data processing service provided for two business units which are billed monthly for IS charges.

Senior Management's Perceptions of IS before Insourcing

The corporate culture, as described by Cam, is autocratic; senior executives make all operating decisions and rarely communicate corporate strategy to lower levels:

> "[Senior executives provide] very poor communication across the business lines into the ranks. I'm a director. I should be able to recite what the directions are for this coming year. I don't know what they are. I asked. Senior managers are all Harvard MBA types—very bright, articulate people when they get in front of the stockholders and analysts, but poor communicators when it comes to dealing within FIRM15. No one trusts them."

In this environment, Randy has difficulty aligning IS strategy with the corporate strategy. As Cam notes:

> "There is not a good flow of information from the top down. I've been here 13 years and I still don't know what our corporate strategy is. Should it be autonomous and let each division do their own thing? Is it centralized? Decentralized? Autonomous units? It's not shared—a couple guys sit upstairs and that's it. It never gets disseminated. They always branch off trying new business ventures and nothing seems to work. The two mainstay companies are now down to a point where we wonder if we will even be around in a couple of years from now."

The lack of communication between senior management and IS has sailed IS off course and consequently damaged IS's credibility. More specifically, applications development is viewed as non-responsive and the data center operations are viewed as too expensive.

Applications Development

During the past five years, the centralized IS function built applications under the fallacious assumption that the mainframe would play a continuing role within FIRM15. The centralized applications development team spent millions on a mainframe-based order processing system. The system is described by participants as a "piece of junk." From the IS perspective, the system development process was a failure because of a lack of senior management direction and user continuity. Cam describes the project as follows:

> "Poor, poor design, the programmers—there was so much turmoil in FIRM15, they were downsizing and firing management and staff. There was no continuity in the development process. We didn't have any good end users to work with. The priorities kept changing. So it's been detrimental to the development process. That is the last development FIRM15 plans to put

on the mainframe. If they put [Division A] on, it will cost $40 000 per month. That's just for that one application, one division. We point our finger at the developers down there and say, 'You guys did a crappy job.' But I know what happened upstairs—they were short changed from the user side."

Another applications failure is a large, mainframe-based manufacturing control system. After 11 years in development, the system is no longer needed because FIRM15 downsized its manufacturing operations. Instead, user managers are looking to purchase an integrated packaged that runs on a smaller platform, such as an AS400.

The push for smaller platforms leaves IS in a lurch. For example, the international importing unit wants to purchase a general ledger system that will run on an AS400. The other divisions are considering their own packages. The centralized IS group worries that incompatible accounting systems will result. The director of IS administration describes the situation:

"The [international import unit] will buy this within the next couple of months. How does that interface with everyone's general ledger? We'll have to write interfaces or find a new way to crunch the numbers at corporate. They'll try to get the other units to use the package instead of the mainframe, but it sounds like they'll let each company do their own thing then try to figure out how to slam it all together."

Cam believes that the applications failures are detrimental to the entire IS department's reputation: "They give us all a black eye." As the adage goes, "It's not IS's fault but it is their problem."

Data Center Operations

Senior management continues to view data center operations as too expensive, even after the insourcing project. Randy is often frustrated by senior management's complaints about costs:

"They are always telling us our processing for payroll is too damn expensive. Then when you say, 'Well have you looked outside?' 'Oh yes, we beat the heck out of them.' So our costs are too high but they can't get it any cheaper."

Randy tries to change senior management's perceptions of the cost-effectiveness of IS by demonstrating constant cost reductions.

"You better be able to keep score and show how you are getting better every year. I think the reports and the numbers is what you keep score with. I don't think there is any question about that."

In summary, the environment in which FIRM15's IS department operates is autocratic and non-communicative. As a result, the IS department's strategies have not been aligned with corporate strategies, leaving accusations that IS is non-responsive and expensive.

The Insourcing Project

The insourcing project evolved over a period of five years. Cam admits, "I think through the natural course of things we fell into this, to be honest." The concept of insourcing was introduced to FIRM15 by a benchmarking service that specialized in identifying specific cost reductions. When Cam attended a seminar by the benchmarking service in 1987, he was skeptical:

> "Everybody is a consultant nowadays. Most consultants don't do you a damn bit of good. They hurt you more than they help you in many cases."

Cam decided to revisit the benchmarking issue the following year after a local company successfully used the benchmarking service to fend off an outsourcing attempt. Even though the benchmarking service compares clients against a best of breed, both he and Randy felt that the benchmarks would confirm that FIRM15's data center costs were very low. The VP of IS thought:

> "Let's get [the benchmarking service] in here to lend some credibility to show that we are not doing a bad job."

Cam concurred that the benchmarks would be favorable, "I wasn't concerned. I thought we were doing a great job." To their surprise, the benchmarking firm reported that FIRM15's data processing unit costs were 35% percent above the reference group average. The benchmarks were supplemented with specific opportunities of improvement. Ironically, Cam previously identified several of the proposed improvements, but could not rally management support to implement them.

> "We were very heavily staffed in data center operations. Part of it was a conscious decision on our part because we have two computer rooms physically separated for contingency reasons. Printing area was heavily staffed, console was heavily staffed, we needed to automate more of the console function. The tape area was heavily staffed. At the time we just had regular tape drives. Those were the primary problems. Most of it was in the operations areas. Technical services was understaffed in their opinion, but we were getting all the work done."

FIRM15 ranked well for data communications, administration, and hardware acquisition costs. According to Cam, FIRM15 was "off the charts" in the area of hardware acquisitions because "we buy rusty old iron."

The benchmarking results were presented to senior management along with a request for cost-cutting investments in automation technology. In the past, senior management refused to fund such projects, but the presence of the benchmarking consultant provided credibility to the request. Cam was glad to receive approval, but is annoyed that senior management did not listen to him previously:

"[The benchmarking service] lent some credibility to IS, having someone else come in, someone independent, look at us and compare us to well run data centers and tell the senior policy committee their findings. They focused on what to automate to reduce staff, which is fine but you have to go out and spend money to reduce staff. We don't have to politic, get additional funds, justify it, if you have a champion like [the benchmarking firm] to go with you to senior management. If you have someone like [the benchmarking service] standing next to you saying, 'Yeah, he should do this,' all of a sudden, senior management opens up a checkbook. And to me, it's infuriating as hell. Why am I on the payroll? Why are they more credible than I am? You should trust me, I'm on your payroll."

With senior management's approval, Randy eliminated eight positions in 1990 and saved $625 000 per year by automating the tape silos, automating the console, and providing on-line report review. Through automation, FIRM15 was able to collapse some of the duplicate functions across both data centers, such as moving to one print site and sharing a tape silo. Cam describes the savings for the projects. For tape silos, he estimates savings through reduced headcounts as follows:

"I'll say I saved $100 000 to $150 000 a year. It wasn't as much as it might be at another shop, only because we don't pay our people. That was one area [the benchmarking service] pointed out to our senior management several times that we are 25–35% below the average salary level than everyone else."

Console automation brought another $100 000 in savings via reduced headcount. Miscellaneous changes accounted for another $125 000 in savings on corporate IS costs. The largest portion of savings, however, came from the reduction in printing costs. Randy installed a system which allowed users to review reports on-line. Users could print selected pages, such as summary sheets, rather than print entire reports. Randy spent considerable time selling the concept to users. The marketing of the concept proved successful as savings on people, paper, and supplies amounts to $300 000 per year.

In the middle of the benchmarking process, Randy instructed the director of IS to fill out a questionnaire by a major outsourcing vendor. At the time, the director ignored the request because he was too busy:

> "At about the time that [the benchmarking service] came in, my boss asked me to—he handed me this great big thing from one of the outsourcers—and wanted me to fill it out. It would take three months and no one on my staff would have been able to do it. It sat on my desk for a month or two. We did the insourcing project thing. I was just getting ready to work on the outsourcing thing, and my boss walked in and said, 'Don't worry about that anymore.' Say what? 'I don't want to mess with that anymore.' "

Although Randy refused to comment on the seriousness of the outsourcing inquiry, from subsequent discussions one can surmise he holds a skeptical view of outsourcing:

> "It's obvious an outsourcer says a unit of CPU costs this. 'We'll give it to for less.' I've been in IS long enough to know unit costs decrease dramatically. Now you sign a 10-year contract at this price. That's proving out."

It remains unclear whether the insourcing project was partly motivated by a defensive action against an outsourcing threat. Cam feels strongly that the two events were only coincidental.

When the benchmarking firm was hired again in 1992, FIRM15's cost reductions placed them around the reference group average. Some of the positive findings of the report were:

- FIRM15 reduced total costs by 10% since the last benchmark
- FIRM15 reduced unit costs by 36%
- FIRM15 reduced headcount by 11%
- FIRM15 added 14 MIPS, 48 gigabytes of (DASD) Direct Access Storage Device

Recommendations for improvement this year included further staff reductions as a consequence of last year's automation. For example, the console automation decreased the number of manually entered commands by 93%. While FIRM15 reduced some of the console staff, the benchmarking firm felt the function was still overstaffed.

FIRM15 also worked on additional automation projects to reduce headcount. For example, FIRM15 bought a package to automatically balance quantities from the allocation and shipping systems. That package reduced headcount by 12 people. As a final cost reduction strategy, plans were made to eliminate the duplicate data centers by going to a hot site.

In 1993, the benchmarking service was hired again. This time, FIRM15's costs ranked well below the reference group average. Instances of the progress made from the last benchmark report include:

- FIRM15 reduced total costs by 3%
- FIRM15 reduced unit costs by 33%
- FIRM15 reduced headcount by 19%
- FIRM15 increased quality in the areas of batch turnaround, number of program abnormally ended (ABENDS), and availability

The benchmarking service recommended some improvements, such as reducing the number of help desk calls, but overall FIRM15 was very efficient vis-à-vis the reference group average. FIRM15 completed cost reduction plans identified the previous year. The second data center was shut down, but when Cam asked for funds for a disaster recovery service, senior management balked:

> "We told [senior management] we were going to go to a hot site. It was a three-year process. We made all these changes. [Senior management] picked on this $120 000 blip in our spending for the hot site. They said, 'We can't afford that.' I said, 'Wait a second folks. It's too late to back out now. We have a major problem on our hands if we don't do it.' "

All told, the three-year insourcing project was a success. FIRM15 reduced the data center headcount from 198 to 125 people and eliminated the duplicate data centers which resulted in savings of 54%. The director of IS summarizes the success of the insourcing project:

> "Within the years we were with [the benchmarking service], we became one of the most efficient MVS shops in the country for our size."

Senior Management's Perceptions of IS after Insourcing

Despite the success of the insourcing project, senior management continues to perceive that IS costs are too high. When Randy and Cam proudly presented their final insourcing results, senior management rejected the benchmarks because the benchmarking service only measures mainframe shops. The director of IS administration explains:

> "After this last report, I walked out of the policy meeting and thought, 'Alright, we've done something real good.' Well after we left, some of the finance guys said, 'Yeah, that's fine and dandy, you look good against MVS shops, but how does that stack up against some other platform? How does that compare to an AS400 shop of the same size?' They wanted to compare apples and oranges. In their mind, it's apples to apples. In a technical way,

it's apples to oranges. So they took a lot of the self-esteem we accumulated on the [benchmark] report and blew it away. They don't care how we look against other MVS shops. They think there are cheaper alternatives, client/server, AS400."

Randy scrambled to find data comparing MVS costs with AS400 costs. The benchmarking service provided some data, but because their AS400 client database only consisted of 10 firms, results are merely preliminary. The benchmarking service concluded that total costs for a 25 MIP shop are comparable in MVS and AS400 shops. The only difference is that the costs are distributed differently. In an MVS shop, hardware costs are lower because of access to older equipment but labor costs are higher because more people are needed to run the equipment. Randy distributed the report around to senior management, along with a summary report of headcounts over the past five years. Senior management again attacked IS. Randy explains:

"I got the information, sent copies all over the building for everyone to look at. I was telling the president, keeping him up on things, 'in the last five years we've dropped 54%.' All he looked at was the end figure that showed 123 people. He said, '123—that's a lot of people.' He didn't even notice that that was 190 five years ago, and every year we get better."

Cam expresses the frustration of not being recognized for the insourcing project:

"We look at it and say, 'Boy, we did a lot of hard work, we did some good things.' We want to pat ourselves on the back by showing it to [senior management]. Then they tell us to turn around and stick it where the sun doesn't shine."

The Future of IS

The future of FIRM15's centralized IS function is uncertain. Rumors circulate that the two business units supported by the corporate data center will abandon the mainframe in favor of client/server technology. Cam feels all centralized IS departments are facing the same fate:

"The mainframe is dead. No more R and D [research and development] invested by software companies on mainframe products. It's all in Windows, client/server. [The president of Unit D] thinks he needs to convert maybe to a big AS400."

Another rumor suggests that senior management will liquidate the two business units. In either case, the centralized IS function stands to lose two-thirds of its business. As Cam laments, "If you walk in here in three years, there may not be a corporate IS."

The IS managers would like to play a more proactive role in shaping the competitive future of FIRM15 but are stymied by a lack of senior management support. The chief executive officer (CEO) of the company believes that IS's role is merely to collect data; the competitive use of information must come from the business units. Cam notes:

"[The CEO] and senior managers both look at information technology as a powerful thing. I know recently, [the CEO] commented, 'IS has all the data and information, we've invested in those areas, they have what you need, you guys in the business units have to learn how to sort through it and make it work to your advantage.' We have the information. I just think it's information overload. They don't know where to go."

This view is unfortunate because the IS managers have ideas on how to make FIRM15 more competitive. For example, the director of IS administration perceives that FIRM15 could improve its market share by getting better merchandise into the stores. Perhaps systems could be used to better track consumer behaviors. But he sighs, "What do I know? I'm just an IS guy."

Randy also possesses ideas on improving the competitive position of FIRM15. He is well versed in re-engineering practices, but notes that IS cannot champion such projects:

"[Re-engineering] has to be driven by the guy running that particular functional area, the purchasing department, the distribution department. So I think those people running the operating companies have to recognize a need for change. If he doesn't recognize it and isn't pushing for it, I don't think it will happen. If IS attempts it without [functional area support], it will fail."

Conclusion

The case of FIRM15 warns us that just decreasing costs will not on its own necessarily change senior management's perception of IS as a cost pit. Indeed, the IS department's reducing costs by 54% only reconfirmed management's perceptions that IS was inefficient. The fact that IS was not considered as strategic to the business, likely helped influence this negative view of IS's efficiency. Clearly then, just reducing costs is an insufficient basis for changing management's perception of IS; it is but one of a number of strategies which could be followed as we will explore later.

FIRM16

Introduction

FIRM16, a public university with four semiautonomous campuses and a centralized administration, epitomizes the loosely coupled organization. The environment is extremely political, with many factions having to buy into decisions—the general public, the state government, the governing board of curators, administration, faculty, and students. Despite the bureaucratic environment, the CIO at the university was able to halt an outsourcing evaluation, achieve insourcing savings of several million dollars, create a unified IS vision, and convince "senior management" that IS is a strategic resource that can be used for competitive advantage to attract students. This case provides many lessons for frustrated IS managers who fear that internal politics will prevent them from achieving insourcing objectives.

The primary source of information for this case was Paul, the CIO. In addition to an interview, he provided documentation including the detailed consolidation plan, president's advisory committee on computing's vision statement, IT report on the future of IS in academic institutions, president's report to the board of curators on the consolidation project, service level agreements, organizational charts, staff reduction report, and all financial information associated with the insourcing project. The case was reviewed for accuracy by a member of the interfaculty council who has had direct contact with the president and the board of curators over the past two years.

University Background

Founded in 1839, FIRM16 has grown to one of the largest universities in the United States, matriculating over 54 000 students. The university is governed by a nine-member board of curators appointed by the governor. The board elects the president of the university system, who presides over the chancellors of each of the four campuses, two of which have medical schools.

Prior to the insourcing project, all four campuses and the two hospitals maintained their own data centers. In addition, a data center to support administrative functions was also maintained at the largest campus. (Note the largest campus will be referred to as the main campus for the remainder of this case.) The focus of this case is on the three data centers that physically resided in the same city—the main campus data center, the hospital data center, and the centralized administrative system data center (referred to simply as "system").

As of 1992, the IS structure of these three units was highly autonomous. Each unit ran their own data center and was organized as follows:

1 The main campus had an assistant vice chancellor for campus computing who reported to the vice chancellor of administrative affairs who in turn reported to the chancellor. The assistant vice chancellor maintained his own data center that serviced the instructional and research needs of the main campus. The data center ran an IBM 170S machine with 16 MIPS and 72 gigabytes of DASD.
2 The head of IS at the medical school reported to the CFO of the hospital. The CFO reported to the hospital administrator who in turn reported to the chancellor of the main campus. The hospital data center supported billing, patient care, and other hospital functions. The data center ran an IBM 300S machine with 58 MIPS and 125 gigabytes of DASD.
3 The system computing facility, which was run by an assistant VP, ran applications that support the entire university—four campuses plus central administration—such as finance, payroll, personnel, the student information system, and the library catalog. The data center ran an IBM 200E machine with 32 MIPS and 138 gigabytes of DASD.

In the autonomous environment, IS expenditures were only planned 12 months into the future. Capital investments were depreciated over a five-year period, which greatly inflated the book value of the university's IS assets. Paul explains the situation at the time:

"Typically all IS purchases around here were amortized over five years and we either depreciated them over five years, we did them over our cost recover mechanism for five years, or we contracted over five years . . . we still have a million dollars on a 170J that isn't worth two nickels."

Each unit also recovered costs in a different manner. According to Paul, for example, the system computing facility was recovered on resource units such as MIPs and gigabytes while "the hospital took it off the top." To summarize, no unified vision of IS existed because each of the university's computing facilities operated autonomously. It is no surprise that in this environment, "senior management"—i.e., the board and the president—viewed IS primarily as a necessary cost rather than as a strategic resource of the "business".

Senior Management's Perceptions of IS before Insourcing

The board of curators is primarily comprised of attorneys who viewed IT as a necessary university cost. A member of the interfaculty council describes the board's view of IS as of two years ago as follows: "The board could not care less about IS. They treated it like they treated the heat or electricity." They did not particularly view IS as a strategic resource because there was no unified IS organization, no IS leader, and no attempt to create a strategic IS vision. Instead, the autonomous units served their own user communities without an integrated strategic plan.

When the new university president took office during the fall of 1991, he faced serious budgetary problems. The state budget, which provides 45% of the university income, failed to keep up with inflation. Faculty salaries were below national averages, student enrollments were dropping by about 5% annually, and fixed costs for utilities and IT were increasing. The board raised tuition by 20% to somewhat offset enrollment declines, but the majority of the budget adjustments were to come from cost reductions.

In the area of IT, the president's main agenda was cost reductions. In particular, he was concerned about the high cost of running three mainframe data centers at the main campus. He felt that the data centers should be consolidated, but doubted that the strong autonomous units would willingly sacrifice their data centers. These circumstances preceded the insourcing project.

The Insourcing Project

The insourcing project actually began as an outsourcing project. At the beginning of 1992, two large outsourcing vendors approached the president and promised savings of over $1 million off the combined $12 million budget for the hospital, main campus, and university IS facilities. The president was highly amenable to the idea and made a preliminary proposal to the board of curators. In conjunction with the outsourcing proposal, he decided to create a new CIO position to overcome the "turf wars" and manage the outsourcing evaluation. He decided to recruit candidates from industry rather than from higher education. In March 1992, Paul was selected as their new CIO.

Paul has 35 years' experience in IT and has worked all over the world. He had a proven record in business and product development. In his last assignment, he marketed outsourcing services for a large outsourcing company. On June 1 of 1992, Paul commenced his position as CIO. Because of his background with the outsourcing vendor, the university IS staff and users assumed he would immediately outsource the three data centers to his previous employer. He says he was "as welcome as Darth Vader." Paul maintains, however, that he had no preconceived commitment to outsourcing. Although there was pressure to outsource, Paul convinced the president to postpone the outsourcing evaluation after studying the situation for one month:

> "When I came in, we had from an outsourcing vendor's perspective the perfect situation . . . we didn't have a plan, we didn't know where we wanted to go. We only had a 12-month budget for applications. We had no view of what the future was going to be, how long we would be on mainframes. Why were we on mainframes and what were our own real abilities to drive down our current costs? So I took outsourcing off the table because we didn't have a plan, a way to deal with the people, or any of the things I thought we needed in place to go do outsourcing. We didn't have metrics. So what service levels would we hold an outsourcer to?"

The president agreed to postpone the outsourcing evaluation on the condition that Paul would deliver the $1 million in savings he promised the board of curators. Paul agreed and decided to develop an IS vision which included cost reductions, data center consolidation, and a detailed technology plan for the next six years. Each of his actions are explained below.

Reduce Current Costs

Paul decided that major cost savings could be achieved before an actual physical consolidation. In particular, he reorganized the IS department and subsequently reduced the headcount, consolidated maintenance support, and reduced software license fees. These actions, which are further explained below, saved the university $1.3 million off the operating budget. In addition, Paul convinced the hospital to buy used equipment rather than new, which reduced the proposed capital budget by $3 million.

Paul felt that the staff could be reorganized and consolidated before closing any of the data centers. A new organization, called university computing services (UCS), was created. The director of UCS, who reports through the main campus, is responsible for operations, production services, technical support, and administration of data center operations. Paul decided to organize the UCS along areas of technical expertise to facilitate headcount reduction:

> "So we've done the organizational consolidation. We got all the people together. We started to organize them more along skill groups instead of all these independent data centers."

Prior to the organizational consolidation, 110 full-time equivalents staffed the three data centers. Through early retirements, transfers, resignations, and terminations, Paul eliminated 24 positions for a total savings of $613 718 per year. The headcounts came from the following functions:

Administrative support	4
Customer support	5
Operations	7
Technical support	8.5
	24.5

In addition to the organizational consolidation, Paul felt hardware and software cost reductions were possible. He noted, for example, that hardware maintenance costs for the university data centers were $976 290 per year. Paul describes the situation:

> "We previously let each organization deal with maintenance separately. In front of consolidating because it took some time to do it, we finally got all three organizations to put out a joint request for proposal. The result of the RFP is we are now going to spend less on hardware maintenance for all mainframe related equipment, CPU, disk drives, tape drives."

By pooling the maintenance requests together, Paul saved $460 912 dollars or 47.2% off maintenance fees.

Paul also reviewed the university's software license agreements and negotiated some better deals. For example, the university spent $80 000 a year for a mainframe database management system which was used primarily for an alumni development application. Paul planned to move the application off the mainframe. He negotiated with the software vendor and became an advanced customer. The software vendor waived the license fee until the application is moved to a smaller platform.

Paul also noted the hospital had budgeted $4 million for a new mainframe to accommodate growth. Paul convinced the hospital to forego their ES9000 computer and instead upgrade their 200S to a 300S at a cost of $1 million. Paul firmly believes that organizations can literally save millions by purchasing used equipment.

Consolidate Data Centers

After Paul reduced costs, he was ready to begin consolidation. He believes that most organizations attribute too much savings to data center consolidation because they include cost reduction items as mentioned above:

"So what we had done, we had driven a lot of costs out before consolidation. Now we have a plan to consolidate. By consolidating we can save another $750 000 dollars, that's all savings simply from consolidation, not throwing previous possible reductions into the pool. Not a lot of organizations have been able to say, 'okay, if I just go try to run these shops efficiently, here's how much I can get out, then here's the additional amount I can get from consolidation.' In most cases, it's all swept up together. So we have a pure picture of what consolidation will do for us financially."

Because of dissention among the three IS groups involved, Paul requested the assistance of a consulting firm to review and verify the university's consolidation plans. The consulting firm had only five weeks beginning in April of 1993 to conduct interviews and develop several consolidation scenarios. The three scenarios were as follows:

1 Consolidate the system and hospital data centers at the hospital data center and upgrade to an IBM 600S.
2 Consolidate all three data centers at the main campus data center and upgrade to an IBM 300S.
3 Consolidate the main campus and the system at the main campus data center and upgrade to an IBM 600S.

Each scenario had unique benefits. Scenario one was desirable because of the similar data processing requirements of the system and hospital—both support on-line business transactions during the day and batch processing at night. Scenario two was desirable because the maximum dollars could be saved if all three data centers were consolidated. Scenario three was the easiest to achieve from an organizational perspective because the IS managers at the system and main campus computing functions have traditionally cooperated to deliver services to essentially the same user community.

The financials for each scenario were calculated over a period of five years. In each case, the university would incur expenses for DASD expansion and mainframe upgrade. The total expenditure in millions of dollars over a five-year period for each of the scenarios is as follows:

No consolidation	33.9
Consolidate system and hospital	31.7
Consolidate all three	31.1
Consolidate system and main campus	32.8

The total one-time costs for each of the scenarios as well as the total savings over a five-year period are shown in Table 3.2.

Table 3.2

	Initial costs	5-Year savings
Consolidate system and hospital	$966 000	$2 122 000
Consolidate all three	$1 290 000	$2 720 000
Consolidate system and main campus	$1 078 000	$1 091 000

After reviewing the scenarios, Paul decided to begin with scenario one, the system and the hospital. This was the easiest to technically implement because both centers run on an MVS environment and have similar on-line and batch requirements. The five-year savings for this scenario are derived from:

1 Reduction of salaries and benefits through specialization and real-ignment of data center functions. Although most of these benefits have already been achieved through the organizational consolidation, an additional saving of $740 000 is projected.
2 Reduction in software license fees by $500 000. The system and hospital use much of the same software, such as MVS and IMS. The university will now only purchase one license rather than two.
3 Reduction in hardware maintenance by $480 000.
4 Reduction in utilities by $500 000.
5 Savings on new hardware costs for upgrades, storage, etc. of $84 000.

The approximate cost of this scenario—$190 000—includes the building upgrade costs. The new data center will have capacity for 120 MIPS.

The consolidation was to be completed by the end of 1993. Paul was still deciding whether to eventually consolidate the main campus computing. He was considering moving many of the applications to a smaller platform, such as UNIX.

In conjunction with the data center consolidation, Paul plans to abandon the archaic chargeback systems and replace them with service level agreements (SLAs). Paul explains:

> "We believe it's in our best interests as we build this plan and as we transition to client server, not to have chargeback and force independent departments to try and make decisions, get out from the chargeback and raise the level of investment across the system."

SLAs will serve as a contract between UCS and their customers. The SLA is viewed as a vehicle to articulate, improve, and commit to delivering quality services. SLAs, which describe the service level and price, are being developed for all services provided by the UCS such as on-line Customer Information Control System (CICS), CMS, and TSO sessions, batch production, data storage, printing, and remote connects. As users' needs change, the SLA can be renegotiated.

Develop a Strategic IS Vision

Paul feels that one of his primary responsibilities as CIO is to create a unified vision of IT. This includes the creation of a vision statement and aligning the IS plans with the university's plans. The president's advisory committee on computing created the following vision statement during June of 1993:

> "The University recognizes computer and information technology are strategic assets that are vital to the University's future. The University will develop computing and information technologies so within five years the University is recognized as a national leader in using computing to maximize higher education's instructional, research, and service missions. The use of computing and information technologies will be an integral part of every student's undergraduate, graduate, or professional degree experience. Student knowledge of computer and information technology tools and techniques will be enhanced via the pursuit of a university degree."

The specific plans to meet this vision include the completion of a university network, a move to client/server architecture, increase in instructional technology, research technology, and upgrade library systems. Each of these plans are briefly summarized:

1 *University network.* The completion of the network which connects all the colleges and campuses is a top priority. The network will enable collaboration for research, teaching, and service.
2 *Client/server architecture.* The university plans to move many systems off the mainframe to client/server architecture. Each application is now being reviewed for possible migration. The consulting firm that reviewed the consolidation plan speculates that the university may abandon mainframe operations after five years.
3 *Instruction.* Some campuses at the university have advanced computer instruction labs where each student has access to a personal computer networked to the instructor's workstation. Some professors are using software such as group decision support systems and hypertext in these classrooms. The university is committed to increasing the use of computers in the classroom by providing faculty with workshops, faculty support in the use of computerized

classrooms, money for new course development, and upgrades to classroom technology.

4   *Library*. Significant dollars (about $3 million) will continue to be spent on library technology. The new library system will integrate the four campuses. This will allow efficient circulation, acquisition, cataloging, and access to library resources. Client/server technology will be used for periodicals and other computerized databases.

5   *Research*. The university plans to provide faculty with technology to facilitate research, such as high speed workstations, massively parallel computing, high resolution graphics, and visualization laboratories.

Senior Management's Perceptions of IS after Insourcing

In the past year, some of the board of curators and the president of the university have begun to take a strategic view of IT. Paul describes the change:

> "If you break it into the general officers: the president, the vice president of academic affairs, the vice president of administrative affairs and the four chancellors on each campus, it's a mixed view, but they have moved that information technology is of strategic importance to the university. That completing our network, integrating more technology into the curricula, trying to plan IS activities in an integrated fashion with voice, video, and data, it's extremely important."

The president, in particular, has bought into the concept that IT is a strategic resource. He has publically stated that he plans to spend the savings from the insourcing project on new IS investments—quite a change of heart from last year when he planned to outsource the entire function.

The change in senior management's perceptions is largely attributed to Paul's leadership in setting an IS vision as well as a member of the board of curators who has begun to champion IS. On Paul's part, he successfully transformed the autonomous IS organizations which were about to be outsourced into a unified function of strategic significance. He accomplished this task despite higher education's political bureaucracy, which he describes as significantly more challenging than private organizations:

> "My experience in business, sooner or later debate has to end and there was always this sense that you had to go do this, this was the corporate will, this was the way to go. In higher education, there is no such thing as the corporate will, therefore, the process for reaching agreement, whether it's unanimous or majority, takes more time and more energy. The amount of talking

and consensus building one has to do in this environment is a lot more than you do in a business organization."

His efforts to build consensus on the direction of IS have obviously worked because the university president has made public statements supporting Paul's strategic IS vision. For example, in a recent edition of the university press, the president described IT as the key to knowledge distribution in the future:

"I am convinced that we are moving toward the day when hard copy periodicals, manuscripts, and books for mass distribution will be a rarity, and the information provided through these conventional forms will be available at our fingertips. Storage will become less and less an issue; expertise and equipment for electronic storage and retrieval of information will be essential."

Paul explained that senior management's perceptions of IS have improved due to a telecommunications committee headed by one of the members of the board. Paul explains:

"He formed a curators' committee on telecommunications. He has been pushing the university on the use of technology to deliver its mission of instruction, research, and service. He's got three curators on the committee that he's now educated pretty well. They are for it. The others, it's more of a layman issue—tell us what you want to do and why."

Conclusion

FIRM16 is somewhat of an anomaly compared to our other cases in that the CIO was able to implement cost reduction strategies without actually going through a formal outsourcing evaluation. Indeed, the CIO went so far as to terminate the outsourcing evaluation. Despite not having the threat of outsourcing to provide the ammunition for adopting service reduction strategies, he was nevertheless able to achieve insourcing savings of several million dollars, while creating a unified IS vision and convincing his management that IS is a strategic resource that can be used for competitive advantage to attract students. The case clearly shows what can happen when IS is empowered to make decisions.

FIRM17

Introduction

Like FIRM16, the senior management at FIRM17 were committed to outsourcing their data center operations to a third party vendor. The IS staff felt that they could reduce costs on their own, but it was only after a benchmarking service corroborated that FIRM17 could reduce costs on their own that senior management reconsidered. In less than four years, FIRM17's data center operations have gone from one of the most costly data centers in the country to one of the least. FIRM17 was able to reduce costs from $18 million to $10.3 million while simultaneously doubling their workload. Unlike most cases where savings come from consolidation, FIRM17's savings were incurred within the scope of one data center. Thus, IS managers operating only one center may read this case to discover new opportunities to reduce IS costs.

Since the insourcing project began in 1988, FIRM17 has suffered much turnover. Of those intimately involved in the outsourcing and subsequent insourcing decision, only Albert, the data center director, remains. He provided the political and contextual details of the decision. In addition, Tony, the president of the benchmarking service who helped FIRM17 identify savings, was also interviewed. He provided significant details and documentation on the insourcing project. Finally, two FIRM17 systems analysts provided information on the company history, organizational structure, and background of the IS department.

Company Background

FIRM17 is a *Fortune* 100 food manufacturing company employing 56 000 people worldwide. In 1992, FIRM17 had annual sales of $7 billion and net profit of $315 million. Throughout most of FIRM17's history, the culture has been described by employees as "family-oriented." During the 1980s, the culture began to change as new businesses were acquired and some traditional businesses were sold. FIRM17 purchased three manufacturing companies that specialized in different businesses [we shall call them Alpha, Beta, and Gamma]. These new acquisitions, along with falling profits due to increased competition in the market, had caused senior management to abandon their family mentality in favor of a hard-lined, cost-conscious style. Albert describes the change in culture:

> "FIRM17 was initially a [food] company. . . . We had sold some businesses in the early 80s and we acquired two companies from the east coast. Prior to that, everyone talked about the FIRM17 family. It was a family-oriented business, very traditional, kind of big brotherly. Everybody liked everybody because you've been around them forever. You've grown up together. When the companies came in from the east coast, they didn't want to be here. They didn't want to be part of the company. They hated FIRM17. It was a totally different environment."

During the 1980s, the centralized IS department, headed by a VP of IS for the corporation, ran the corporate data center and performed managerial functions such as capacity planning and technology standards. The applications staff were assigned to the different business units, but reported through the VP of IS. The VP of IS reported to the corporate controller who in turn reported to the corporate chief financial officer (CFO). The CFO reported to the chief executive officer.

During this time, the IS department had a chargeback system based on resource units such as CPU seconds and gigabytes of DASD space. The unit price recovered the fixed costs of hardware and software licenses. This chargeback system motivated business units to request as much software as they liked because the cost would be spread over the entire company (see our discussion of the restaurant check analogy in Chapter 6).

During the acquisitions in the 1980s, FIRM17's centralized IS organization absorbed the new processing load in their MVS shop, bringing the total number of MIPS to over 180. The absorption into the corporate data center caused many political battles because the newly acquired firms wished to maintain their own data centers. Senior management forced them to close their data centers, which set up an adversarial relationship between corporate IS and the new business units. Albert characterized his new users as "captives":

> "In 1986, [Alpha and Beta] didn't want to come [to corporate IS] in the first place. They didn't want to close their data centers—a control thing, 'my car is faster than your car' thing, and my old VP had out-politicked them. He didn't sell them, he manipulated them. That's the reason why I say they were more like captives than customers."

The VP of IS tried to treat the new businesses professionally by signing a three-year, fixed price contract.

During the same period, FIRM17 sold off a company that was one of the biggest data center users. Rather than offer to become the company's outsourcer, so to speak, the VP of IS wanted to sever ties. Albert considered this decision a mistake for two reasons. First, the data center could have made a profit. Second, the company opted to outsourcing elsewhere and claimed to save a half a million a year over FIRM17's IS costs, which damaged IS's reputation. Albert describes the situation:

> "Due to a bad decision on the part of my old VP, what he was thinking— these people aren't strategic, they are a different company. There was a feeling within FIRM17 we need cut ties and burn bridges and get on with our lives. Like after a divorce. These people never complained about service

or price. They were big users, in many ways, they were a perfect customer. They had only a couple things a week they cared about. And we had it hardwired to execute those two things routinely with no trouble. The rest of the week, they didn't care what we did to them. They were the perfect customer. Anyway, they migrated off and claimed to have saved $500 000 a year. They had to say that. What they didn't say was that they had to hire 12 people which ate their savings."

This incident planted the seed that outsourcing could reduce FIRM17's IS costs.

Senior Management's Perceptions of IS before Insourcing

As will become apparent, one of the outcomes of the outsourcing evaluation was the recognition that the centralized IS function did not understand how senior management perceived IS. During the 1980s, the VP of IS mistakenly assumed that service excellence was senior management's top priority for IS. Working under this assumption, the VP of IS spent significant resources to reduce response time and provide expensive backup and recovery systems. Albert describes his boss's push for service excellence:

> "Over the years we had done a lot of things in the name of service excellence. I used to have a bunch of things in my office about excellence. The VP of IS quoted Tom Peters and all these things in the name of excellence. And a lot of extra costs had been incurred trying to be excellent. It turns out that my predecessors and others had defined excellence in their terms. Excellence is redundancy, extra software, all of those, if you were in a company who valued IS like an airline reservation, those would have been excellence."

As the VP of IS later learned as a consequence of the outsourcing evaluation, senior management did not view IS as a strategic resource. Instead, they worried more about IS costs than about service excellence. Albert notes, "There was a feeling that this was a rat hole to pour money down." As a consequence of the misalignment of IS goals with corporate goals, senior managers perceived IS as too expensive and began to consider outsourcing.

The Insourcing Project

As with many insourcing projects, it was first prompted by an outsourcing threat. After the three-year contract with one of the acquired companies [Beta] expired, the VP of corporate IS wanted to increase the price of Beta's contract to recover the costs of their growth, which had tripled in volume. The president of the group rejected the new contract and decided to outsource instead. As Albert explains, the president of Beta told the VP of IS:

> "We don't like you guys anyway, you cost way too much, you want to increase our prices, our profits are down, we want to go outside."

As the president of Beta commenced an outsourcing evaluation, the VP of IS planned a response. According to Albert, the VP of IS could not say, "I wish you luck, enjoy your savings," since for the other customers IS costs would increase because fixed costs would be spread over less volume. Instead, the VP of IS hired a benchmarking service to assess the corporate data center's service excellence. The benchmarking service focused on service quality such as response time and availability. Plotted against the benchmarking service's entire database of clients, FIRM17 fared favorably. Armed with the benchmarking report, the VP of IS falsely assumed he could compete with an outsourcer.

In the meantime, the president of Beta prepared a request for proposal (RFP). He asked the data center director to pull certain tapes off the computer, presumably to determine volumes for the RFP. The data center director obliged, but noted to himself that Beta only pulled 40% of their volumes. As Albert recalls:

> "They got what they asked for, but what they asked for wasn't what they wanted. Since they wouldn't tell me what they wanted it for, I didn't volunteer."

The Beta company prepared a one-page bid and found several outsourcers willing to charge less than the price of FIRM17's new contract proposal. According to Albert, the VP of IS finally "called in the artillery fire." He decided to expand the outsourcing contract to include the entire data center. He told management that if outsourcing could reduce IS costs for one business unit, it should reduce costs for all the units. Of course, this was merely a political maneuver because the VP of IS assumed outsourcing would not reduce costs if the entire data center was included in the evaluation. Once it was decided to expand the outsourcing proposal, the VP of IS was fired.

The old VP of IS was replaced by a manager from the business side of the company who knew very little about IT. He was told to "straighten out" the outsourcing evaluation. He began to call some outsourcing vendors, none of which responded to the outsourcing query. Albert explains:

"Early on, he came over, he called some outsourcers—he said, 'We have X amount of computer, X amount of disk, my budget is X, can you do it cheaper?' He had no idea what he was doing, but he made some early calls. They get a lot of these calls and it's people trying to justify their existence. They say, 'we're not interested.' They hang up. So he was naive enough to say, 'okay.' And hung up. He decided this is a cost effective organization."

The controller and business unit leaders, however, continued to push for a formal outsourcing evaluation. Albert was brought into IS from one of the business units and appointed head of the outsourcing evaluation project. He describes his assignment as follows:

"I got to be captain of the *Titanic*. So they gave me the captain's hat and said, 'There are the icebergs . . . have at it.' "

As leader of the project, Albert was concerned about several things: losing his key staff before the outsourcing evaluation was completed, educating himself on how outsourcers propose to save their clients money, and wondering whether FIRM17 could reduce costs on their own. Albert handled each of these concerns as follows.

Albert worried that the outsourcing evaluation would prompt key staff members to seek employment elsewhere, thus degrading IS service quality. As Albert explains:

"[We needed] to keep the service quality up. It's one thing to go through an outsourcing evaluation for costing, because it's an open market, a commodity, all this stuff and I believe that to a degree, but it's another thing if the quality is so low you can't run a business, you don't care what it costs, you have to do something. So the major risk was if the service dropped, [the business units] were going to leave regardless of the cost outcome, because you are not going to do business with someone who hates you. So, keeping the key people here and happy, kept the overall department going."

To protect his key staff, Albert created an internal "save the data center task force" manned by his key technical employees. As part of a retention package, they were given $2000 bonuses every three months. In return, the employees promised not to tell anyone about the retention package.

The task force, in addition to retaining key employees, also served the purpose of investigating the possibility of reducing costs through insourcing. Although Albert felt outsourcing was a foregone conclusion because of the politics involved, he took two steps to ensure the insourcing bid would be fair. First, he requested the assistance of a corporate financial analyst who had no vested interest in the outcome. Albert describes the analyst's role:

"His job was to bring the facts to light in an unbiased manner and ensure the analysis was above board. His job wasn't at risk, he wasn't a customer, he had no vested interests. He gave us credibility in the end that we could not have gotten another way."

Albert also brought in another benchmarking service whose philosophy and methods were radically different from FIRM17's previous benchmarking service. First, this benchmarking service focuses on cost efficiency, not service excellence. Second, the benchmarking service compares clients to a best of breed reference group rather than their entire database of clients; best of breed comparisons provide a better view of the client's competitiveness in the market. Third, the benchmarking service guarantees to identify concrete cost reductions rather than just delivering a set of reports. Compared to the previous benchmarking service that identified FIRM17 as cost-effective, this benchmarking firm claimed FIRM17 was highly inefficient. Albert used the benchmarking report to help prepare the 50-page RFP as well as the internal bid.

The insourcing bid proposed to reduce costs by 40%. Savings were driven by a change in philosophy from service excellence to cost efficiency. All the redundant hardware, software, and people were to be eliminated. Data operations management was to be significantly reduced. Automation software was to replace technical staff. The general allocation chargeback system, which motivated inefficient use of services, was to be eliminated.

As the internal task force prepared their bid, Albert investigated the outsourcing market. But this was 1988—just before Kodak brought outsourcing into vogue. Because he ran a 180 MIP center, Albert concluded that outsourcers should not have significant economies of scale over his shop. He reasoned that both his and an outsourcer's unit costs decrease over time and suspected that outsourcers bid less than their costs in the first year to secure the contract. In future years, they compensate for the loss as unit costs decrease and profits increase. When he explained the concept to senior management, they responded as follows:

"The guy doing it [championing outsourcing] was a controller. He had no grasp of anything technical. I told him if you give me a five year contract, I'll give you a fixed price. He looked at me and said, 'but your costs go down every year.' I said, 'Sure—what do you think an outsourcer does?' There was no conception that that was related."

The RFP went out in the fall of 1988. When four outsourcers responded, the VP of IS was surprised. As Albert explains:

"I talked to him later, he said, 'I don't understand, I tried to do this and no one quoted me numbers like this.' Even one of the salesman said, 'No one took you seriously. We get a lot of those calls.' "

FIRM17 entered into heavy negotiations in September. Two vendors promptly dropped out—one of which promised to increase service excellence even though they could not reduce IS costs. As Albert was well aware, FIRM17's outsourcing decision was not based on service quality. The remaining bidders bid $1 million less than current IS costs of 18 million. After a few rounds, the outsourcing vendor most determined to win the contract dropped their bid to $15 million. Eventually, they dropped their bid to the same as the internal bid, around $12 million. As Albert noted, "Essentially their price was whatever it needed to be to get the contract."

Albert's bid was slightly more favorable from a financial viewpoint because costs would significantly drop off as the inflated book value of IS assets depreciated. Albert told management:

"For the first year, costs were similar, but then I had things dropping off with depreciation. I said, 'If you can hang with us [we'll save you more].' Not all those were cash off, some were depreciation. That's where the financial analyst helped clarify this stuff."

Senior management accepted the internal bid and strong-armed the business units to maintain processing at the corporate data center. Albert explains that Beta was particularly displeased but conceded to management:

"[Beta] only stayed with us to be a good corporate citizen. They firmly believe they could have saved a million on the outside. The other [business units] said, 'If you do all these changes, your quality will go down so low, you can't function like this . . . you'll have to add costs or outsource.' "

Once Albert won the bid, he had to deliver on the promised 40% savings. Albert accomplished this by changing the entire philosophical orientation of the data center from service excellence to cost efficiency. As part of the philosophical change, he changed the chargeback structure to motivate efficient use of resources, eliminated unneeded services, reorganized the department to eliminate redundant employees, empowered the remaining staff, eliminated the redundant hardware and software his predecessor installed to protect service, automated functions, changed his acquisition of policy from "just-in-case" resources to "just-in-time" resources, standardized service options, and reduced DASD. Each of these actions, of which many were often identified and facilitated by the benchmarking service, is described below.

Change the Chargeback Structure

A major philosophical change was the abandonment of the general allocation chargeback system in favor of an unbundled pricing strategy practiced by most outsourcing vendors. Albert describes the switch:

> "[Outsourcing vendors] price like a Sunday paper car—you get a Ford Mustang for $4000. Then if you want a radio, good tires—by the time you are through, it's a $13 000 car. And so we changed our philosophy to the same thing. Our internal customers can buy very basic data center services at a Sunday paper price."

Users now purchase a block of computer time that comes with a standard set of software. If a business unit wants any application beyond that, Albert charges them for his exact cost of the software license fee. By unbundling the software, much of the software disappeared because users could not justify the cost to their managers. Instead, many users converted their idiosyncratic systems to the standard platform. Albert had many discussions with business unit leaders about removing certain software:

> "We had conversations such as, 'Ramis and Focus are the same language— I'm doing almost the same thing with them. It's just two different departments. If I converted my Ramis into Focus, you mean I wouldn't have to pay this $50 000? Well then I want to do that.' "

In some instances, business leaders cooperated and decided to split the costs for additional software. In essence, the new accounting system forces the business units to justify software rather than push the responsibility on IS.

Eliminate Unneeded Services

As a consequence of the change in philosophy to cost efficiency, several functions were eliminated. For example, Albert had four employees who monitored the chargeback system and created the bills based on usage. Under the new accounting system, these people were no longer needed.

Albert also eliminated the staff that performs long term capacity planning:

"Long-term capacity planning isn't valuable because company plans change so quickly. We have a 6–12 month general pattern—that's enough."

Thus, any service that was exclusively devoted to service excellence was reduced or eliminated. Users simply could not justify these functions once they knew exactly how much they cost.

Eliminate Redundant Employees

Albert realized—partly because of the benchmarks—that his data center was overstaffed. The previous VP of IS felt that functional redundancy was a key to service excellence. Albert, however, posed the following questions:

"Is excellence in redundancy or in doing a good job on things customers care about? A manager on every shift for every five people? Or do you need to make it clear to people what they are supposed to accomplish and then turn them loose? . . . If we organize like this, we can eliminate two managers, combine redundant functions. And we did all of that without impact to service quality . . . no excess outages."

Albert thus reorganized the department and eliminated several managerial positions.

With the help of the benchmarking service, Albert also reduced the number of systems programmers. The president of the benchmarking service explains:

"They had a tremendous amount of systems programmers to fine tune the data center. In order to prove themselves as a valuable asset to somebody, these people that we saw as redundant, were loading the machine as much as they could. They tuned things that didn't need to be tuned."

The redundant systems programmers were eliminated.

Empower Remaining Workers

When the department was run under the service excellence philosophy, quality assurance checks on system programming changes, migrations, and Job Control Language (JCL) changes were extensive. Under the new philosophy, Albert eliminated several people associated with these functions and instead made the staff responsible for the quality of their work. For example, Albert reduced the systems programming staff to only 5 people whereas other shops of this size may employ 20 people. Albert describes the change:

"Increasingly, we hold the person responsible for the quality of their cut-over. If they feel the need, they have access to testing, if they don't they can cut it over. If it fails, they will incur a penalty, but we are no longer big brothering it. Now there's an MVS team, they go through all the work and decide who will do it and how they will test it. The actual cutover time is documented, but we don't mandate big test plans."

Some of the systems programmers did not like the new environment and left the company. Of the remaining five programmers, Albert has full confidence in three of them, but notes that the other two have installed changes with errors. This is a consequence that FIRM17 is willing to live with.

Eliminate Redundant Hardware and Software

Albert removed the millions of dollars in equipment his previous VP of IS installed to protect response time. Although response time subsequently suffered, senior management did not complain. Albert conveys a conversation he had with the controller:

"When we were through, one of the controllers, he said, 'You cut my bill by a couple of million dollars.' [Albert said], 'yeah.' [The controller said], 'My response time is a little more erratic . . . if you made the response time slower, could you save me a couple more million dollars?'"

Automate Functions

The benchmarking service noted that FIRM17 could save significant money through automation. Through automation, FIRM17 would be able to further reduce their staff. According to the president of the benchmarking service, the automation of data communications, console operations, and network monitoring saved FIRM17 $400 000 annually.

Move to "Just-in-time" Resources

When the data center was primarily concerned with service quality, IS management bought additional backup resources in case they were needed. Under the new philosophy, Albert purchases additional resources only when they are actually needed. He explains:

"We try to buy in my motto 'Just-In-Time-MIPS,' rather than 'just-in-case.' We used to buy in reserve, thinking we'll probably need this. Now we'll buy it at the last possible minute. Well, the way market prices drop, this is perfect. The just-in-case leads you down the path of redundant equipment and maybe extra capacity. Those things are okay if you are in the right business, but the business we are in, we don't want to do that."

Standardize Service Options

The benchmarking service noted that FIRM17 spent a lot of money meeting the idiosyncratic needs of their users. For example, users could request special paper to print out reports which may vary by color, size, and logo design. The data center had employees devoted to manually changing the forms for each print job. By standardizing the forms, FIRM17 saved $115 000 annually.

Reduce DASD

Under the service excellence philosophy, users stored any data they wanted for as long as they wanted on DASD. Under the new philosophy, data not used for a given period of time was migrated off to tape for an amazing annual savings of $500 000. By optimizing the remaining DASD space, an additional $90 000 was saved.

Summary of Savings

Albert emphasizes how the change in philosophy drove the cost reductions:

"So, the real tragedy is the IS definition of excellence had nothing to do with the business definition of excellence. Had low cost, reliable service been my predecessor's definition of excellence, all this might not have happened. But responsiveness was his key measure."

Although Albert described the savings from a managerial perspective, the benchmarking firm allocated the dollars associated with the savings they identified as follows:

Reduce staff	$1 800 000
Reduce dead DASD	500 000
Reduce MIPS	400 000
Move from impact to laser printing	300 000
Automate data communications	300 000
Reduce the number of print forms	115 000
Optimize network software	90 000
Optimize disk space	90 000
Reduce printing supply costs	85 000
Outsource COM production	80 000

Automate network	60 000
Automate network monitoring	40,000
Total savings identified	
by benchmarking service	3 860 000

Although the benchmarking service accounts for about half of the dollar savings, it does not include the savings achieved from actions such as changing accounting systems. In total, FIRM17 reduced IS costs by 40% over a four-year period. The budget, which was once $18 million, is now about $10 million. The benchmarking firm that rated FIRM17 as a poor performer in 1988, presented FIRM17 with their best of breed award in 1992—FIRM17 had become the lowest cost performer compared with their database of 300 clients. Several trade magazines published the award and the VP of IS threw a party for the data center personnel. Although the insourcing project was a success, Albert enjoys few residual glories.

Senior Management's Perceptions of IS after Insourcing

One might suspect that reducing IS costs by 40% and winning national recognition for efficiency would influence senior management's perceptions of IS. Unfortunately, the president of Beta continued to believe outsourcing would have saved money and senior corporate management continues to pressure IS to justify their costs. Thus, Albert never experienced a "halo" effect from the insourcing project.

As far as the president of Beta was concerned, he still maintained that he could have saved more money through outsourcing:

> "The division who wanted to outsource continued to feel that they could have saved $1 000 000 for themselves alone if they had outsourced. Now I happen to know that we weren't comparing apples and apples. They hadn't sized everything, but by that time, emotions had been so polarized, nobody was talking about facts any more. We were talking emotions."

To counteract the president of Beta's outsourcing myths, the IS department created reports showing what outsourcing would have cost. Albert explains:

> "Another of my bosses who has also since gotten fired, he used to periodically have me prepare charts that show, had they signed, the best deal they got had they signed—it comes out to a ridiculously astronomical figure. That is accurate. It shows they never could have afforded to have grown the way they did. The business would have evolved differently."

Given that the reports were created by IS, the president of Beta viewed them with skepticism. It was not until he hired his own consultants to evaluate outsourcing that he believed insourcing was a cost efficient option:

> "Well the [president of Beta] had [a major consulting firm] in for some other reasons and the president called them in and said, 'Hey guys, I'm in this pissing match with the VP of IS, would you go and tell the guy I can get it cheaper outside?' Well they poked and prodded and examined, and I couldn't talk to them because of the politics. Anyway, they got it through to the president, they came back and told him, 'You guys are getting a good deal. You can't get it any cheaper on the outside.' So this was an unbiased consultant. Well, actually, he was biased because the guy that was paying wanted to outsource. It was a pissing match. That's what it seemed like.' '

Senior corporate management also expects Albert to demonstrate effectiveness every year. As Albert laments, "I've got to win every year." Albert notes that senior management expects concrete numbers to demonstrate efficiency. Albert explains what one business unit leader told him:

> "He kind of was up front, he said, it's the same as with the data center, you can tell me you are good, and you probably are, but I don't have any other data points that I can compare it to. You may be or may not be, I don't know how to judge."

Albert uses benchmarking and informal outsourcing evaluations to provide corroborative evidence of his efficiency. He felt that winning the benchmarking award for cost efficiency in 1992 would certainly convince senior management, but one senior executive complained that the benchmarks measured the wrong items. Albert explains:

> "He was disappointed because what they did, given an MVS data center, your costs are good. He doesn't care. He wants to know given you have a consumer products business of $2 billion—how are your costs? He was really disappointed with the benchmark because it was a narrow technical benchmark. He wants something that monitors applications, data centers, telecommunications, and business processes. For a company of your size in this business—is your inventory variance about right? Things like that."

Albert plans to continue using the benchmarking service, although he may increase the time between benchmarks.

Albert also uses a strategy that failed his boss—he informally calls outsourcing companies to "keep close" to the market. He reports to management the results of these informal inquiries. When Albert was asked how could he consider these informal inquiries as valid when he admitted his boss's informal inquiries were dismissed by the vendors, he responded that he knew more about the outsourcing market. For example, when he requested a "ball park" figure from a vendor, he always reduced that number by about half; Albert reasons that vendors always give inflated preliminary numbers. The informal outsourcing queries, besides convincing management that IS is effective, also motivates the IS staff, "I've used outsourcing as a club—it's a reality that our people have to be competitive."

The Future of IS

As noted in other cases, a successful insourcing project does not provide residual glory for IS managers. New challenges are constantly arising, especially in the area of downsizing to smaller platforms. Like many IS managers, FIRM17 is facing the issue of the role of the mainframe during this decade. Albert foresees that a centralized data center function will continue to exist, but will be devoted to supporting peer-to-peer (i.e. client/server) platforms.

At FIRM17, division users have purchased local area networks (LANs) with their discretionary funds. Fueled by optimistic vendors, users saw LANs as a way to reduce IS costs and gain control over their IS. Many of the LAN purchases were made without IS input. The result: users were disappointed with LAN security and manual backup procedures. More and more FIRM17 users are looking to Albert's organization for help. He now maintains 50 servers within the data center:

> "People call us and say, 'Can we put our server in your data center?' They worry the power will fluctuate, they don't want to hire someone at night to backup, or shut down the LAN during the day to backup. I offer them another option. I think we'll have a data center, some of these LANs may be consolidated. If there are 46, may drop to 30 or 20. We'll have a data center in the future with controlled access, air conditioning, power, and security."

With the change in platforms, Albert sees the mainframe as a big server. He describes the current integration between LANs and the mainframe:

> "New applications at FIRM17 are essential, they use the mainframe as a big server. They enter an order, validate it, price it, then they shift it to the mainframe and ask, 'Is there enough inventory? When's it going to ship?' Just use the mainframe for the back end of the process. Those applications, the mainframe is not involved in every keystroke, but may be a big server. So I think data centers will survive."

Albert has embraced the change in technology enthusiastically, providing vital support services to LANs. He foresees the day when all data centers will be like Microsoft's data center—a centralized place to service peer-to-peer technology.

Conclusion

Like FIRM15, FIRM17's senior management continue to have doubts about the efficiency of IS even though its IS costs are benchmarked to be best of breed. Even with this objective data, management continues to believe that somehow IS could be done less expensively. Apparently, since IS is not perceived as a strategic component of the corporation, senior management refuses to take IS seriously. So like FIRM15, just reducing costs is not enough to fundamentally alter management's perception of IS. Other tactics are needed such as a politically astute CIO who is well connected to senior management.

FIRM18

Introduction

In 1991, FIRM18 participated in our research project on outsourcing decisions. At that time, FIRM18 had just rejected two outsourcing bid proposals in favor of an aggressive insourcing bid which promised to cut annual data processing costs from $32 million to just $20 million. We revisited FIRM18 during the summer of 1993 to determine whether their insourcing objectives were achieved. Indeed, they were—FIRM18 exceeded their insourcing proposal by reducing costs to $18 million. In addition to a data center consolidation which greatly reduced headcounts, they implemented novel approaches for software licenses and chargeback systems which other IS managers may find insightful.

In 1991, two managers were interviewed for this case. James, corporate manager of planning and administration, was a member of the steering committee in charge of the outsourcing evaluation. Matthew, manager in a pipeline subsidiary, wrote a thorough report on FIRM18's outsourcing decision for an MBA class. In 1993, three additional IS managers were interviewed. Murray, corporate manager of technology development, was responsible for implementing the insourcing proposal. Lou, manager of software strategies, created the insourcing proposal along with the other members of the internal response team. Bret, manager of computer strategies, initiated many of the cost-saving strategies used to achieve insourcing objectives. In addition to the interviews, the following documents were gathered: the RFP, an insourcing progress report, the internal bid, quantitative and qualitative bid analysis results, benchmark results, chargeback bill, annual reports, organizational charts, and published articles on the insourcing decision.

Company Background

FIRM18, a *Fortune* 100 company that employs over 52 000 people in 60 countries, produces oil, natural gas, and industrial chemicals. Financially, FIRM18 flourished during the 1960s and 1970s, but suffered severe losses in the latter 1980s. To make dividend payments from 1985 to 1990, FIRM18 had to acquire a $9 million debt. In 1990, after losing almost $2 billion the previous year, the senior management decided to restructure the company by concentrating on their core competencies. By selling off non-strategic businesses, such as their coal division, FIRM18 increased their competitive position and enjoyed positive earnings in 1991. In 1992, the company suffered another financial loss on sales of $10 billion, which the CEO attributed to the weak economy and worldwide overproduction in petroleum products. The CEO responded by cutting annual operating costs by $300 million and capital spending by $150 million. Because petroleum and chemical companies cannot dictate the price of their products, cost reductions are the primary means to ensure competitiveness.

Until the past few years, FIRM18 operated highly autonomous divisions each with their own data center. IS service in each division was satisfactory as determined by peer benchmarks. The divisional IS managers implemented most of the business units' requests for software, so there was high satisfaction with IS performance. Murray describes the situation:

> "IS at FIRM18, the divisions had had a lot of autonomy. They had their own data centers. If they could cost justify it or they felt in their business plan they wanted to control their destiny, they did what they wanted to do. We had a loose federation if you will, some standards, a common network so we could talk from data center to data center over a network, but there was a pretty strong autonomy. There were no dissatisfactions in performance *per se* in terms of the product that we produced. Availability was fine, we had historically done some peer group benchmarking and we were at or beneath the medium."

In 1991, FIRM18 operated three of these autonomous data centers. The largest data center provided services for corporate accounting and finance, oil and gas, and the pipeline. According to an internal document, this data center provided "all things to all people" and was seen as the Saks Fifth Avenue of data centers. The second largest data center supported chemicals. This data center was more cost-conscious and supported fewer products, but was responsive to the idiosyncratic needs of the chemical business. This center was viewed as the Walmart of data centers. The last data center primarily supported the coal business, which was just sold this year. In total, all three data centers operated 200 MIPs.

The chargeback system for these data centers was a general allocation system. When users requested a new software package, costs would be spread over all users, thus encouraging excessive software demand. According to Murray, monthly chargeback bills did not motivate the divisions to cut usage. Instead, users explained away billing aberrations with such excuses as "there were more billing days in a certain month" or "the rates changed." Bret sums up the chargeback system as "a mystery for users and a source of embarrassment for IS." Senior management's view of IS at the time seems to be partly attributable to the chargeback system.

Senior Management's Perceptions of IS before Insourcing

According to participants, senior management at the corporation viewed IS as a cost burden while divisional managers viewed IS favorably because their needs were aptly serviced. James describes the CEO's view of systems prior to insourcing as follows:

> "All they (senior management) see is this amount of money that they have to write a check for every year. Year after year after year. Where is the benefit? IS says, 'Well, we process data faster than we did last year.' They say, 'So what?' IS says, 'Well, we can close the ledger faster.' And they say, 'So what? Where have you increased revenue? All you do is increase costs, year after year after year and I am sick of it. All I get are these esoteric benefits and a bunch of baloney on how much technology has advanced. Show me where you put one more dollar on the income statement.'"

Senior management believed that IS was too expensive and suspected that savings could be achieved through data center consolidation. The CFO noted, for example, that the largest data center employed 24 systems programmers and the next largest data center employed 12 systems programmers. Through consolidation, the CFO figured he could reduce system programming costs by $1 million. The divisional managers, on the other hand, balked at the idea—they liked having control over their own data centers. In 1988, Murray heard the CEO of chemicals say:

"If it cost me five million more dollars to have this in my business unit and be able to control it and make it responsive to my needs, it's worth five million dollars to me."

Murray said senior management abandoned the idea because "for one million bucks, it wasn't worth the drama. The politics were too severe."

The Outsourcing Decision

In 1991, Matthew, a pipeline manager, claimed that FIRM18 considered outsourcing as a way to reduce IS costs for three reasons. First, his management believed the published reports that outsourcing could reduce IS costs by 25–50%. Second, he suspected that vendors had contacted the CEO and were offering him tremendous savings. Third, he states that management perceived that IS was costing them too much money, over $130 million per year ($32 million of which was data processing). Two years later, Murray corroborated these reasons with more detail.

In April of 1990, the corporate chief operating officer (COO), read in *Fortune* magazine that Kodak reduced IS costs through outsourcing. Murray explains the COO's reaction:

"The COO of the parent—the number three guy, if you take chairman as top, president as number two, COO as number three, made a statement after reading in *Business Week* and *Fortune* and every other magazine about Kodak outsourcing. He said, IS costs too much. He read that you ought to be able to get 25 or 30% savings if you outsource. So, whether he believed it or not, he said, '25%, that number looks like this. I think we should be able to do the same thing.'"

Senior management created an outsourcing steering committee, comprised of the CFOs from the major divisions. The committee was chaired by the director of IS, although he was forbidden to vote. At first the committee limited the decision to the three data centers. James describes the committee's function:

"The steering committee was assigned the responsibility for doing all of the analysis, review, whatever needed to be done, and then to make a proposal to (FIRM18) senior management saying this is our recommendation: we should outsource and we should outsource using vendor X, or we should retain it in-house and here is why."

Soon after the committee was formed, outsourcing vendors descended upon FIRM18 promising significant savings. The vendors requested information about FIRM18's operations, costs, and headcounts. At first, senior managers just sent the vendors to the data center sites and instructed the IS managers to cooperate. When Murray received such a call, he responded:

> "I got a call from the IS director, 'so and so is coming to your data center.' I said, 'That's interesting, What am I supposed to do?' 'Well, give them all your leases, give them all this stuff—whatever they ask for.' I said, 'Absolutely not. This is no different than a business decision to sell a business. I propose, what I think we should do is learn from our brothers who sell oil and gas properties regularly, how do you do that? Every bidder has to be treated the same way, an arm's length relationship.' "

In addition to these informal visits, one vendor convinced the steering committee to expand the outsourcing decision to cover all IS functions—data processing, telecommunications, system development, maintenance, and support. The vendor asked senior management, "Why limit savings to 25% on data processing when you could save 25% on the whole IS budget?" The corporate COO was particularly enthusiastic about expanding the scope of the decision. The division leaders, however, requested that outsourcing be accomplished in phases. The steering committee agreed to limit the decision to the data centers. If outsourcing worked well in these areas, the rest of the functions could be outsourced later.

The steering committee, which swayed with the wind, decided to hire an outside consulting firm to help them develop an RFP and to benchmark existing operations. The consulting firm had previously helped other clients develop RFPs and evaluate outsourcing bids by normalizing them to ensure fair comparisons.

The IS manager convinced the steering committee to allow an internal response team to develop their own bid. Senior management was skeptical . . . if IS could reduce costs on their own, why have they not already? The strong autonomous units had previously stonewalled consolidation, but clearly senior management's commitment to cost reduction could overcome internal politics. Murray explains the plea for the internal response team:

> "The IS management said that there is no reason we should be excluded from the party. You cannot assume, it's not fair to say that we'll just do what we've been doing. We ought to have the same freedom to make decisions that these outsourcers are making. So IS management in each of the divisions caucused. We put together a team."

The internal response team was chaired by the head of data processing from the largest data center. Lou served on the team, as well as representatives from the other data centers. The team was removed from their positions and moved to an out of state location for three months to work on a bid in isolation.

James notes that the committee displayed no favoritism towards the internal IS bid:

"The internal bid committee was treated exactly like the outside vendors. They didn't have any information given to them that the others weren't given. They were to respond in the same length of time that the outside vendors were."

The internal team made five assumptions about their bid. First, their bid had to win on costs. They assumed the steering committee would not select the internal bid if it cost even one dollar more than the vendor bids. Second, they would use the consulting firms' target number of $20 million. Based on the benchmarks, the internal response team believed their bid would be competitive at this price. Third, they abandoned the philosophy that hardware was a strategic asset. Instead, they adopted management's view that hardware is a commodity. This change in philosophy would help them abandon their allegiance to certain products and hardware vendors. Fourth, they were going to change the philosophy from excellent service to cost efficiency. Rather than tweak every piece of software to meet idiosyncratic needs, software would be used as is. Fifth, automation was seen as a key strategy for reducing headcount.

Before they could prepare a bid based on these assumptions, the internal response team wanted users to commit to their volume for the next five years. In the past, capacity planning was rather informal, based on historical data. Murray recalls:

"In the past, we said, well we grew out of the last one in so many months, the next machine is so much of an increment, the growth path looks like this, the current machine will last this long. That was about as state of the art as we got."

The internal response team explained that users had to commit to their volumes over the next five years or else the bid would be invalid. As Murray explains, "those lines of business understood that they were signing in blood." The vendors were also given the growth estimates.

The RFP, which was completed in the summer of 1990, requested bids for a five-year contract on data processing. Although many RFPs require vendors to assume responsibility for the entire IS staff, FIRM18 did not require that the staff be transferred. As long as a vendor responded to the base RFP, FIRM18 welcomed alternatives as far as the transfer of people, hardware, and software was concerned.

The RFP contained only volume data to prevent vendors from "backing into a number." Because the internal response team was aware of FIRM18's costs, some may contend that they had an advantage over outside bidders. Bret denies this allegation because the internal team did not know the vendors' cost structures:

> "Yeah, but they know what their cost structure is too. EDS knows what they can do it for as much as you know what you can do it for. You don't know what their costs are, they could have given you a much lower bid. So I would contend, that's the right way to do it. You are selling yourself short if you give them all your costs, they won't give you their best number."

Of the three outsourcing vendors invited to bid, only two responded. One vendor refused to bid because the scope of the outsourcing evaluation excluded applications support and development. One vendor, who will be referred to as Vendor A, submitted a bid that indicated a 32% savings in data processing costs. The other vendor's bid—Vendor B—submitted a bid that was actually 9% higher than current IS costs. The internal bid committee submitted a bid that reduced IS costs by 43%.

James explained the discrepancy in bid amounts. The internal bid committee was able to reduce costs by proposing to consolidate the three data centers into one. Vendor A proposed the same action, which is why its bid is commensurable with the internal bid. Vendor B proposed that FIRM18 dismantle all its data centers and run its systems through the vendor's data center. The cost to convert systems to Vendor B's center increased the price.

In addition to comparing costs, the steering committee also made a qualitative assessment of the bids based on nine factors, including the quality of service, contract flexibility, and control over technical decisions (see Table 3.3).

For each factor, the bids were rated on a Likert scale with three choices: advantage over current operations, no advantage (i.e. equal to current operations), or disadvantage over current operations. FIRM18 emerged as the preferred candidate because it had the greatest cost advantage and no noted disadvantages. Vendor A and Vendor B were both deemed as disadvantages on the contract flexibility factor—the steering committee feared that all outsourcing contracts are too binding. In addition, Vendor A's culture clashed with FIRM18's culture. Vendor B's costs were too high.

The insourcing project was successful because senior management supported a change in IS philosophy. Rather than have IS service

Table 3.3   *FIRM18's qualitative bid comparison*

Criteria	Firm18	Vendor A	Vendor B
Cost	Advantage	Advantage	Disadvantage
Service level	No advantage	No advantage	No advantage
Flexibility	No advantage	Disadvantage	Disadvantage
Control	No advantage	No advantage	No advantage
Security	No advantage	No advantage	No advantage
Technical expertise	No advantage	No advantage	No advantage
Business expertise	No advantage	No advantage	No advantage
Consulting skills	No advantage	No advantage	No advantage
Cultural compatibility	No advantage	Disadvantage	No advantage

localized needs, IS would operate as a low cost provider of computer services. Lou explains:

"Organizational philosophy, it was changed. We were not going to be all things to all people. We were not going to be a service organization. The company at this point in time wanted low cost computing power. So we weren't going to go out and study neat things."

Most importantly, senior management supported this change in philosophy and empowered IS to implement necessary strategies to reduce costs. Murray explains:

"This is critical: this is the first time someone handed an IS guy a stick. In the past, I know what happened in [the largest data center] because we were serving lots of lines of business, if a company came and said, 'I want this new piece of software, I need it.' Bingo, we went out and bought it. That doesn't happen anymore. In fact, the opposite happens. They couldn't just go buy something for their special needs, we wouldn't pay for it."

Bret concurs that the insourcing project was successful because senior management gave IS the power to implement cost cuts:

"With a real tight management core, we didn't have all these levels any-more, there was three of us under Murray. When we thought of something innovative we could do it. Like Murray would say, 'Why do I need all these monitor vendors?' We'd go think about it. Then we said, 'Let's go do this.' Then we did it. We didn't have to go to [senior management] or the users, we had the stick. With three or four of us, we made 90% of these macro level decisions. Decisions were made real easily. I'd walk into Murray's office and say, 'Let's try this.' And we would—there were no studies. That was a big philosophical change. We were able to try things. We put the rigor into the task instead of trying to justify and make pretty the idea itself."

Once empowered by senior management's support, Murray and his staff implemented many cost-saving strategies. A new chargeback mechanism was implemented, data centers were consolidated, a "fixed-fee" service including a "meat and potatoes" software portfolio was offered, new hard-nosed deals were negotiated with software and hardware vendors, and the remaining staff was empowered. Each of these changes are described below.

Change the Chargeback Structure

As previously noted, the chargeback system before the insourcing project motivated excessive usage for two reasons. First, divisions that requested software paid less than actual cost of the software because license fees were spread across all data center users, regardless of who actually used the package. Second, when chargeback systems focus on costs instead of volumes, users are billed on items they may not directly control. For example, IS costs may decline because FIRM18 acquires a new business allowing the fixed costs to be spread over more volume. Division managers may take credit for these cost reductions, saying, "I reduced IS costs by 5%." Obviously, they had not initiated any cost reduction practices. Conversely, if IS costs went up—perhaps due to a sale of a business—division managers would say costs increased because IS charged higher rates. Once again, the user's bill fluctuated based on no action of their own.

Murray radically changed the chargeback system from a monthly general allocation based on costs to a daily report based on usage. The daily report contains a one-page summary of the computer consumption units (CCU) actually used by each of the seven divisions versus what each division committed to use. The report is distributed over e-mail to the seven CFOs.

The change in the chargeback mechanism motivated more efficient resource usage because: (a) divisions had a billing system that reflected their actual behavior, (b) daily reports allowed divisions to react to usage variances immediately, and (c) each division was pressured by other divisions not to exceed their allocated units because everyone's costs would increase. These three effects are explained below.

Under the new billing system, the divisions had a chargeback system that reflected their actual computer usage. If they used more, they paid more. If they used less, they paid less. Murray explains:

> "We got people away from cost. They would take unit times rate and they would look at what is hitting my budget. You don't control costs. You control the piece that is constant, the capacity. Rates change. Rates go up or go down. So if you use the same thing, someone says my IS budget went down. They had nothing to do with that. That's because I lowered the cost of the service. They didn't do a damn thing to impact their bottom line. So we

said, 'We'll worry about cost. You guys worry about consumption.' Get them to focus on the metric that they can control."

With a daily consumption report, the CFOs immediately investigate cases where actual usage exceeds projected usage. Perhaps, for example, an accountant made several errors and resubmitted a batch job several times. Such an accountant would be reprimanded. As Bret explains:

"The [users] lived in fear of their CFO. He wanted to know who it was who put him over. That helped us a lot because we were no longer the bad guy."

The daily report also spurred competition across divisions. If one division exceeds their CCUs, the other CFOs pressure them to reduce usage. Bret explains:

"Interesting phenomenon, it happened accidentally, we weren't shrewd enough to have done it this way. Since we had everyone on one page, there got to be some competition, peer pressure, 'Hey you are over, I'm under, you drive my cost up, you better get your act together.' "

The chargeback system was successful because it transferred the responsibility for computer usage from IS to users. For example, if IS has to buy additional capacity because a division exceeded their growth estimates, the division is blamed, not IS. Murray explains:

"We put the responsibility on them, if we have to go out and buy more capacity, we are not the bad guys, they are. So the unwritten rule is, if one division uses more than what was budgeted and causes the data center to upgrade, the person who is going to talk to executive management is the line of business that caused the data center to go over."

Consolidate Data Centers

The data center consolidation was accomplished in only four short months: the insourcing decision was made August 3, Murray was brought in on August 25 to implement the decision, the new organization was announced September 1, the staffing of the new organization was announced September 13. By October, the first data center was consolidated. By December the third data center was consolidated.

Murray feels that FIRM18 was able to consolidate much faster than a vendor could for three reasons. One, FIRM18 had considerable experience opening and closing data centers. This was the order of the day to accommodate all the businesses acquired and sold during the 1980s. Two, their robust network allowed them to easily dismantle processing. As Murray explains, "just pick the processor up, move it, and turn the network backwards, leave all the local lines coming into a front end processor but move the computer over to here." Three, FIRM18 retained the personnel who understood how the systems were integrated. Bret believes that a vendor would never be able to consolidate that quickly because they do not understand how a client's systems are integrated.

The consolidation allowed for a significant reduction in headcount. Before the consolidation, 20 managers ran the three data centers. Under the consolidation, only four managers run the entire operation. Most of the people savings, however, came from the technical staff. In total, the technical staff was reduced from 123 to 63. These headcount savings came from the elimination of redundant functions. For example, rather than employ three IMS programmers, FIRM18 now employs one.

The consolidation also reduced software costs. Before the consolidation, each data center had two licenses for each database product—one for production, one for test. At some sites, there were even quality assurance versions. After consolidation, Murray only ran two versions of each product. Ideally, he would like to standardize to one database product, but the cost of conversion is prohibitive.

Standardize Non-billable Software: the "Meat and Potatoes" Software Portfolio

Murray strongly believes that judicious management of "non-billable" software offers tremendous savings. He estimates that 50% of CPU load is for non-billable software such as operating systems, schedulers, and security. Through standardization, the "non-billable" portion of the workload could be reduced to about 20%.

Upon consolidation, Murray realized that his non-billable load was outrageous. As one might suspect, FIRM18's three separate data centers each had their own software portfolio. Even when products were the same, different data centers often employed different versions of software. Murray mandated that there would only be one version of one tool to support one function:

> "The software portfolio across these three divisions—they had each done their own quirk. We had to aggressively get down to a subset of one. You have one business problem, you have one tool to solve that—not three not six."

Rather than three scheduling systems, for example, FIRM18 would support one. The same was true for the security system, the database tools, programming workbench, import tools, and utilities.

The software standardization process was not easy. The data center staff was comprised of people from all three of the previous data centers—each with their own preference for software. Murray describes the choice of one such application:

> "We had JES3 and JES2. We had religious wars over which was better. It was a fundamental decision to convert to JES2, as unpopular as that was. That meant the (largest) organization was changed—it was the JES3 shop. [The other two data centers] were JES2. More importantly, the surviving data centers outside of US—if this thing survived, you still have responsibility for them—were all JES2 shops. So it was obvious it was going to be JES2. Also, the JES2 license was cheaper."

Negotiate a Comprehensive Software License Agreement

Murray implemented an innovative cost saving mechanism to reduce his software costs from $4 million to $2 million. He noted that buying software products from 250 vendors was extremely inefficient. To reduce costs, he created one huge RFP for all the software products. Rather than cherry-pick the best tools from multiple vendors, it would be less expensive to buy one portfolio from one vendor:

> "Before there were 250 different vendors, 250 different interfaces . . . we just said it will be simpler to support, simpler to operate [with one vendor]. They may not have a product that is best of breed, but across their entire product breadth, it will get the job done, it will be a lower cost, and we will work with that strategic vendor if there are some weaknesses in the product line. It ought to be an attraction to the vendor. They will have a premier showcase account because we'll have all their products. Some of that ought to be translated back to us in lower costs."

In the RFP, Murray noted that the benefit to the vendor would be a guaranteed maintenance stream over a five-year period. He had no money to purchase new products, so the vendors would have to basically install the software free of charge. Because the size of the contract was substantial—about $1.5 million annually, several vendors responded. To cover his software needs, Murray actually contracted with three vendors.

Murray's software strategy was successful from a financial standpoint. In addition to dollar savings, Murray claims that his staff no longer wastes time entertaining software vendors who try to sell their latest products. On the downside, Murray thought he would have more influence over product improvements because he was such a large account than actually happened.

Purchase Just-in-time Computer Resources

When the leases on the current machine expired, Murray decided to replicate his software strategy to reduce his hardware costs.

Murray created an RFP for a five-year, fixed price supply of MIPs and gigabytes. The vendor selected provided a guaranteed monthly price to provide most of FIRM18's hardware. Included in the contract is the 14% growth rate committed to by users. If FIRM18 exceeds these growth expectations, FIRM18 has an option to purchase additional MIPs or gigabytes from the vendor or from another source. This way, Murray has the power to negotiate the lowest prices if resource consumption exceeds current estimates.

In addition to acquiring the CPU and DASD from one vendor, Murray also created one RFP for maintenance on auxiliary equipment such as the tape drives and front end processors. When one vendor offered him a 25% discount off their list price, Murray pushed them down to a 40% discount. Murray is not sure that the vendor's corporate headquarters even knows about the deal because he signed "side agreements" with the vendor's local management.

In total, Murray saved $3 million per year on hardware costs by entering into five-year agreements with the two vendors.

Manage Contracts More Closely

In the past, contracts were administered rather loosely. If a vendor sent a bill, FIRM18 promptly paid it. Murray noted, however, that many bills were erroneous. For example, vendors may send bills to transfer software after an acquisition. The vendor's new contracts may have a transfer clause, but FIRM18 may have signed an older contract without this clause, thus they were not legally bound to pay such a fee.

Today, Murray has a contract specialist on his staff who rigorously reviews old contracts and creates custom documents for new contracts. The contract specialist has reduced costs because FIRM18 specifies contract terms on items the vendors are usually silent on, such as upgrade fees, maintenance fees, transfer fees, and scope of use.

Empower the Remaining Staff

Under the new philosophy, managers are workers and workers are managers. For example, when the data center had to be rewired to accommodate the consolidation, Murray spent the night pulling cables rather than hiring a person at $100 an hour. Murray explains:

"When people showed up and saw me lifting tiles, pulling cable, the message got through. They understood real quick that this was a hands on approach. We demonstrated, everybody counts, every hand counts."

In addition to managers working more on tasks, workers are now responsible for much of their own supervision. Murray implemented the concept of self-directed work teams. Teams are assembled with the right skill set, assigned a task and a time limit, then told to accomplish the task. Murray does not appoint a team leader nor tell them how to accomplish the task.

In summary, Murray exceeded insourcing objectives by reducing costs from $32 million to $18 million. He allocates the savings as 60% from people savings, 25% from hardware savings, and 15% from software savings. Given the project's success, one might assume that senior management might change their views on IS function. Unfortunately, IS is still seen as a necessary cost burden, even though they now believe that costs are as low as possible.

Senior Management's Perceptions of IS after Insourcing

Senior management views the insourcing project as a financial success. However, they still tend to view IS as a necessary cost. Murray explains:

"IS in [FIRM18] is not looked at as a strategic asset or resource. I firmly believe that. I've had the top guy tell me that. What he said is that we are—I won't say a necessary evil—but we are a business requirement, a cost to be minimized."

Murray has tried to sell the concept of strategic systems to management but they ignored him. For example, Murray had an idea to build an expert system to give away to architectural engineering firms. The expert system would specify the use of FIRM18 products where appropriate. He even built a working prototype, but management dismissed the idea. Murray laments, "You give up after you try a couple of those."

Because IS is still viewed as a cost to be minimized, Murray notes that the future of IS is uncertain. Under the current regime, costs are contained by basically "running the legacy systems into the ground"— there is no new mainframe development. What will happen to IS in the future when LANs replace mainframe computing? Will an outsourcer be able to provide this technology for less than Murray's group? Only time will tell.

Conclusion

FIRM18's approach to insourcing and its results are illustrative of what other organizations might be able to achieve—cost reductions in the order of 45%. Indeed, IS management was even able to exceed the cost reductions noted in their insourcing proposal. In addition to their primary cost reduction strategy—data center consolidation which reduced headcount significantly, they obtained considerable further cost reductions by implementing novel approaches for software licenses and chargeback of services. However, like FIRMs 15 and 17, these cost reductions have not fundamentally altered senior management's perception of IS—it is still seen as a cost burden, albeit a necessary one.

FIRM19

Introduction

FIRM19 is one of the largest diversified telecommunications companies in the United States. Although many people consider IS to be a strategic asset for telecommunications companies, FIRM19's senior management decided to outsource the function after learning of Kodak's success story. After FIRM19 employees convinced management to allow the internal IS department to submit a bid, an internal response team prepared a bid that eventually won. The internal IS department was able to reduce their high labor costs by finally having the power to negotiate with their unionized data center employees—either the union would cooperate or lose the entire work site. A year and a half later, most insourcing objectives have been met, although the road has been rocky due to several organizational and cultural changes within FIRM19.

Seven FIRM19 employees were interviewed for this case. Katherine was the IS manager at the time of the outsourcing evaluation. Elizabeth, a lawyer, drafted the legalese of the RFP and was a member of the executive team charged with evaluating the bids. George, an IS manager previously under Katherine, served as the focal point for answering vendor questions and was also a member of the executive evaluation team. Jerry and Stewart, George's subordinates, were members of the RFP and internal response teams and later charged with implementing the insourcing proposal. Ken was the data center manager during the outsourcing evaluation. Mario is the facilities management director who currently has IS in his chain of command.

In addition to the interviews, the following documents were gathered: FIRM19 vision brochure, portions of the RFP, the internal bid, bid evaluation criteria, bid analysis, annual reports, organization charts, and articles published in the trade press.

Company Background

FIRM19 is a diversified telecommunications company that has enjoyed strong financial growth in revenues and net profits recently. In 1992, FIRM19's revenue was over $0.5 billion, which represented almost a 20% increase in profits over the previous year.

FIRM19 operates three major businesses: a local telephone company, a deregulated network and long distance company, and a regulated local exchange company. Until recently, the three lines of business each had their own data centers because regulations instituted by the regulatory commission made consolidation financially infeasible. Thus, the IS functions across the companies were totally autonomous with no central leader establishing the direction of IS.

The local telephone company—the division studied for this case—runs a 32 MIP, 120 gigabyte shop at company headquarters that services 1500 users. Labor costs were extremely high because the local telephone company has an office labor union which also staffs the data center. The labor union rules forbid data center managers to touch the hardware and software, required a manager on every shift, and required both a manager and a worker to be called in for emergencies. Although Jerry, the data center manager in 1991, had tried numerous times to negotiate better terms, the union rejected his proposals. To try to compensate for the high labor costs, FIRM19 tried to minimize hardware costs by searching for bargain prices on used equipment.

The IS department at the local telephone company has two chargeback systems. For development, users are charged for analyst time. For data center operations, there is only a general allocation system. George, an IS manager, explains why data center costs were never tied to usage:

> "We've never charged by job, by I/O. The operations are shared stuff, so it's argumentative who should pay what part of a CPU, backup system, database . . . so it's difficult to explain to a user. The problem is this, why do we want to have chargeback? We said we want our users to have incentives to use IS resources—that's a pricing game. I talked to several companies, if you put pricing in place so that they minimize the use of expensive things, you do not advance. You don't get into new technologies. Where is your R&D? How does that fit into the formula?"

As noted in the four previous cases, general allocation chargeback systems provide incentives for excess usage—when one unit requests software, the costs are spread across all units. The chargeback system, therefore, may have contributed to senior management's perceptions that IS was too expensive.

Senior Management's Perceptions of IS prior to Insourcing

Despite the information intensity of the telecommunications industry, senior management had until recently viewed IS as a cost burden to be minimized and not as a strategic asset. George, an IS manager, explains the president's view of IS:

> "One of the questions I asked was, 'How do you view IS, Mr President, particularly in the operational center as an asset to your corporation? Of potential value?' For the most part, business people don't see it that way. They see it as cost. So, unless you understand the potential of IS and where the technology is going, it won't give you a competitive edge."

Because IS was viewed merely as a cost, senior management constantly challenged the IS department to justify their costs. Jerry, the data center manager prior to insourcing, explains:

> "As a line item in the budget, IS expenses were going up. We were constantly being challenged. We had a new business unit president who came in from the deregulated side of our business who really challenged us and pushed for an environment to really look at the cost of IS."

Jerry responded to management pressures by demonstrating that unit costs were going down by 20% annually, even though total IS costs were increasing due to growth. Jerry and George did not, however, compare FIRM19 costs against outside companies because senior management did not believe in benchmarks. As George explains:

> "When we put it forward—and we did that several times—we thought benchmarking was a good way to go. It just did not land. It was not a believed thing. Benchmarking produces a bunch of reports. 'Oh look at that, we are in the fiftieth percentile.' What does that mean? Whenever you talk to executives they say, 'well, you are better than so-and-so' or 'so-and-so are better than you,' the first thing is, 'Well we are different. We are unique.' It's almost like you jump to an excuse. So they didn't feel that benchmarking provided the hard facts."

Because senior management did not believe in benchmarks, George and Jerry's justification for IS expenses was based solely on the decreasing of unit costs. Their inability to demonstrate the value of IS placed them in a weak position when senior management started entertaining the possibility of outsourcing.

The Outsourcing Decision

In the fall of 1991, the division president of the local telephone company decided to outsource IS after learning about Kodak's success and being approached by an outsourcing vendor. Elizabeth, the lawyer charged with creating a contract to seal this handshake deal, explains:

> "The division president was approached by [an outsourcing vendor] and had been sold on how wonderful outsourcing was. Kodak had done it. Kathy Hudson is a visionary. It's working out great for Kodak. It's a wonderful way to reduce costs. Go with it."

Elizabeth refused to draft the contract. In her role as ethics coordinator, she told the president that the proposed deal was against company policy:

> "I attended a meeting on behalf of one of the other attorneys who was going to draft the contract in FIRM19 because the decision had been made to do what Kodak had done with very little analysis. At that meeting—I'm also ethics officer for the company—I explained very bluntly that we have internal bidding practices that mandate that any goods or services over $7000 must be competitively bid. This would certainly be in excess of $7000—I refused to draft the contract unless it was bid. I said over my dead body. It was explained to me that was not the direction the president wanted to go, I explained I'd be happy to discuss that with the division president."

Ironically, it was Elizabeth, a lawyer, who halted the outsourcing decision and not Katherine, the IS manager. Katherine was virtually silent on the issue despite the fact it was her unit about to be outsourced.

The division president agreed in late October of 1991 to a more formal investigation, although he wanted a fast decision. FIRM19 had one month to create an RFP. Jerry, who was on the committee charged with creating the RFP, said that FIRM19 hired an outside consultant to help create an RFP and to explain how outsourcing vendors operate:

> "What we did, we brought them in for three days of intensive brain picking, laying out the pitfalls, what should we look for. We knew generally the pitfalls, how the vendors really price it, what we would expect to see, what we would put in there to protect FIRM19. [The consulting firm] helped us understand how outsourcers price it, what it really means and how do we construct a bid to protect us."

The RFP requested bids for 5, 7, and 10 years and contained volume information, growth projections, and current information on the costs of hardware and software. Labor costs were not provided because FIRM19 feared it would condition the vendor bids.

Meanwhile, an internal response team was assembled to create an internal bid, with Jerry as committee chair. When asked whether there was a conflict of interest for Jerry to be on both the RFP committee and the internal response team, Elizabeth responded:

> "It was an ethical issue to have Jerry on the internal response team yet help with the RFP and analysis. My advice was that the entity all of our loyalty goes to is FIRM19. Whatever will aid it in the long run is what we do, not that we would give confidential information to one of the bidders, but it's okay to use internal people to get the best bid we can."

To help ensure that the internal response team would be treated the same as outside vendors, George, an IS manager, implemented a procedure that all questions about the RFP—whether from a vendor or the internal response team—would be funneled through him in writing. Every three days, George assembled the questions and answers and distributed the entire document to all the bidders. George explains:

> "A lot of the bidders were concerned we'd give unfair treatment to the internal response. We assured them that we wouldn't do that. I treated Jerry like all the other bidders—like a dog not worth talking to. Jerry would pop in my door and say, 'How are we doing?' He'd get the same answer as everyone else, 'We'll let you know.' "

Another precaution was taken to ensure fair treatment of all bidders— senior management was forbidden to talk to the vendors. George feared that vendors would contaminate the decision process by wooing senior executives:

> "We were careful—all telephone calls had to go through me, the executives were off limits. Even the CEO was told not to speak to these companies on the subject of the RFP."

The internal response team concentrated on preparing a bid that would reduce their high labor costs caused by the union contract. In the past, FIRM19 had not been able to negotiate favorable terms with the union, but the outsourcing evaluation provided the stick that IS previously lacked. Jerry explains:

> "One of the things that the internal response team did was meet with the union folks. We met with them and said, 'We have to lower costs or we

won't be competitive. You will lose your work unit.' That was a reality. The union president—we outlined some things we wanted to see flexibility on so we could reduce our costs."

Jerry was indeed able to negotiate a much better deal with the unions. He did not cut salaries but he changed the rules on overtime and the division of work. For example, supervisors can now touch the machines, a manager does not need to be called in for emergencies, and workers can multi-task rather than specialize.

The internal response team proposed to reduce costs by $3.4 million over a three-year period by eliminating 18 of the 39 people currently staffing the data center and by using existing resources more efficiently. The 18 positions, which account for $2.3 million in savings, would be eliminated through a reorganization and software automation:

11 people	Reorganize the department to eliminate redundant functions and unnecessary supervision
4 people	Exploit unused portions of existing data center support tools. For example, the job scheduling module of the master console operations software would be activated to eliminate the need for constant human monitoring
1 person	Purchase a report distribution system. This system will print all reports for one customer in a bundle instead of having a person manually sort reports
2 people	Purchase a problem management/rerun system to efficiently handle production abends. This system would automatically correct catalogs and determine those datasets that must be recovered, determine where in a jobstream to restart processing, and rerun the job

An additional $1.4 million would be saved through data center environmental improvements, on-line review of reports, overtime reductions, and CPU/DASD technology savings. Examples of annual savings from these measures are:

$17 000	Reduce lighting in the data center
$12 000	Increase the temperature in the data center by three degrees
$ 3000	Power down systems not used at night

$59 000   Eliminate security guards because they should be covered by the building group

$33 000   Review reports on-line, a feature of the report distribution system

The internal response team noted that all of these savings were contingent upon management's commitment to purchase the software needed to eliminate the staff.

After the RFP was distributed on December 7 of 1991, FIRM19 held a bidders' conference so that the vendors could ask questions about the RFP before their six-week deadline. Five vendors and the internal response team attended the conference. In the end, only two vendors and the internal response team submitted bids.

FIRM19 established three teams to evaluate the bids: a financial evaluation team, a qualitative factors team, and an executive evaluation team. The financial team, comprised of two financial analysts, was responsible for the net present value calculations of the bids. The qualitative factors team, comprised of five managers, considered non-financial issues such as the impact on service levels and the risks of signing a long-term contract. The executive evaluation team, comprised of George, Katherine, and Elizabeth, reviewed the reports from the first two committees and created the decision criteria and weights with which to evaluate the bids. The committee used the following 18 criteria and their associated weights to evaluate the bid:

Criteria		Weight (%)
1.	Price	35
2.	Personnel	10
3.	Service levels	10
4.	Contract administration	4
5.	Disaster recovery	4
6.	Software	4
7.	Supplier information	4
8.	Security and confidentiality	2
9.	Audit	2
10.	Technology	2
11.	System transition	2
12.	Term	2
13.	Reversal	2
14.	Remedies	2
15.	Shared processing	2
16.	Additional contract provisions	2
17.	General	1
18.	Value added	10

In order to ensure a fair evaluation, Katherine, the IS manager, insisted that the decision criteria and weights not be altered after the bids were received. George fruitlessly objected:

"There's a catch 22 to doing an RFP this way. She set down the rules that we are going to establish these weightings and we are not going to change them. Yet, every RFP I've ever done, you learn something when you see responses back, it affects the way you think about them, and that affects your weighting. Okay? So I was at odds on that. But the weights didn't change."

Although price was by far the most important factor in the decision, FIRM19 has always treated their employees fairly. As an indicant of data center employees' job satisfaction—there was zero turnover in 1991. The executive team, therefore, assumed responsibility for redeploying the displaced workers in other areas of FIRM19 if the vendors did not want them. Ideally, employees would be given meaningful jobs at comparable wages.

The evaluation teams asked the bid respondents to present their bids in a series of three- to six-hour meetings documented by a stenographer. Elizabeth claims the meetings provided an indication as to what type of business partner each vendor would make:

"How well in the meeting did the vendors respond to our questions? Were they prepared? Not that we expected polished presentations, but did they know what they were talking about. Again, being indicative of the effort they would put into the relationship."

Elizabeth became wary of one vendor during the meeting because they wanted to eliminate the clause about alternative dispute resolutions. She interpreted that request as follows:

"There was a large vendor that said, 'We don't want that. We'd rather go to court.' My interpretation of that, they have a deeper pocket than we do, so this is an indication that they would be willing to drain us in the event of a dispute. We would have no flexibility, like a David and a Goliath. This is an indication of how they would treat our relationship. Is this what you want to get into long term? Those things were indicative of the trend for the long-term relationship."

After the bidders' meetings, the stenographer's notes were transcribed and distributed to the qualitative factors and executive evaluation teams. George corroborates Elizabeth's explanation about how the evaluation teams analyzed the transcriptions:

"Although financial numbers can tell a lot, it will have the most influence on the people removed vertically. Everyone else wanted it made on subjective

aspects—quality of service, how do we provide services? How do we inter-
act with the outsourcer? The transcripts were sent to the executive team and
the qualitative team. Then we formed our judgements."

When both the financial and qualitative teams recommended that the
RFP be awarded to the internal bid, the executive team concurred. In
January of 1992, the decision was announced to award the bid to the
internal response team.

The Insourcing Project

Eighteen months later, the insourcing proposal has been deemed a
financial success. In fact, the IS department exceeded their projected
savings by deploying workers ahead of schedule. Unfortunately,
other aspects of the insourcing proposal have been less successful—
management has not invested in the automation software, nor has the
IS staff been able to negotiate better contracts with the hardware and
software vendors. The implementation of the insourcing proposal did
not go exactly as planned because of many changes within FIRM19,
such as a corporate restructuring, a new CIO, the planned death of
the mainframe, and self-managed work groups. As will be shown,
these changes—which did disrupt the implementation of the insourcing proposal—have nevertheless actually been beneficial for IS
overall.

Reorganize the Data Center

The data center was reorganized to eliminate redundant functions and
unnecessary management. Under the new organization, workers now
multi-task instead of specialize. Jerry explains:

> "We increased the responsibilities of the senior craft person. [We no longer]
> restricted the craft levels to specific tasks, such that any craft person can do
> any craft position. We don't have a level that says, 'I can only do this.' We
> said, 'You will train and you will learn or you will not be here.' "

In addition to multi-tasking, Jerry eliminated unnecessary supervision:

> "On each of the second and third shifts, we had two management people.
> One person dedicated to supervising the staff in the data center, one in the
> operational support role. We proposed to eliminate the strictly supervisory
> role on the second and third shift. With the tools we were going to be
> adding, we would free up enough time from the operations support person
> to assume a portion of management responsibility."

Soon after the reorganization, management started redeploying workers ahead of schedule. Because of FIRM19's commitment to offer displaced workers meaningful employment within other areas of FIRM19, management had to transfer employees when opportunities arose. Mario, the new facilities management director, explains:

> "I came in after they went through all this. We are going to take 18 people out of this organization—make it work. It's been working, they also took the opportunity because this was a union shop, that we would find positions for them. When the opportunity came along, they grabbed at the opportunity and sent the person because there was another job for them. So they sent them before the mechanization got there."

Automate Operations

Although the insourcing proposal called for software automation to displace workers, almost none of the software has been implemented. Participants identified three reasons: (1) management's belief that the department can run short-staffed without software, (2) a new CIO, hired as a result of a corporate reorganization, who does not want to invest in mainframe automation, and (3) the data center workers' disbelief that software proposals will be approved by management. These three reasons are explored below.

Although the insourcing proposal called for software automation *prior* to redeployment, early redeployment transferred people before the software designated to replace them was bought. For example, three operators were redeployed nine months before the console automation package was scheduled to be implemented. The remaining staff was overburdened and service levels declined. Stewart, a member of the internal response team and Jerry's subordinate, blames declining service levels on the lack of software automation:

> "In the first six months, we had a plan laid out. But we had opportunities to redeploy these people ahead of time based on openings in other departments. But we weren't ready to implement the products yet. We are running three operators short. The operators remaining work more overtime, our service level goes down because we haven't had the tools we based our benefit on . . . That has affected the morale of the people left. They work long hours, there are mistakes. Our service levels aren't great now because we are running with fewer people with just as much work. We make stupid mistakes which cause reruns and upset customers."

IS management is having trouble acquiring the funds to purchase the software because senior management feels that the data center is functioning without it. Mario, the new facilities management director, explains:

> "That's the current struggle. Then of course, we have new management and trying to piece it all together and say, 'I want to spend $70 000 now for two people we got rid of last year.' "

Stewart continues:

> "Now comes my dilemma. Management sees us, 'You've been running a year and a half at this manpower level, why do you need these tools? You've proved you can run it like that.' Yeah we are running, but customer service suffers."

Stewart also explains how frustrated his staff is:

> "My staff [thinks of management], 'you bought off on redeploying people, why aren't you buying off on the product I told I needed to justify that? . . . You are awfully quick in taking away my peers and leaving me with long hours. When it comes to products that will make my job easier you tell me you can't do it.' That's how they see it."

In addition to management's reticence to purchase software, major organizational and cultural changes have also interrupted the implementation of software automation.

In 1993, FIRM19 reorganized the entire company in preparation of acceptance of a proposal submitted to the regulatory commission. As part of the new organization, IS departments across the business units have been consolidated into one division. Once the plan is approved, IS will become a wholly owned subsidiary that sells IS services to the sister companies.

A CIO position was created to head the new IS organization. The CIO, appointed in January of 1993, has a strong technical and entrepreneurial background. George describes him as follows:

> "He'd appreciate the characterization—he's an entrepreneur. Fairly young man, he started to run and successfully managed several companies. He was a consultant to our firm last six months of last year to one of the business units. He's one of these get-it-done people. They saw an opportunity to take IS from where it was to where it needs to go."

The CIO certainly changed the direction of IS from a mainframe cost center to a service-oriented department based on client/server architecture. The CIO envisions the death of the mainframe within three years. George explains the new push for client/server:

"We were going at this 30 mph last fall, last winter we picked up a new CIO, we are going now at 174 mph. So we have whiplash. Those of us who said it was a good idea can't hear our voices because we are moving faster than the speed of sound."

George, Jerry, and Stewart are less optimistic than the CIO that the mainframe can be fully replaced by client/server technology within the next three years. Jerry expresses their sentiments:

"Our CIO would like to get rid of that, but there are some things right now only the mainframe can do the way we would like it done in terms of security. Quite frankly, we are looking at things to put there that make sense, like network backups which are horrendous in our 40 server, 70 gigabyte LAN environment. We have people every night starting manual backups of servers. We have management software on the mainframe [that could do this automatically]."

Despite the IS staff's doubt about the speed of the LAN conversion, senior management believes the mainframe is dying and are therefore reluctant to invest money in mainframe computers. Thus, management has a second reason to not purchase the software designated to displace workers. Stewart explains:

"Now the de-emphasis on mainframes, they don't want to spend any more money on the mainframe. So how can we justify these new products? We've de-emphasized the mainframe and gone client/server route. The [insourcing] proposal was based on the mainframe and the importance is not there anymore. It's affected our decisions in other ways. We aren't implementing a lot of the things we wanted to implement as far as the internal response. We changed our decision. What we tried to do 2.5 years ago, is not the same business decision we would make today based on our changes and strategic corporate goal. It's tough to take the letter of the law we proposed and merge it into our new strategic plan."

Jerry agrees with Stewart that mainframe expenditures will be harder to sell to senior management:

"I think the test for the business justification is as viewed for mainframe products is more stringent now than it would have been a year ago. The time horizon for the MVS based mainframe is in question much more so than prior to this year. This adds to Stewart's frustration. People are frustrated that they are being called to show a payback in a shorter period because—well I don't think the mainframe will go, maybe our conception of it. At the same time, you have to adjust planning to what's likely. You can't build a four-year payback into something that won't be here in two years."

Stewart and Jerry are trying to motivate the staff to build a business case for some of the software proposed in the insourcing bid. They feel management will invest in software if it has a short payback period. The staff, however, are overworked and do not believe it is worth their time to justify new products. Jerry explains:

> "The frustration I see in people—they throw their hands up. They say, 'You never do anything we propose anyway so why should I bother revisiting this?' Sheer frustration."

Stewart adds the following comments:

> "In the operations area, we were charged with implementing a lot of suggestions concerned with automation—console operation, tape library automation, restart automation, JCL automation, the manual functions that the operations staff perform—report distribution. As such, we still haven't implemented because we are so shorthanded we don't have time to do the work to make the business case to do it. We want to do it. We see the benefit, but we don't have time to throw it together and implement it because we are shorthanded."

In summary, management's belief that the department can run short-staffed without software, the CIO's abandonment of the mainframe, and the data center workers' belief that software proposals will be rejected have contributed to the failure to implement the automation portion of the insourcing proposal. In addition to these factors, a change in FIRM19's culture towards empowered workers has also disrupted the insourcing project.

Empower Workers

FIRM19's culture is changing—cross-departmental task forces and self-managed work groups are replacing the previous hierarchical structure. Within the data center, self-managed work groups now supervise their own work. The consequence of this cultural change has been difficulty in implementing some of the insourcing proposal. The self-managed groups have tried to argue against the insourcing proposal, claiming that FIRM19 needs to retain more staff. Stewart explains:

> "We spent a lot of time the first year in the self-managed work groups trying to disprove the internal response and have more people while the management team was trying to implement the internal response and downsize. Two opposing forces."

Jerry concurs that implementing the self-managed groups and the in-sourcing proposal at the same time was a mistake:

> "At the time this implementation went in, the operations area was just forming self-managed work groups. I think, it was a major mistake to at-tempt such a revolutionary thing like that in a time frame when you know you are reducing the work force. That had a lot to do with the delays. But it was the biggest mistake that I see. It was a process that had just begun to start. I just don't think you can do those two things at the same time . . . how do you do [redeploy] when you are evolving into these self-managed teams? They undermine each other."

Although the self-managed work groups had a detrimental impact as far as the insourcing proposal, FIRM19's management believes that the change in culture will lead to a more responsive and productive work force in the long run.

Negotiate Better Hardware and Software Agreements

Another cost-saving strategy that Jerry and Stewart tried to implement was lower hardware and software costs through better negotiations with vendors. Although their hardware and software costs were al-ready low, they thought that the outsourcing threat would provide the same stick with the vendors as it did with the union—either offer us a better deal to help us win the bid or risk losing us as customers. Unfortunately, the vendors did not respond positively. Jerry explains:

> "We explored partnerships with our software and hardware vendors to try to build partnerships, particularly the hardware vendors. We basically brought them all together and laid out, 'hey you are our suppliers now. We would like to have you support us in putting together this internal response. What can you do for us in a partner, long-term arrangement?' I can summar-ize, I got back weasel words, specific proposals for replacing DASD with X—they didn't get the message. They didn't know how to respond to what we were looking for. We were trying to get creative with them. 'Commit with us to this.' They couldn't do it. They couldn't get [their corporate headquarters] to understand the potential."

In the end, Jerry and Stewart did not need the vendors to support their internal bid.

Senior Management's Perceptions of IS after Insourcing

Senior management's view of IS has dramatically changed during the past few years, but this change is attributed to the new organizational structure and the new CIO, not necessarily the insourcing project. In fact, senior management has turned over so much, participants are not even sure the new senior managers are aware of the insourcing project. Jerry assembled a status report to present to management in December of 1992, but it was difficult to identify savings vis-à-vis the new organization:

> "The status report was December 31 of last year. We came in, the savings were greater than anticipated. Part of the restructuring of IS, we are changing the way we do budgets and reporting. We've lost visibility to some extent because we are in a different organization now. Things are starting to get recorded differently. Reporting back to the budget as we did last year is next to impossible. Quite honestly, we record progress but not to targeted dollars."

Jerry believes that senior management has changed their perceptions of IS, but they still focus on costs:

> "So, the corporation is changing and I'm coming back to believe that IS is now viewed by senior management as still an expense from a standpoint that they'd like to get the expense down to a smaller percentage of revenue. But I think it's viewed as an asset, as a way to get where we want to go. That's different from 2½ years ago."

When the market plan is approved and the IS department is made into a separate company, IS managers will be better able to explore IS as a competitive weapon. Elizabeth describes some of the new technologies that may be developed:

> "In the future, especially personal communications networks—Dick Tracy phone watches, a phone number assigned to a person. The phone number will follow a person—that would all be hooked into the data center in some fashion. That's strategic."

Conclusion

In sum, the insourcing project was a financial success overall—the IS staff actually exceeded their proposed savings. Despite some setbacks in the area of software automation, IS management believes that the FIRM19 is in a much better position to adopt to corporate changes because of insourcing. What if FIRM19 had signed a 10-year contract? Would the vendor facilitate the move towards client/server technology? How could the IS department be spun off to a separate company? How would outsourcing fit into the proposed strategic role of IS? If FIRM19 had signed with an outsourcer, it may not have had the flexibility to adapt to new organizational structures and strategies. Unlike

FIRMs 15, 17, and 18, senior management now views IS positively and not as a cost burden. While reducing IS costs no doubt helped in the formulation of the new positive perception, the business acumen of the new CIO probably had the most influence.

FIRM20

Introduction

FIRM20 is one of the largest energy companies in the United States. A financially weak position in the mid 1980s led management to consider ways to trim budgets in all areas of the business. IS was no exception. Outsourcing seemed to offer the potential for reducing IS costs and management initiated an evaluation. Two external and one internal bids were received, the internal bid eventually won. While the actual cost savings turn out to be difficult to pin down, the insourcing decision is felt by management to have been the right move. With a reduced staff level, IS support for the business is higher now than ever before and the IS activities continue to grow at a significant rate. Additionally, changes in the business environment have been capably handled by the IS department using new technology platforms which might have been cost prohibitive had they outsourced.

Two FIRM20 employees were interviewed for this case. Jack, the director for IS planning, was interviewed on two separate occasions. He was responsible for much of the outsourcing evaluation although the decision to insource was made by the president of FIRM20. Bill the new CIO was also talked to. Although he was not working for FIRM20 during the outsourcing evaluation period, his thoughts about the psyche of the company helped to clarify management's view of insourcing and outsourcing. In addition to the interviews, documentation about the company and its decision to insource was obtained. This helped to corroborate the interview data.

Company Background

No matter what criteria are used in assessing FIRM20's size, it always comes out ranking as one of the top five energy companies. Be it in terms of size of customer base, revenue, or number of employees, FIRM20 is among the largest. FIRM20 is really a holding company comprised of five operating entities and formed in the 1920s. It has a customer base of over 2 million, an operating revenue in excess of $4 billion, and employs over 16 000 employees.

The company has grown through a small number of large acquisitions. While the industry was once a fairly stable one, recent government regulations have turned the industry on its head and caused a tremendous growth in competition—something the industry was neither accustomed to, nor knew exactly how to respond to. The growth in competition has also had a significant effect on the bottom line of the companies in the industry. Companies in the industry, particularly in the 1980s, struggled. The days of easily making profits were gone. Coupled with the increased competition, FIRM20 had found itself—during the latter part of the 1980s—in a period of severe financial constraints brought about by government regulations, high interest rates, and large debt. It was because of these conditions that FIRM20 found itself, according to Jack: "in a period where we had a very tight cash squeeze." Any way that costs could be reduced, had to be seriously considered. The company implemented a policy of tying employee compensation to aggressive cost reduction targets for all areas of the business. It was against this backcloth that FIRM20 looked seriously at outsourcing. Although outsourcing was to be considered Jack felt: "that there was some concern that continued throughout our overall assessment of outsourcing about turning over critical business practices and processes to a third party." Nevertheless, the outsourcing evaluation began.

Senior Management's Perceptions of IS prior to Insourcing

Senior management at FIRM20 while supportive of IS now, was not always so positive. The strong interest in ways to drive down costs is consistent with the view that management felt that IS costs had gotten out of hand. The outsourcing evaluation was one way to see if costs had indeed been excessive.

At FIRM20, IS was not specifically perceived as "strategic" to the business although it was felt be an important component of doing business in the industry. But it was important enough to be willing to spend money on new hardware and software as it became available, at least in the early days. Jack explains:

> "We had been one of the pioneers, one of the beta test sites with CICS and along with several other [companies in the industry] had been one of the first to put up an on-line customer system. And it was almost as if the corporation said 'enough pioneering, let's sit back and rest for a while and exploit what we've got.' And its real reluctance to invest in IS with the result that there was a tremendous amount of pent up demand. In 1979 we were just beginning to come out of that lengthy period where the company had been so reluctant to invest significantly in information systems."

But even though the company started investing again in IS during the 1980s, senior management still did not view IS favorably. It might have had something to do with IS's centralized position while the rest of the organization was decentralized. For FIRM20's operating companies, centralized functions were seen to be burdensome and bureaucratic— they were not favorably looked upon. Jack comments:

> "We've had some real tough decisions to make because quite honestly the IS organization didn't enjoy outstanding credibility in the company. And I guess the other thing that's relevant from a historical perspective is that IS was the one piece of FIRM20 that was fundamentally centralized [while the rest of the company was decentrally organized]."

Another reason why FIRM20's management may have had a negative view of IS was the way the operating companies were charged for IS services. They were allocated costs based on the decision of an IS advisory board, but the allocation scheme was never clear to the operating units. They were charged for services but the rationale for the charging scheme as well as what IS activities were being measured and charged for, was not articulated. Such IS allocation schemes are prone to cause problems. Jack states:

> "We had always kept track of projects [but had difficulty apportioning IS costs to departments] . . . the old metrics (e.g. CPU minutes) ceased to be as valid. The engineering folks burned lots of cycles, didn't store much on disks, maybe kept some things on tape. Didn't necessarily print a whole lot, at least not proportioned to the cycles they burned. They . . . got one consolidated number and were getting hit with disproportionate bills. The customer folks were getting a free ride in a lot of cases, although they didn't think so. So we were under a lot of pressure to change the process, but the chargeback has been a fact of life and everybody wanted their charges reduced."

In allocation chargeback schemes such as this, user departments increasingly question what they are being charged for, and fight to have their portion of the allocation bill reduced. When the budgets of the departments at FIRM20 got squeezed, Jack noted that "they'd come knocking on IS's door and say 'give me everything I asked for, in fact I'd like more but at a lower cost.' "

Yet the departments paid their IS costs with "inside" money, i.e. not like money they had to spend on outside products and services. This led Jack to conclude that in reality: ". . . our end users just really don't care what their costs are, 'cause they're not accountable for them."

Because IS costs were simply allocated and the user departments had no understanding of what they were paying for, there was little appreciation for IS. IS was simply viewed as *an overhead,* and as such, everyone wanted the costs to be reduced. The business units rallying cry was: "[let's] . . . get rid of that overhead."

If the view of IS being seen as corporate overhead was not enough of a drain on its credibility, FIRM20's IS group had another problem to contend with: the low esteem accorded its IS director. According to Jack: "The credibility of the IS executive is extremely important to getting things done," and unfortunately the IS director at the time of the outsourcing decision lacked that credibility. In some sense, this might have been reason enough to persuade management to outsource at the outset, but they were willing to let the formal bidding process go forward, and rationally and unbiasedly evaluate all alternatives.

The Outsourcing Decision

FIRM20, from the outset, took the outsourcing evaluation process seriously. It was not perceived as a passing fad. Jack states:

> "We were very serious. We weren't doing it just to get senior management off our back. If there was a better way to do the business, we were committed . . . We weren't very excited about it quite honestly, but we were committed to doing what was right for the company."

At the time FIRM20 considered outsourcing, it was running two IBM 3090s with a processing capacity of about 150 MIPS. They had approximately 450 IS people, about 200 of which worked in data center operations. In considering outsourcing, they looked exclusively at data center operations. Jack states: "We really had major reservations about applications development because that really represents business processes but we thought telecommunications was a possibility." In the end they decided not to extend the outsourcing analysis to telecommunications because "we run our own fiber network" and to turn this over to a third party "was too complicated, and it wasn't worth doing in the early stages." The door was left open to possibly consider it at some later time though. Jack says: "Basically the approach we took was look at data center operations exclusively. Let's prove that it's economical and then once we've gotten that established then we can look at telecommunications."

FIRM20's outsourcing evaluation began in April 1989 which made them one of the early adopters of formally considering outsourcing. Jack states: "Kodak had gotten all the press I guess mid '89 with their deal so we can't claim to be quite a pioneer, but we took a serious look shortly after. Driven by a lot of things, the fact that Kodak had done it was a consideration. I wouldn't say a major one, but it certainly was a consideration." FIRM20 had felt that even though their data center operations costs were thought to be among the lowest in the industry, it was sensible for them to consider any vehicle for reducing costs. If outsourcing could reduce costs, then surely they should investigate it. The first step was to gather data about others who had evaluated outsourcing in the past. Jack explains:

> "As we started looking around talking to other companies we ran down about 18 companies that I guess, if memory serves me right, it was 12 that had outsourced and 6 that had looked at it and decided not to. So it was possible to find some large corporations that had . . . but hadn't gotten a lot of press."

As FIRM20 looked at the situation and looked at the companies that had made outsourcing decisions, they saw a number of motivators. What they did not run across in their preliminary fact-finding exercise, was a company that had outsourced simply and solely to cut IS costs over the long term. There were always other factors; a second consideration which was key. Either there were *political issues*—it was a tool to force some scale economies and consolidations into the interorganizational bickering discourse; or IS did *not have credibility*, or it was *difficult to hire staff*; or a company was faced with some sort of need for an *immediate cash infusion* and an outsourcing deal was a way to get money quickly. In the end, they came to believe: *"that the outsourcing arrangement was simply a way to restructure cash flow."*

For FIRM20, neither the issue of politics nor immediate cash infusion nor difficulty in hiring staff was a key concern, their prime objective was to be more competitive in the long term. Jack says:

> "But our concern was not short-term savings, not to take a decreasing price performance curve and flatten it. Our concern was much more to be competitive in the tenth year than it was to be price competitive in the first year of the deal."

In order to achieve this goal, Jack felt it would be necessary to specify their wishes directly in any contract they would sign:

> ". . . [we would] put into the contract that they guarantee us that they would continue to maintain a price performance advantage over what we could have done internally. That's difficult to measure but basically the mechanism that we had put into our RFP that would have gone into the contract was basically a mechanism that let the market determine what was a fair price. Based on a provision that if someone came in with a price that was 10% better, first time the company that had the contract had the right to meet

that price. Second time that happened, though, it was our choice whether they continued having met the reduced price or we switched suppliers. So we basically said that you're not guaranteed 10 years unless you stay on that continually reducing price performance curve. That was our sole motivator and we did not find any company, not to say that there weren't ones that had, but we didn't talk to anybody that outsourced solely because they felt that the third party could do it cheaper and sustain that on a long-term basis."

FIRM20 spent about two months on this preliminary fact-finding/ data-gathering phase. The results suggested that while FIRM20's reasons for considering outsourcing were not the major focus of those organizations embarking on outsourcing, there was nevertheless enough evidence to continue the analysis. The next step in the evaluation process involved inviting two leading vendors to offer preliminary outsourcing bids on FIRM20's data center. It was felt that these two vendors were sufficient since the purpose of this phase of the outsourcing process was simply a "test of concept," i.e. to see if evaluating outsourcing made sense. Jack prepared a short document detailing FIRM20's data center workload and operating environment. This was given to the two vendors. These preliminary bids were solicited to not only see if money could be saved, but to see whether the vendors were really interested. Jack says: ". . . we asked them to convince us up front if it was worth our spending the time and effort to amass all that detail for them." Interestingly, the preliminary bids did not differ that dramatically from the final bids received.

The preliminary bids which came back from both vendors suggested that cost savings were possible. Based on this, the company decided to formally evaluate outsourcing.

The next stage was to put together a formal RFP detailing all services and levels of support which would have to be provided. Because they lacked experience in putting such a document together, they enlisted the support of a consulting firm who had been involved in such activities in the past. The consulting firm not only helped in the preparation of the RFP, but they also benchmarked FIRM20's data center operation with others. The result showed that while FIRM20's costs were generally reasonable, there was some scope for cost savings, mainly through data center operations automation, upgrading DASD technology and practices, and restructuring operations staff. Data center consolidation, a typical strategy for reducing IS costs, was inappropriate for FIRM20 as they had already centralized the entire IS function.

Although FIRM20 was aware of these cost-saving strategies and indeed had planned on implementing most of them in the future anyway, the benchmarking confirmed their suspicions that there was considerable advantage in implementing them sooner rather than later. It was decided that FIRM20's IS organization should compete in the outsourcing evaluation exercise by preparing a bid of their own. The bid would be based on improved cost figures accrued through the adoption of these cost-saving strategies. Bids based on the RFP invitation were solicited.

Jack states: "We put together an RFP, called a bidders' conference and invited three groups: [two prominent outsourcing vendors] and our data center operations folks. So the same RFP was given exactly the same deadlines to respond. We just ran the whole process as if they were another provider." There was to be no favoritism. To ensure that there was no bias all bidders were treated the same—they all had to respond to the RFP by the same date, and they each had the same information as the others. At the bidders' conference, the RFP was explained and any queries which any vendor had, would be shared with all others. These queries were submitted in writing, and were circulated to others as well as FIRM20's responses.

Each bidder was given detailed information about the data center operations. "We gave them a complete inventory of our hardware, all the lease terms. We gave them lists of all the employees and their salary information in aggregate, we didn't identify individuals. They knew all the numbers." This was felt to be important because "what we were expecting them to do was pick up the people and we have some provisions in there in terms of guaranteeing benefits and the like." FIRM20 did not want to have any surprises when it came to any transitioning of staff. Furthermore, as Jack notes: "I think people that believe the competition don't have a good handle on what your cost structure is are kidding themselves."

Jack, as director of IS planning, was given the role of running the outsourcing project:

> "I worked directly with our VP and with the president of the services company. And they pretty much gave me free rein to run this thing. So, when we put the RFP out, I was very coolly treated over at the data center, there were a lot of folks who felt I was the enemy. I was maybe a little better than [named outsourcing vendor], but not much. It was a very awkward arrangement all the way around, I mean yes, I personally would've been in a very awkward position had it happened. But an awful lot of friends would've been in an equally or worse positions at least from their perspective at the outset. So it was a real gut wrenching time, but we were convinced that if there was a better way, it was our obligation to the corporation to [explore it]."

FIRM20 did not want any surprises or be accused of holding back any pertinent information. Jack notes:

"And what we wanted to be sure, when we put that detail on the table, was that when we walked away from all those lease obligations that whoever picked it up understood what they were taking on, that we wanted to try to avoid, it hadn't happened at the time, but we wanted to try to avoid some of the controversies that arose subsequently with Computer Associates at EDS."

FIRM20 was not only open about their leasing and cost arrangements to the bidders, but they were also very up front about the outsourcing evaluation to the IS staff. The preliminary outsourcing assessment surrounding the two outside vendors was done in confidence. Just three people were involved: Jack (the director of IS planning); the director of IS; and the president of the services company. But, as Jack says:

"once they gave us some reason to believe that there was an opportunity to save money, and we would go through the formal process, we told everybody at the data center what was going on. This is not the way some companies do it, but we were one of those companies that was up front with the people from the outset. We told everyone here's what we're going to do; here's how we're going to work the headcount down. So if you were on the list to be let go you knew it. And we focused a lot of attention on giving those people the opportunity to train for other options; jobs in the company or get skilled up so they would be more competitive in the market place if they left and in several instances those who were on the keep list found other job opportunities; created vacancies and people moved into vacant spots before their separation date was reached. Other people found jobs in the company, others found other opportunities elsewhere and left. We let people know what the expectations are a year, year and a half in advance. One of the management challenges was to keep people motivated, but one of the clear understandings everybody has is you've got a job for x amount of time as long as you perform. You stop performing you're out of here just like any other employee who doesn't perform."

The outsourcing decision proceeded as follows. All three invited to bid, submitted bids. Surprisingly, all three were very close in terms of overall cost but FIRM20's internal bid was marginally cheaper. Since FIRM20 did not develop formal evaluation criteria by which to evaluate the various bids (such as some of the other organizations in our study), the actual choice of the winning bid was based—at least overtly—on overall cost. However, when pressed, Jack noted that there was an additional criterion which was surely factored in, at least subjectively, in assessing the bids. It was risk. This relates to the difficulty in predicting the nature of technology in the future and worrying about being locked into a vendor's standard technology for a 10-year period. A firm loses flexibility in such an arrangement and this likely had some bearing on the decision to stay inside.

Although the internal bid was ultimately chosen, the decision process involved a number of stages. First, the three bids were reviewed for about two weeks to make sure they were complete, comprehensive, and unambiguous. Since Jack was to be involved in the presentation of all three bids, especially the two external bids, to an IS advisory board, he needed to make sure he understood them. Second, the bids were objectively presented to this advisory board comprised of senior management from the various operating companies. Third, the president of the company was informed of the views of the advisory board, and he then made the decision. Fourth, FIRM20's board of directors formally approved the decision made by the president.

The actual presentations to the IS advisory board involved Jack making the case for outsourcing while the director of the data center presented the case for insourcing. Jack took more of a neutral role, stressing the advantages, as he saw them, of going outside. He focused on the cost figures presented in the bids and suggested additionally that outsourcing would allow FIRM20 to focus on its core business. Against these potential benefits, Jack cautioned about reversibility, i.e. how difficult it would be to rebuild a data center after outsourcing it to a third party. Although there were some instances where this had been done in the past in other organizations, Jack wanted to make sure that no one would underestimate the effort and resources this would entail. Jack also cautioned the board about the hazard of realizing cost savings through outsourcing in the long term. Ten years was a long time and with changing technology and changes in FIRM20's future workload it might be difficult to realize cost savings. He could envisage that the outsourcing contract would have to be renegotiated with some regularity, and this could be a costly process.

The presentation of the internal bid by the data center manager, was not so neutral. He emphasized where cost savings could be obtained in the data center and why it made sense to stay inside. His job was made easier by two basic facts: (1) the internal bid was the lowest of the three (although not by much), and (2) if he could not deliver on his promise to reduce costs, the board could easily reverse their decision and simply outsource.

In the end, the recommendation of the IS advisory board, subsequently followed by the president, and then formally agreed to by the corporate board, was to keep IS inside, and their rationale for the decision was fairly clear. The internal bid was better in the sense of lower cost and it was much less risky. They could always reconsider outsourcing if the data center did not deliver the cost savings proposed. But if they had outsourced, there was a general feeling that flexibility would be lost. In particular, they worried about the loss of leverage when it came time to either renew or renegotiate the contract. With no internal data center, they could only negotiate from a position of weakness.

While the choice of the winning bid turned out to be fairly non-polemical because the decision was to stay inside, it would have been somewhat different had the choice been to take one of the two external bids. Jack states: "We probably didn't absolutely have to get more approval [from the corporate board] since we were staying inside. . . . If we had decided to go outside, it would definitely have been seriously reviewed by the board as we were making this kind of commitment to go outside. We wanted our internal customers to agree that they would take that risk."

FIRM20 was intent on obtaining data center cost savings over the long run. In order to ensure this occurred, benchmarking was to be undertaken regularly. FIRM20's costs would be compared with other leading companies and would be expected to be among the leaders. This would require the data center staff staying on the leading edge of achieving price performance gains over the 10-year period. Additionally, the data center director's job performance would be evaluated based on how well the data center was achieving its cost reduction goals spelled out in the insourcing proposal.

It is clear that in the case of FIRM20, the outsourcing decision process was driven by long-term considerations and not short-term gains. An interesting and unplanned side-effect of the outsourcing evaluation is what has happened at the data center. According to Jack and confirmed by Bill (the new CIO), the staff now see themselves as in-house entrepreneurs—they have the freedom to aggressively pursue cost-cutting measures as there is a strong incentive (job performance evaluations) to improve on the insourcing bid's cost reduction levels. They have sped up the data center automation project and have continued to reduce staff. They have also become more aggressive in hardware and software lease negotiations.

The Insourcing Project

Throughout the bidding process, FIRM20's internal data center group felt good about themselves, feeling their costs were among the lowest in the industry. Informal, anecdotal evidence suggested that FIRM20's IS was cost-effective, hence there was initial reluctance to bringing in a consultant to perform a benchmarking assessment. Nevertheless, they eventually acquiesced bringing in a noted benchmarking firm. The result showed that while overall costs were good, there were savings to be had through automation. The outsourcing evaluation process brought forward the date in which they were to implement data center automation, from initially one year, down to six months. It eventually became three months. So as Jack notes: "[outsourcing] dramatically accelerated the process." Additionally, the benchmarking assessment pointed out that a number of their equipment leases which were thought to be satisfactory, were not as good as they had thought. FIRM20's management knew the reason for the poor leases. They were signed when the company was in very serious financial shape, and the leasing companies clearly had the upper hand in such a situation. But the benchmarking results showed them, according to Jack, "that was a more severe problem than we had anticipated and so one of the things that we did as part of the data center's bid was to restructure some of those leases."

In order to drive down costs, Jack notes that:

"we ended up working with [one of the leasing companies] to come up with a leasing arrangement that gave us some flexibility to expand or contract but still restructure some of these particularly burdensome leases. Now in retrospect, we've got some real reservations about the wisdom of doing that because price performance in technology particularly the service side has improved dramatically and we'd really like to get rid of one of the mainframes if we weren't still locked in. So, in retrospect, what really would have been the smartest move for the corporation would've been to say OK, we've proven that we ought to stay inside, but let's not really take up anybody's offer."

In FIRM20's case, the outsourcing decision was not the sole impetus for implementing cost reduction strategies in IS. Jack contends that many of the cost-saving measures were embarked upon prior to the insourcing bid. "[Because we had stayed inside] it was business as usual. Some of the cost-saving measures had been triggered even before the bid was submitted. Processes had begun to be automated. We hadn't begun to lay people off yet, but the automation project was finished at the time the bid was submitted. And we had started to achieve those benefits and some people were laid off by the middle of May (1989). Others were scheduled throughout the remainder of the year. Some on into the early part of 1991."

Management at FIRM20 are very happy with the insourcing project, noting that a number of benefits have been achieved. These can be divided into the following areas.

Cost Reductions

Cost reductions (no concrete figure given) were generated largely from staff reductions and reduced hardware costs. On the staff reduction side, Jack says: ". . . as a result, I guess directly of the outsourcing proposal, we reduced staff at the data center by about 25%." And the reduction in staff is continuing.

Software turned out not to be a big contributor to savings; 66% of the savings came from reduced staff, about 33% from less money spent on hardware. Jack states that the data center continues to reduce head-count, even though the workload has increased significantly—25–30%. In a nutshell: "What we've seen overall, we've got additional capacity, appreciable increase in workload. We're running the data center today with less than half the staff we had."

Tape automation has also played an important role in driving down costs while allowing an increase in workload. Jack states: "The last big increment came as a result of putting automated tape libraries . . . we are to the point where 90% of the tapes are automated."

Overall, IS costs at FIRM20 are felt to be excellent. The belief is backed up by the latest benchmarking figures performed by one of the leading benchmarking firms which show that FIRM20's IS costs are 37% below the norm.

Empowerment

Another strategy which was implemented as part of the insourcing project was to empower the IS staff. They were given more autonomy and authority to make decisions on their own. Further, they imple-mented a policy of having quarterly "Quality Meetings" where they get people together and talk about what's going on in IS. According to Bill, this has caused a remarkable improvement in team spirit. He says: "so we operate a lot as one team. It is a dramatic change . . ."

Standardized Platform

A third area which has led to improvements in IS has been the imple-mentation of standards and the use of a standardized platform. Jack states: "We need to download and you just sit there watch and in less than a minute it will download 20, 30, 50 modules that I need to get current and I'm on my way. You see last year it took five minutes just to get logged on to the system. So we're able electronically to deliver software to the desktop because it's a controlled standard environ-ment. And the productivity gains from managing those otherwise di-verse environments, the benefit to the business is just tremendous."

Flexibility

Flexibility was a key concern in the reason to stay inside. Had one of the external bidders won the contract, Jack believes things would be radically different:

"It probably wouldn't have looked like it did at the end of '92. We wouldn't have any of that backbone, I don't believe, or very, very little of it. We would have a lot of fragmented independently developed systems. We wouldn't have been able to do what we're doing and what we're about to do."

Additionally, there was the issue of risk which was part of the reason to want flexibility. Jack states:

"I think senior management recognized that there was some risk and we were very acutely aware that the nature of this technology was so volatile that it was extremely difficult to predict for even 2 or 3 years much less 10 with any degree of confidence . . . companies that have gone to [outsourcing vendors], it's very difficult for them to make the transition to the new technology."

Jack continues:

"And whether it's 2 years, 3 years, 5 years, you're increasingly going to see involvement in renegotiating to cover the kinds of technology situations that were unforeseeable when you struck the deal; and it is a truism with any contract, especially with an outsourcing contact, that you've lost all your leverage once you've signed the deal because in this case all your expertise is gone as well."

From the flexibility perspective, Jack summarizes FIRM20's belief:

". . . our recognition is that this is very rapidly evolving technology and any long-term deal, whether it's an equipment lease or an outsourcing deal, represents tremendous risk and the risk goes up the longer the term of the arrangement. Stay flexible, that is the best strategic decision from the technology perspective; posturing your company to leverage technology at the lowest cost, you've got to stay short term."

CIO Position

Another change to IS that came about as a result of the insourcing project has been the creation of a CIO post in the corporation. Prior to the insourcing bid, IS had a director, but the status of that position was clearly not as great as the new post. The new CIO has more of a strategic role in the company, and is responsible for helping to set the strategic direction for FIRM20.

Service Levels

The cost savings accrued by the implementation of the above-mentioned strategies have come at a price. Service levels, or perhaps it might be better to discuss them in terms of the quality of service, have likely dropped due to insourcing. Jack states:

". . . he [the CIO] is very seriously talking about owning the software on the desktop and telling people what they can run and what they can't run . . . he's talking and nobody's greatly exercising; I'm sure a lot of people aren't very happy, but nobody's voicing any concern. He's talking about pulling all the [particular type of software] products off, or at least dropping support for them."

Jack appreciates that services to the operating units have likely gone down, but he feels that the same would have happened if they had outsourced. "But I think what it represents . . . and one of the things we were concerned about, is what you end up with an outsourcer is their average service. You're not going to have outstanding service relative to their clients to the extent that you want to really differentiate yourself from the market; you may be at a disadvantage with that kind of average."

Senior Management's Perceptions of IS after Insourcing

Senior management's overall perception of IS after the insourcing project seems to have improved markedly. While it is impossible to prove that insourcing was responsible for the improved attitude towards IS, both Jack and Bill believe it was instrumental in the general positive perception they feel they now have. Jack says: "[it has] changed the environment that IS works in within this business. And that has made a real difference."

Of course, all is not perfect at FIRM20. Jack notes: ". . . there was a very definite tension between various organizations out in the field and central IS [in the past]. It's not gone entirely, but it's an order of magnitude less than it used to be. It's much more of a one company atmosphere. . . ."

Perhaps an example of the positive perception that senior management has about IS comes from the corporation's CEO. In the past, nothing was ever formally said about the value of IS in the business. But in this past year's annual report, the CEO wrote: "We are working smarter—not just harder—as we use new information technology . . . [it] is critical for our future."

CONCLUSIONS

As can be noted in our six cases, insourcing provided IS management with the opportunity to drive down IS costs and to be competitive with outside vendors. One might suspect that such cost reduction successes should lead senior management to change their negative perceptions about IS since internal IS costs would be comparable to outside options. Yet, in three of the cases (FIRMs 15, 17 and 18) senior management continues to perceive IS as a cost pit.

Consider, for example, FIRM18 where according to one IS manager: "All [senior management] see is this amount of money that they have to write a check for every year. Year after year after year. Where is the benefit? . . . Show me where you put one more dollar on the income statement."

From this quotation, FIRM18's IS is not strategically recognized by senior management—they view the entire department as a cost burden. Yet, the IS manager feels it does not deserve such a reputation. He states: "The IS organization have a tremendous amount to contribute if they ever get out of the back room and be perceived as having an opportunity to participate in the resolution of problems rather than being one of those problems."

A similar situation occurred at FIRM15. Although IS reduced costs by 54% senior management continues to perceive IS negatively. Indeed, the IS department's reducing costs only reconfirmed management's perceptions that IS was inefficient. One of the IS managers expresses his frustration: "We look at it [the insourcing success] and say, 'Boy, we did a lot of hard work, we did some good things.' We want to pat ourselves on the back by showing it to [senior management]. Then they tell us to turn around and stick it."

Again, like FIRM18 senior management does not appear to consider IS to be of strategic importance—IS's role is merely to collect data. The competitive use of information comes from the business units. Yet IS feels it could contribute strategically. For example, the director of IS administration believes that the company could improve its market share by getting better merchandise into the stores. Perhaps information systems could be used to better track consumer behavior. But he sighs, "What do I know? I'm just an IS guy."

A major lesson from these cases is that while cost reduction (combined with proof of comparable costs to outside vendors) is an apparent necessary condition for this formulation of positive senior management perceptions of IS, it is not a sufficient condition. Other factors are also necessary. In FIRMs 16, 19 and 20, the hiring of a business-minded CIO helped sway management perceptions about IS. In FIRM16, for example, not only did the CIO achieve insourcing savings of several million dollars, but he did this while creating a unified IS vision and convincing his management that IS is a strategic resource that can be used for competitive advantage to attract students. Similarly, in FIRM19, senior management now views IS positively and not as a cost burden. While reducing IS costs through insourcing no doubt helped in the formulation of the positive perception, the business acumen of the newly appointed CIO likely had the most affect.

In the case of FIRM3 (from the outsourcing study), the political savvy of the IS director, as well as his intimate knowledge of the corporation's business, significantly contributed to shaping senior management's supportive attitude towards IS. They firmly believed that IS was strategic to the business.

In sum, the insourcing cases alert us to the fact that just decreasing costs on its own will not necessarily change senior management's perception of IS as a cost pit. Indeed, reducing costs may only confirm senior management's perceptions that IS was inefficient to begin with. And if IS is not considered as strategic to the business, it will only help influence this negative view of IS's efficiency. Reducing costs is but one of a number of strategies which can be followed to help align the perceptions of senior management and IS, as will be further explored in Chapter 7.

4

The IS Manager's Role in Insourcing

INTRODUCTION

IS managers play many roles in insourcing projects from initiator of the decision, creator of cost reduction tactics, and implementor. This chapter focuses on the creative role participants assumed in identifying and implementing tactics to reduce IS costs. Through their successes and failures, other IS managers may gain insights on how to reduce their own costs.

Participants identified cost reduction tactics that focus on the three major IS cost drivers: people, hardware, and software. Participants noted that insourcing decisions should focus on cost drivers rather than esoteric aspects such as "service quality" and "technical competence"; they felt that reducing the cost drivers was the only way to slash IS budgets. In particular, because personnel costs are the greatest proportion of IS costs, participants focused on headcount reduction. For example, most of the savings from data center consolidation can be attributed to reduced personnel. In addition, some participants found innovative ways to reduce hardware and software costs. Participants' tactics to reduce IS cost drivers are categorized as follows:

1 Automation
2 Chargeback
3 Data center consolidation
4 Departmental reorganization
5 Employee empowerment
6 Hardware negotiations

7   Just-in-time resources
8   More efficient resource usage
9   Service elimination
10   Software negotiations
11   Software standardization

Table 4.1 identifies which tactics were used by which participating companies and indicates whether the tactic was successful. In most cases, participants quantified the savings achieved by these tactics either in terms of dollars or headcounts. In some cases, however, participants could not specifically isolate savings to particular tactics, thus savings are described more theoretically.

Table 4.1   *Cost reduction tactics used by case participants*

Tactic	FIRM 15	FIRM 16	FIRM 17	FIRM 18	FIRM 19	FIRM 20
Automation	X		X	X	X	X
Chargeback			X	X		
Data center consolidation	X	X		X		
Departmental reorganization		X	X		X	
Employee empowerment			X	X	X	X
Hardware negotiations		X		X	X*	X
Just-in-time resources			X	X		
More efficient resource usage	X		X	X	X*	
Service elimination			X			
Software negotiations		X		X	X*	
Software standardization			X	X		X

* Tactic was not successful.

Each of the 11 tactics are described in detail below.

AUTOMATION

Several participants decided to reduce labor costs by replacing people with automation technology. While the investment in automation technology increases software costs, a net gain is achieved through personnel displacement. In particular, participants found that automating the following functions leads to reduced costs: console operations, tape silos, report distribution, network monitoring, and problem management. Each of these areas are explained below.

Console Operations

Many of the participants employed computer operators around the clock to monitor computer consoles. Operators were required to continually scan the pages of operator messages for items requiring an action, such as restart a program, schedule a job, or mount a computer tape. With constant monitoring, computer operators could not leave the console to perform other tasks. With console automation technology, the software package sifts through the operator messages and notifies the operator only when a specific action is required. This frees the operators from constant monitoring and allows them to perform other tasks in the data center. FIRMs 15, 17, and 19 all implemented or planned to invest in console automation to reduce the number of computer operators:

- FIRM15 saved $100 000 per year in reduced headcount.
- FIRM17 also saved money through console automation, but they failed to attribute an exact dollar amount to the savings. (Instead, FIRM17 bundled the $400 000 annual savings from automation to include console automation, data communications, and network monitoring.)
- FIRM19 planned to reduce headcount by four people through console automation, although senior management has not yet invested in the technology.

Tape Silos

Although some vendors tried to sell participants robotic tape technology, participants found that a compromise between totally manual tape libraries and totally robotic tape libraries offered the most cost efficient tactic for tape management. FIRM18 provides an apt example.

FIRM18 had 16 operators mounting 90 000 tapes per year. Tape mounts were very slow because the tape library was designed with long, narrow aisles. By redesigning the tape library with input from the operators, they configured the library to minimize the distance between the tapes and the tape drives. They also shortened the shelves so that the operators can scan the entire room. FIRM18 invested in big screen TVs that can be viewed from anywhere in the library. Operators can now see what tapes need to be mounted without having to physically walk to a monitor. In addition, FIRM18 invested in some automatic loaders which allow operators to load tapes before a shift. Through the redesign and automation, FIRM18 reduced the staff from 16 full time operators to 4 operators and 3 contractors. As far as service is concerned, an IS

manager at FIRM18 explains that the new tape design and partial automation allow workers to mount a tape as fast as a robot:

> "The other thing in terms of the mount time, on average, we mount a tape as
> fast as a robot does. A robot will mount a tape, on average, in 45 seconds,
> whether it's a scratch tape that hasn't been used or go get a specific one, on
> average, we do a scratch tape in 12 seconds because they are in an auto
> loader, it takes the next one and stuffs it in. And we do demand mounts in 63
> seconds. For a weighted average, we are in within two to three seconds of
> what the robot does."

FIRM20 achieved similar savings through tape automation. The director of IS planning states:

> "The last big increment came as a result of putting automated tape libraries.
> We are to the point where 90% of the tapes are automated."

Report Distribution

Many data centers employ a person to continually monitor printers.
Their main task is to separate reports into the appropriate user box.
Some participants found that they could eliminate a person through
report distribution software that automatically batches a given user's
reports. FIRMs 18 and 19 both invested in report distribution. FIRM19
planned to reduce headcount by one person on the graveyard shift. An
IS manager from FIRM19 explains:

> "The reports that come off the mainframe, the operator has to split them apart,
> try to figure out, 'If this is XYZ, it goes here to second floor.' Then put it in his
> bin. The report distribution system—the first phase, all of Joe's reports for one
> night were bundled into one package and put a bin number on it. Joe gets 15
> reports from 20 different jobs—the software does that now."

Network Monitoring

According to a benchmarking firm, most companies can reduce labor
costs through automatic network monitoring. Without such software,
operators may have to manually enter as many as 400 commands per
1000 terminals per shift. Through automation, the number can be reduced to about 160 commands. FIRM17 was able to save $60 000 per
year in labor costs by investing in a network monitor.

Problem Management

FIRM19 plans to reduce headcount by two employees through investing in problem management software. Prior to automation, computer

operators had to determine which datasets to uncatalogue and where in the jobstream to restart processing when an ABEND occurred. With automation, the problem management system would automatically correct catalogs, determine where in a jobstream to start reprocessing, and rerun the job.

Taken as a whole, the participants estimate the annual savings from automation as follows:

FIRM15	$625 000
FIRM17	$400 000
FIRM19	seven workers (dollars figures were not given)

CHARGEBACK

Chargeback systems appears to be the IS albatross. IS managers have a difficult time overcoming internal politics to implement fair chargeback systems. Instead, users demand more and more services with seemingly little consequence to their monthly "bills." Consider, for example, a recent complaint expressed by Richard Huber of Continental Bank on chargeback systems in general:

> "Perhaps half of Continental's problems with in-house services stemmed from overuse. For instance, the most routine documents were always sent to the legal department for reviews. 'Better safe than sorry,' people would say, while thinking, 'and besides, it's just an internal cost, not real dollars.'" (Huber, 1993)

Prior to outsourcing or insourcing, participants employed a general allocation system in which the entire IS budget is shared among all business units based on their usage. With general allocation systems, users are often motivated to excessively consume resources. As our restaurant check analogy (discussed in Chapter 6) shows, each person is actually motivated to order more food and beverages because part of the cost will be covered by the other parties. The same is often true with general allocation chargeback systems. If one business unit purchases a software package, such as a new Database Management System (DBMS), the cost will be spread across all the business units, thus motivating excessive software demand.

Two participants felt that their general allocation systems promoted excessive resource consumption, but had previously been unable to change the chargeback structure due to internal politics. When senior management finally empowered them to make a change, two companies—FIRMs 17 and 18—created chargeback systems that made users responsible for their own computer consumption.

FIRM17 created an unbundled allocation system in which users buy a block of computer time with a modest set of standard software. If users want any additional software, they must pay the IS department for the exact cost of the software license fee and maintenance. Thus, the costs associated with software used by one unit are no longer spread across the whole company. If two units decide to both purchase a piece of software, they negotiate among themselves which unit will pay which portion of the costs—the IS department no longer determines the allocation algorithm.

FIRM17's unbundled allocation system made the users take responsibility for their systems. They began to negotiate among themselves to eliminate redundant software. Throughout the software spectrum, users banded together to purchase one software package for one function—one spreadsheet, one e-mail system, one report writer. Of course cases exist where individual units decide to purchase software not included in the standard software set, such as a DBMS, but these software packages are cost justified by the business units not IS. An IS manager at FIRM17 reiterates the change in user behavior as a result of the new chargeback system:

> "If they can make the business case that they need SAS [Statistical Analysis], their prices are essentially our costs. But it's unbundled. What happened was a lot of the software disappeared. Everyone said, 'gee, I can't justify that.' We used to have the VM [Virtual Machine] operating system. Then we went to unbundled pricing and someone said, 'it's ridiculous to pay $200 000 a year for VM.' Before we were selling CPU seconds and they'd say, 'I want my CPU seconds to have the VM operating systems.' And that raised the price of everyone's CPU seconds. When outsourcers come in, they sell you a logical 3084 for a fixed unit, and it isn't until later you realize all the little kickers that aren't included. So I've tried to change the charging philosophy to reflect my out of pocket costs."

FIRM18 created a unique chargeback system in which users only see volumes, not prices. Senior management made the IS department commit to a certain dollar budget and made users commit to a certain volume. An IS manager describes why the user's chargeback system is based on consumption rather than cost of consumption:

> "[Users] don't control costs. [Users] control the piece that is constant, the capacity. Rates change. Rates go up or go down. So if [business units] use the same thing, someone says my IS budget went down. They had nothing to do with that. That's because I lowered the cost of the service. They didn't do a damn thing to impact their bottom line. So we said, 'We'll worry about cost.

You guys worry about consumption.' Get them to focus on the metric that they can control."

The IS department now generates a *daily* usage report distributed to the seven CFOs of the business units. If the CFO sees that volumes were exceeded the previous day, he or she immediately investigates and the culprit is reprimanded.

"They (the users) lived in fear of their CFO. He wanted to know who it was who put him over. That helped us a lot because we were no longer the bad guy."

If a business unit exceeds volumes to the point where IS must purchase additional resources, the business unit—not IS—must request funds from senior management. Like FIRM17's chargeback system, FIRM18's chargeback system makes users responsible for their own IS costs.

DATA CENTER CONSOLIDATION

By far the greatest opportunity for savings is through data center con-solidation. All IS cost drivers—people, hardware, software, and facilities—can be significantly reduced through consolidation. As noted before, many IS managers recognize the potential savings of consolidation, but oftentimes cannot overcome political opposition among business unit leaders. With an outsourcing threat, however, IS is empowered to consolidate—either the internal IS department will consolidate or an outsourcing vendor will consolidate for them. The following examples are highlighted from the cases.

Before FIRM16 consolidated, it maintained three data centers on the same campus to service three different academic units. Due to political infighting, FIRM16's president believed consolidation would be im-possible. At first he considered outsourcing—let the vendor do the consolidation—but instead he created a CIO position which managed all three data centers. With the CIO's power, he was able to overcome political obstacles and consolidate the three data centers into one to achieve estimated savings of $2 122 000 over the next five years.

Before FIRM18 consolidated, it maintained three data centers in three separate cities to support three divisions. Like FIRM16, FIRM18 had tried several times to consolidate but business unit politics stone-walled implementation. When senior management finally empowered IS to outsource via an outsourcing evaluation, the three data centers were consolidated into one. Although FIRM18 did not isolate the savings for consolidation, participants view this tactic as instrumental in slashing their IS budget from $32 million to $18 million.

Before FIRM15 consolidated, it maintained two data centers *at the same site* to provide disaster recovery for each other. This strategy was implemented by a previous IS manager who convinced senior management that two data centers were less expensive to maintain than subscribing to a disaster recovery service. (What would happen if a flood, fire or earthquake hit the site?) Through the insourcing project, FIRM15 gradually consolidated the tape libraries, print sites, console operations, and CPUs. Although a specific dollar amount was not associated with the savings, the cost was only $125 000 for a disaster recovery site in the next state—much less than the cost of maintaining their own hot site.

DEPARTMENTAL REORGANIZATION

Participants believe that departmental reorganization offers many companies opportunities to reduce personnel costs by eliminating redundant workers. Typically, data center operations involve many skill sets from highly technical (systems programming) to highly mundane (tape mounters). As a result, data center personnel tend to specialize in particular technical areas. Although specialization was efficient before data centers became more automated, today highly specialized jobs lead to inefficiency. Through departmental reorganization, narrowly defined job titles are eliminated and replaced with generalists through cross-training. For example, computer operators may operate printers and tape drives, systems programmers may perform their own quality assurance checks, and supervisors may actually operate machines. The following examples are highlighted from the cases.

Through a reorganization, FIRM17 reduced management, particularly on the night shift. As the data center manager noted, "why need a manager to supervise five people on a night shift?" They also reduced some of their technical staff. For example, the data center manager proudly notes that FIRM17 employs 8 systems programmers whereas other data centers of his size employs 20 programmers.

Of all the participants, FIRM19 saved the most through departmental reorganization—they eliminated 11 out of 39 positions through a reorganization. Prior to the reorganization, a powerful labor union instilled rules that required excessive specialization as well as excessive supervision. For example, union rules specified that if a worker was called into work during an emergency, a supervisor must also be called into work—all on overtime pay. Another example, supervisors were not allowed to touch the machines. Thus, FIRM19's labor costs were extremely high due to the specialization of tasks imposed by the labor union. Not until the outsourcing evaluation when the union faced the risk of losing the entire work site, did they allow FIRM19 to reorganize the department, create generalist positions, and eliminate unnecessary supervision and redundant tasks.

FIRM16 also achieved saving of $613 718 annually through a reorganization prior to consolidation, but the savings came largely through the organizational consolidation rather than shifting from specialists to generalists. The CIO explains:

> "So we've done the organizational consolidation. We got all the people together. We started to organize them more along skill groups instead of all these independent data centers."

Thus, FIRM16 achieved savings by having one organization support three data centers before physical data center consolidation. The CIO of the university wanted to associate these savings with reorganization rather than consolidation; he believes it is important to separate the benefits so that companies realize they can still achieve savings through departmental reorganization even if they do not wish to physically consolidate their data centers.

EMPLOYEE EMPOWERMENT

Employee empowerment is the tactic of making the employee responsible for his or her own work so that less supervision is required. Rather than have a manager dictate what, when, and how to accomplish work, employees determine this for themselves. Four participants implemented this tactic with mixed success.

FIRM17 trained their employees to be responsible for their own work. Empowerment actually led to reduced labor costs because FIRM17 eliminated their quality assurance personnel by making programmers responsible for the quality of their own work; programmers may decide to test their programs or not test their programs according to their own professional judgments. An IS manager from FIRM17 explains:

> "Increasingly, we hold the person responsible for the quality of their cut over. If they feel the need, they have access to testing, if they don't, they can cut it over. If it fails, they will incur a penalty, but we are no longer big brothering it."

Although employee empowerment was successful from an economic perspective, participants from FIRM18 note that programmers now implement systems with more errors. Management, however, is willing to tolerate the decrease in quality in return for lower costs.

FIRM18 feels that its employee empowerment has been successful because it motivated creative and efficient behavior through competition. Participants explained that employees create their own self-managed work teams that compete for tasks by submitting bids to management. For example, management may request a bid to investigate the economic feasibility of client/server technology. Employees assemble bids in response. The winner(s) are released from some of their current responsibilities to work on the client/server project. As an IS manager from FIRM18 explains, the winning group decides how to manage the project themselves:

> "We have advertised what we have to do. We have let people volunteer, literally bid for the job and do interviews. We had a four-month project. We took them out of their normal work and put together a special team and we came back and said, 'Okay, it's you three people. We are not going to figure out how to run your team. We are not going to tell you who is in charge. You know what we want done. You know when it's supposed to be done. You figure out how to do it.' "

The competition promotes creativity, but one wonders what will happen when management requests a bid for a task no one wants to perform.

FIRM19's employee empowerment has not been as successful as the other cases, primarily because it was implemented during the insourcing decision. The staff could not embrace the concept of self-managed work groups while implementing other insourcing tasks such as departmental reorganization. An IS manager from FIRM19 explains the situation:

> "At the time this [insourcing] implementation went in, the operations area was just forming self-managed work teams. I think, it was a major mistake to attempt such a revolutionary thing like that in a time frame when you know you are reducing the work force in that same time."

Thus, FIRM19 believes that empowerment may have reduced supervision costs if it was implemented after the other insourcing tactics.

FIRM20 implemented empowerment as part of its insourcing program. They gave the remaining IS staff much more freedom and authority to handle tasks as they saw fit. They were, however, held accountable for their actions. Every quarter, IS teams reported their progress in "Quality

Meetings." The CIO claims ". . . we operate a lot as one team. It is a dramatic change." Teams that led to further IS cost savings translated into positive job performance ratings, and higher pay. Failure to meet performance expectations resulted in negative evaluations.

HARDWARE NEGOTIATIONS

During the past decade, participants noted that hardware vendors have less power over users due to increased competition and connectivity among different manufacturers. Whereas customers once rarely entered into hard-nosed negotiations with hardware vendors, customers now fiercely bargain for significant reductions on hardware price lists. In addition, the used mainframe market offers some participants bargain prices. Some of the participants' successes and failures in dealing with hardware vendors are reported below.

Buy Used

All participants agree that the used mainframe market offers significant discounts. In our outsourcing study, for example, the IS manager from FIRM8 leased a used CPU for only $4000 a month. He believed that IS managers can significantly reduce hardware costs by using older technology:

> "As long as we stay on the trailing edge of technology—and I've been pushing this concept to management—we have an opportunity to capitalize on cheaper computing costs." (Lacity and Hirschheim, 1993)

An IS manager at FIRM15 follows the same tactic to reduce hardware costs:

> "Our acquisition costs, especially on the hardware side [are low]—we've been running rusty old iron here for many, many years."

An IS manager at FIRM18 commented that the used hardware market is even driving down costs on new technology:

> "The new mainframe market may lower [the advantage of the used market]. The used mainframe market is competing with the new mainframe market—vendor discounts are 30–40% on new equipment."

Thus, bargains seem readily available in the used and new hardware markets.

Upgrade Used Hardware rather than Purchase New Hardware

The CIO at FIRM16 employs a strategy of upgrading existing equipment rather than purchasing new equipment. For example, the CIO noted that the campus hospital had budgeted $4 million for a new mainframe. He convinced the hospital to upgrade rather than purchase a new machine. The CIO explains:

> "The hospital would have normally gone to buy more equipment. We told them they had to go buy used equipment. Instead of spending 4 million on a new ES9000, they spent a million to upgrade from a 200 to 300S."

Create a Bundled RFP

In dealing with hardware vendors, the size of the account appears to determine, in some sense, the relative power of customer and vendor. Participants found that by bundling an RFP for all hardware maintenance, they were in a better position to negotiate because the bidding vendors each wanted the sizable account. Two examples are highlighted from the cases.

FIRM16 saved $400 000 annually off hardware maintenance by bundling the hardware maintenance across all four campuses into one account. The CIO explains:

> "We previously let each organization deal with maintenance separately. In front of consolidating, because it took some time to do it, we finally got all three organizations to put out a joint RFP. The result of the RFP is we are now going to spend—hardware maintenance on all mainframe related equipment, CPU, disk drives, tape drives, we were currently spending $976 000, we [now pay $476 000]."

FIRM18 employed the same tactic. An IS manager at FIRM18 explains that he saved 40% off a list price by bundling a maintenance RFP:

> "We got better than 40% off list price. That was unheard of. This was due in part to the new [hardware vendor] organization—some local autonomy to make decisions . . . A very strange deal . . . We have side agreements . . . We are doing things and being charged outside of the standard piece of paper. They went as far as they could with that, then local management did some things on the side."

FIRM18's IS manager was able to negotiate such a good deal because the vendor was anxious to get the large five-year maintenance contract.

FIRM19 also tried to negotiate with their hardware vendors but were less successful than FIRM18. The IS manager tried to explain to the hardware vendors that if they did not lower costs, then FIRM19 may outsource to a third party and the vendor would thus lose the whole account. An IS manager from FIRM19 explains that hardware vendors "didn't get the message":

> "We basically brought them all together and laid out, 'hey you are our suppliers now. We would like to have you support us in putting together this internal response. What can you do for us in a partner, long-term arrangement?' I can summarize, I got back weasel words, specific proposals for replacing DASD with X—they didn't get the message. They didn't know how to respond to what we were looking for. We were trying to get creative with them. 'Commit with us to this.' They couldn't do it. They couldn't get [names of hardware divisions] to understand."

Perhaps FIRM19 failed at hardware negotiations for the same reason FIRM18 was successful—the size of the RFP; the dollar value of FIRM19's RFP may have been too small to woo vendors.

Negotiate Contracts

Another finding from the outsourcing study which was corroborated with the insourcing study is that contract negotiations are a key determinant of customer satisfaction. In the past, customers merely signed the vendor's standard contract, which always favored the vendors. Many times customers were charged fees for upgrades, maintenance, transfers, and scope of use. FIRM18 put a stop to this—they now have an IS contract administrator negotiate their contracts because a lawyer was not, in their minds, as qualified. An IS manager from FIRM18 explains:

> "[The IS contract administrator] has over this three-year period, he has been delegated sufficient authority from the legal department to read a contract. If the dollar level is X, he has the authority to pass on the legalese of the contract because he is recognized—he brings up things that the lawyer doesn't. A lawyer specializes in general business law doesn't understand our business. Our guy is living it, breathing it, day in day out."

FIRM20 has taken a much more aggressive role in contract negotiations and renegotiations. In particular, the director of IS planning notes that vendors are no longer able to rope FIRM20 into long-term contracts. Rather, FIRM20 negotiates short-term contracts with renegotiation options to reduce their risk. The director of IS planning notes:

> "Our recognition is that this is very rapidly evolving technology and any long-term deal, whether it's an equipment lease or an outsourcing deal,

represents tremendous risk and the risk goes up the longer the term of the arrangement. Stay flexible is the best strategic decision from a technology perspective."

JUST-IN-TIME RESOURCES

Many IS managers purchase computer resources "just-in-case" they are needed. For example, IS managers may want to upgrade before capacity is exceeded or may buy more DASD in anticipation of increased demand. This IS inventory, while considered an element of service excellence, is costly.

To reduce costs, IS managers can move to "just-in-time" (JIT) resources in which the inventory carrying costs are minimized. In the spirit of the Japanese concept of JIT inventory, some participants achieve JIT computer resources by postponing upgrades and purchasing MIPs and DASD at the last possible moment. JIT is particularly relevant to the IS arena because of the IS maxim "the longer you wait to make a purchase, the cheaper the price."

FIRM17 used to maintain a large inventory of excess hardware in anticipation of user demand. For example, they maintained a store of excess DASD. The IS department also purchased new machines when old machines still had capacity because they feared that response time would suffer if purchases were postponed. After the insourcing project, this strategy of "stocking up for a rainy day" was abandoned. Now, FIRM17 purchases resources at the last possible moment. FIRM17's IS manager explains:

> "We try to buy in my motto just-in-time-MIPS, rather than just-in-case. We used to buy in reserve, thinking we'll probably need this. Now we'll buy it at the last possible minute. Well, the way market prices drop, this is perfect. The just-in-case leads you down the path of redundant equipment and maybe extra capacity. Those things are okay if you are in the right business, but the business we are in, we don't want to do that."

FIRM18 also reduced hardware costs by moving to "just-in-time" inventory. FIRM18 bundled an RFP for a five-year contract for MIPs and DASD. The hardware vendor would supply additional resources as needed. An IS manager from FIRM18 explains:

> "The hardware side, we said, we've got to find an arrangement with a supplier that is literally a fixed price arrangement. We know exactly what we want to buy—MIPS and gigabytes and DASD farms and processors. We have to find somebody who would be willing to across multiple years, multiple machines, bid something. Our understanding—at that point, not

too many deals have ever been done that way . . . to say for five years, here's what we want to buy and that's everything, lock stock and barrel—that approach had not been [done]."

FIRM18 accepted a bid from a hardware vendor that significantly reduced hardware costs. The vendor even offered a 14% growth factor for free.

MORE EFFICIENT RESOURCE USAGE

When senior management pressures IS staff and IS users to reduce costs, they often respond by conserving use of existing resources. Participants found ways to frugally use printers, DASD, and utilities. The following examples are highlighted from the cases.

Printing

Excessive user printing can cost millions of dollars per year. In most organizations, users are free to print with no financial repercussions. Two organizations gained significant savings by charging users to print and offering them on-line report viewing as a hardcopy alternative. In addition, print costs were reduced through form standardization and paper supply negotiations. Examples from the cases include the following.

FIRM19 plans to purchase a system that will allow on-line review of reports. Rather than have users print massive reports they do not need, users will first review output on the screen and only print the summary information they need. FIRM19 plans to save $33 000 per year through on-line report review.

FIRM15 achieved more dramatic savings of $300 000 per year through on-line report view. An IS manager explains:

"In printing, we just started doing on-line viewing. At the time [the benchmarking company came in], we had just got the package and had started to explore that, get users to look at it on-line. Because our print volumes were very high. Since then, we've cut at least 50% off printing volumes with on-line viewing."

FIRM17 reduced print costs through form standardization. Prior to standardization, users were free to select among many forms that provide virtually the same function. For example, two forms may be identical except one has a color logo while the other has a black and white logo. Multiple forms for the same function increased printing costs by requiring multiple order transactions and a dedicated printing operator to change forms. Through form standardization, FIRM17 was able to significantly reduce printing costs.

FIRM18 achieved reduced printing costs by creating an RFP that bundled all their paper and supplies. Rather than purchase forms, paper, and supplies from multiple vendors, FIRM18 has contracted with one vendor for all their printing needs. An IS manager from FIRM18 explains how savings were achieved:

"By aggregating paper, we were able to buy paper as much as 40% cheaper by taking all domestic requirements to the paper suppliers. We probably had four or five suppliers before, let's put all of this on the table, we have to find one supplier who can handle our business in every geographic location. These print sites are in excess of one million pages per month. These are not little printers in the corner."

Due to the size of the order, the vendors bid rock-bottom prices.

DASD

Every participant reduced the cost of DASD by moving old datasets to tape and by optimizing DASD storage. Although IS managers feared that the users would object, most users did not even notice that their datasets were migrated off DASD. The migration allowed several participants to cancel orders for additional DASD—a dollar saved is a dollar earned.

Utility Bills

FIRM19 was determined to reduce IS costs to the lowest possible levels. Although most people conserve energy in their home, IS management at FIRM19 noted that employees often waste electricity in the office. They proposed to reduce the electric bill by $32 000 annually by dimming the lights in the data center, increasing the temperature in the data center by three degrees to reduce air conditioning costs, and powering down systems not used at night.

SERVICE ELIMINATION

The president of a benchmarking firm we interviewed noted that insourcing projects should lead to the elimination of unneeded services. Despite his claim, only one participant, FIRM17, specifically mentioned this tactic.

After IS management at FIRM17 changed the IS philosophy from service excellence to cost efficiency, they found they could eliminate several services associated with service excellence. For example, they eliminated four people who previously monitored the chargeback system. Under the simplified unbundled pricing system, the chargeback monitoring function was no longer needed. With the move from "just-in-case" resources to "just-in-time" resources, FIRM17 could eliminate the two capacity planners because long-range estimates were no longer required. The IS management also eliminated redundant hardware and software used to protect response time. Response time suffered somewhat, but senior management applauds, rather than complains. The data center manager explains:

> "When we were through, one of the controllers, he said, 'You cut my bill by a couple of million dollars.' I said, 'yeah.' The controller said, 'My response time is a little more erratic . . . if you made the response time slower, could you save me a couple more million dollars?' "

SOFTWARE NEGOTIATIONS

In the same way that savings can be achieved through negotiations with hardware vendors, software savings can be achieved with software vendors. Two examples are highlighted from the cases.

FIRM16 reduced software costs by negotiating with some software vendors to become advanced customers. The CIO explains one successful negotiation:

> "To give you another example, the initial budget for this fiscal year, FY94, having at $80 000 for [a database management system] on the mainframe. We told the [software vendor] guys we aren't going to muck around with [a DBMS] on the mainframe. We went and cut a deal with [the software vendor] and our alumni development thing and [the software vendor] waived the rights. We are going to be an advanced customer, we will move the alumni system off the mainframe, they waived the right to [the mainframe DBMS] until we move to a smaller platform."

Thus, FIRM16 no longer has to pay the license fee for the mainframe DBMS because they agreed to become an advanced customer—analogous to a beta site—for the vendor's LAN DBMS.

FIRM18 also instituted a unique strategy—they bundled all their system software needs into one giant RFP. FIRM18 participants rationalized software and reasoned that software vendors would be willing to provide free software in exchange for a monopoly on the maintenance fees. Rather than continue to buy software packages from 250 vendors, they now purchase all their software from only three vendors. Admittedly, some of the products are not "best of breed," but the total software portfolio costs FIRM18 $2 million less annually. An IS manager for FIRM18 explains:

> "[The software vendor] may have a product that is not best of breed, but across their entire product breadth, it will get the job done, it will be a lower cost, and we will work with that strategic vendor if there are some weaknesses in the product line."

FIRM18 also applied the same strategy to software contracts as hardware contracts. Rather than sign vendor contracts, an IS contract administrator negotiates fees for upgrades, maintenance, transfer of licenses, and scope of use.

FIRM19 tried the same procedure as FIRM18 but without success. They may have had the same problem they did with their failed attempt to negotiate better deals with their hardware vendors: the account may be too small to woo vendors.

SOFTWARE STANDARDIZATION

To reduce software license fees, several participants standardized their software portfolio. Rather than have multiple packages perform the same function, users were only offered a "meat and potatoes" portfolio in which one tool is selected to support one function. If users want additional software, they are charged the full price of the license and maintenance fees. Although software standardization can significantly reduce costs, users often resist having their favorite packages eliminated from the portfolio. Once again, senior management support is critical to successful implementation.

As explained in the chargeback section, FIRM17 created a CPU block of time with standard software. The data center manager explains that to compete with an outsourcer's costs, internal IS departments have to mimic their strategy of offering only a standard set of "no frills" software:

> "[Outsourcing vendors] price like a Sunday paper car—you get a Ford Mustang for $4000. Then if you want a radio, good tires—by the time you are through, it's a $13 000 car. And so we changed our philosophy to the same thing. Our internal customers can buy very basic data center services at a Sunday paper price."

FIRM18 also created a standard set of software upon consolidation. Each of the three data centers previously used different operating systems, schedulers, security systems, monitors, tools, and utilities. As part of the consolidation plan, the three data centers had to agree to adopt one package for one function. The IS manager describes these software decisions as "religious wars":

> "The other thing they said is that the software portfolio across these three divisions—they had each done their own quirk. We had to aggressively get down to a subset of one. You have one business problem, you have one tool to solve that—not three, not six . . . We had religious wars over which was better."

FIRM20 also developed a set of standard application packages they would support. The result has been the ability to electronically deliver upgrades of the software directly to everyone's desktop. It has led to significant productivity gains for the company.

CONCLUSION

Participants reduced IS budgets by focusing on IS cost drivers: people, hardware, and software. By far, staff reductions achieved through automation, data center consolidation, and departmental reorganization offer the greatest opportunities for savings. Participants, however, were also able to reduce their hardware costs through tougher negotiations with vendors, reduced IS inventory (JIT), and using existing resources more frugally. In the software arena, participants reduced costs by implementing chargeback systems, reducing the software portfolio, and negotiating with software vendors.

While senior management applauds IS savings, the reader may note that service degradation was often a consequence. For example, software standardization may cause users to relinquish their favored software packages for what might be perceived as inferior products; JIT resources may cause users to wait for needed resources; chargeback systems may squelch research and development; hardware negotiations may cause business units to use slower technology. One participant summarizes an overall lesson learned from insourcing: "Users are not the decision-makers." Senior management's drive for IS cost savings has shifted the balance on the IS cost versus service pendulum —a theme which is taken up in Chapter 6.

5
The Role of Benchmarking Services in Insourcing Decisions

INTRODUCTION

Many companies, as noted in our two studies, hire benchmarking services in conjunction with outsourcing and/or insourcing decisions. Benchmarking companies may be asked to assess IS performance, create an RFP, and/or to identify ways in which the internal department can reduce costs on their own. To assess IS performance, benchmarking services collect a client's data, normalize it, and create reports which plot the client's performance against a selected reference group extracted from the service's client database. Although the reports do not identify the companies in the reference group, benchmarks provide some objective assessment of IS performance. A benchmarking firm may also use the benchmarks to help define service levels in conjunction with an RFP. Finally, benchmarking services may also provide information on the "best practices" used by other clients in the database. The benchmarking firm may use "best practices" to prescribe cost reduction tactics.

Participants, however, report mixed satisfaction with benchmarking services. Satisfied benchmarking customers claim:

- The benchmarking service helped the internal IS department identify specific cost reduction tactics.
- The benchmarking service provided IS with the needed credibility to convince management they could reduce costs on their own without outsourcing.

Dissatisfied participants claim:

- The benchmarking firm indicated that IS cost and service performance was excellent, leaving IS managers with the impression that they could compete against an external IS vendor. The IS managers were shocked to learn that the IS department was not cost competitive.
- Senior management was unimpressed with the quality of the benchmarking results. Instead, for example, senior management viewed the benchmarks as abstract technical measures which are irrelevant to business concerns.
- Mimicry of "best practices" does not necessarily work.

Through the lessons shared by practitioners, this chapter describes criteria for selecting benchmarking services that facilitate outsourcing/ insourcing decisions. In particular, the following questions are addressed:

- How do IS managers benchmark?
- Why should IS benchmark?
- What should IS benchmark?
- How can IS select an appropriate benchmarking firm?

HOW DO IS MANAGERS BENCHMARK?

The participants in our study consult a variety of sources to compare their performance with external companies (see Tables 5.1 and 5.2). Companies benchmark in four ways:

1 IS managers informally compare cost and service data from a network of peers, typically in the same city or same industry.
2 IS managers informally compare current costs to an outsourcer's costs.
3 IS managers—but more typically senior executives—initiate formal outsourcing evaluations to compare internal costs with a vendor's costs.
4 IS managers hire benchmarking services to compare their IS departments against a database of previous clients.

These four methods are further explained below.

Informal Peer Comparisons

IS managers in 18 of the 20 companies participating in our combined insourcing and outsourcing studies use a network of peers to

Table 5.1   *Case studies classified by source of benchmarks*

Source of benchmarks	Number of sites
Informal peer comparison	18
Informal outsourcing queries	9
Formal outsourcing evaluations	16
Benchmarking services	7

Table 5.2   *Case studies classified by type of benchmark services*

Company pseudonym	Type of benchmark(s)
FIRM2	Data center operations Applications development and support
FIRM17	Data center operations Network and telecommunications
FIRM3	Data center operations
FIRM18	Data center operations
FIRM20	Data center operations
FIRM15	Data center operations
FIRM19	Customer satisfaction/IS effectiveness
FIRM21	Data center operations Customer satisfaction/IS effectiveness

informally compare IS performance. IS managers place great validity on informal peer comparisons because they know and trust their peers. A corporate manager of technology development from FIRM18 adds that peer comparison provides information on *why* costs may differ:

> "So-and-so has some unearned residual that was rolled into a lease and that's why their technology costs are high."

He believes that formal benchmarking services do not explain differences in the data because the benchmarks are created against a blind reference group.

An IS manager from FIRM1 (see Lacity and Hirschheim, 1993) uses informal peer comparisons because he feels that the $50 000 cost of benchmarking services is too high. Instead, he takes "a poor man's approach" to benchmarking by exchanging cost information with IS peers from other companies that operate in the area.

Whether the issue is trust or cost, most IS managers rely on peers to evaluate IS performance. Typically, IS managers continually monitor peers to provide constant feedback on IS effectiveness.

Informal Outsourcing Queries

IS managers from nine of the companies periodically (on average once a year) call outsourcing vendors to test the market. Unfortunately, most outsourcing vendors do not seriously attend to such calls. For example, a new IS manager at FIRM17 tried to understand the IS department's costs by soliciting informal outsourcing bids. As his data center manager explained:

> "Early on, he [the new IS manager] came over and called some outsourcers. He said, 'We have X amount of computer, X amount of disk, my budget is X, can you do it cheaper?' He had no idea what he was doing, but he made some early calls. The vendors get a lot of these calls and it's people trying to justify their existence. They say, 'We're not interested.' They hang up."

According to participants, senior executives tend to discount informal outsourcing queries. Instead, they place more faith in formal outsourcing evaluations.

Outsourcing Evaluations

Of the 20 companies, 16 conducted formal outsourcing evaluation to assess/improve IS cost effectiveness. Outsourcing evaluations, by far the most rigorous way to benchmark, entail creating an RFP, soliciting vendor bids, and comparing bids against internal costs. Senior executives tend to view this method as the most reliable because it compares apples to apples and requires bidders to commit to their costs. Outsourcing evaluations, however, are extremely disruptive to the organization and are typically only conducted once or twice per decade.

Benchmarking Services

IS managers from seven of the companies hire benchmarking services every year because they provide more formal comparisons than peer review or informal outsourcing queries. Benchmarking services collect data, normalize it, and create reports which plot the client's performance against a selected reference group extracted from the service's client database. Although the reports do not identify the companies in the reference group, participants theorize that senior executives view benchmarking services as a more objective way to assess IS performance than informal comparisons.

Of the four sources of benchmarks, this chapter focuses on the rate of formal benchmarking services for four reasons. First, benchmarking services provide a wealth of comparative data in which to compare performance—some benchmarking services have as many as 400 companies in their client database which provides ample opportunities for comparisons. Second, external benchmarking firms are perceived as more rigorous than informal peer evaluations or informal outsourcing inquires. Third, external benchmarking services are perceived as less disruptive than formal outsourcing evaluations. Fourth, as the benchmarking industry continues to grow, practitioners will need to understand how to differentiate among services to avoid jumping from service to service (as some case participants experienced).

WHY SHOULD IS BENCHMARK?

According to participants, IS managers may benchmark for the purpose of obtaining a good report card or to identify improvements. When benchmarks are used for soliciting a good report card, senior executives often fail to be impressed by the results because they are not viewed as objective. Instead, senior executives seem most impressed when the benchmarks are coupled with concrete, feasible recommendations for improvement. Each of these reasons for benchmarking is discussed below.

Benchmarking for a Report Card

Although benchmarking for a report card appears politically motivated, participants feel this is a valid reason to benchmark. As the president of a benchmarking service indicates:

> "The climate is so defensive that a lot of people are willing to pay money to benchmarking companies only to get an alibi that they are doing at least as good a job as somebody else."

This is not to suggest that IS managers are poor managers. They may be convinced that their IS department is cost effective based on their years of experience, network of peers with other IS managers, trade reports, and the like. The problem is trying to convince senior management. Some IS managers use benchmarks to sway senior management's perceptions because they believe "objective" measures are more effective than informal anecdotes. Unfortunately, many participants report that senior executives do not view the benchmarks as objective because IS managers typically hire the benchmarking service. As several participants noted, almost anyone can find a consultant to corroborate IS managers' effectiveness or efficiency claims.

"If you want a bunch of graphs that say you are pretty good, you can buy those. If you want improvement ideas, you can buy those. You can buy a combination. So many people don't know what they want to buy. I think benchmarking hurts because it gives a false sense of security, or a false sense of insecurity." (Data center manager at FIRM17)

Benchmarking for Improvement

Several participants claim that benchmarking services identified concrete cost reduction tactics which allowed the internal IS department to create an internal bid that beat vendor bids:

- An IS manager from FIRM17 used his benchmarks to cut data center costs by 45% over a three-year period.
- An IS manager from FIRM18 used his benchmarks to consolidate data centers and reduce headcount from 143 to 67 people in one year.
- An IS manager from FIRM15 used his benchmarks to reduce data center headcount by 37% over a three-year period.
- An IS manager from FIRM20 used benchmarking to speed up the automation project the IS organization had embarked upon which led to headcount reductions of 25%.

How did the benchmarking services accomplish these improvements? They first determined the participant's performance vis-à-vis a reference group. Then, the benchmarking services identified areas of strengths and weakness and recommended improvements. For example, one benchmarking service noted that FIRM15 had more console operators for a given size shop than the reference group. The benchmarking service consultant believed the additional headcount was attributable to a lack of console automation. The benchmarking service then estimated the cost of automation and the associated decrease in headcount. Thus, the participant was given this and other specific recommendations for improvement.

In addition to identifying specific improvements, a benchmarking service may encourage clients to swap success stories. The president of a benchmarking service explains:

"What we encourage as a second step is for clients to talk to each other and we will do the matchmaking, saying, 'You need to talk to this guy, talk to this company about this aspect of what you are doing here because they have mastered that. They have taken that to perfection.'"

Thus, many participants believe that benchmarks can be used to identify and adopt the best practices. However, other participants and benchmarking experts debate the usefulness of mimicry. For example, an applications manager at FIRM21 notes that benchmarks merely describe the characteristics of good IS departments. This does not imply that cost or service improvements will follow if an IS manager imitates these characteristics:

> "[The benchmarking service] doesn't recommend mimicry. They are just saying, if they model high performers, that is what they look like. It's going to be different [for each company]."

Participants' disagreements reflect sentiments debated by benchmarking experts. Dissenters argue:

> "How can benchmarks yield a competitive advantage if you are only learning what your competitor already knows? Aren't we just bringing companies up to the same level of mediocrity?" (Linsenmeyer, 1991, p. 35)

> "A practice that works for one company may harm another." (Richard Swanborg of Ernst & Young in Sullivan-Trainor, 1993, p. 72)

Thus, many participants—as well as benchmarking experts—disagree whether benchmarks can be used to identify and adopt the best practices. The best argument in favor of benchmarking for improvements is from case participants who actually used benchmarking services to identify and improve performance.

WHAT SHOULD IS BENCHMARK?

In this study, participants employ benchmarking services for data center operations, networks and telecommunications, and applications development and support. In addition to these functional benchmarks, two participants purchase user-oriented benchmarks for IS effectiveness/customer satisfaction. All participants feel their benchmarks include both quality and efficiency measures, although benchmarking services seem to favor one aspect over the other. Table 5.3 contains a sample of measures the benchmarking firms use in developing the participants' benchmarks.

Data Center Operations

Participants that use benchmarking services to assess effectiveness feel that data center benchmarks are the most mature. Many benchmarking services provide comparisons with hundreds of clients on cost and service measures related to data center hardware, software, and staff.

Table 5.3 Benchmarks for various IS functions

Customer satisfaction/IS effectiveness	Data center operations	Networks/telecommunications	Applications development and support
Headcount	Allocated DASD storage	Availability	Analyst/programmer turnover rates
IS costs as a percentage of revenue	Availability	Average connect time	Average age of systems
IS leadership style	Batch turnaround time	Average bytes per call	Average development cycle time
IS involvement in strategic planning	Costs per MIP	Cost per kilobytes per mile	Average size of applications
Management to worker ratio	Hardware costs per MIP	Cost per person	CASE tool productivity
Organizational structure	Management to worker ratio	Cost per device	Cost productivity based on fuction points
Perceived system quality	Overall utilization	Cost per call	Defect per 1000 function points
Perceived system functionality	Personnel costs per MIP	Cost per minute	Length of the backlog
Perceived quality of IS staff	Prime shift utilization	Management to worker ratios	Management to analyst ratio
Perceived analyst knowledge of user needs	Response time	Number of failures	Number of programming languages supported
Perceived IS management knowledge of user needs	Software costs per MIP	Utilization/capacity ratio	Number of customer complaints
Perceived information content	Total data center costs		Percentage of new development vs enhancements
Perceived contribution of IS to user goals			Percentage of time spent in each SDLC phase
Policy flexibility			Percentage of custom-made software vs packaged
Standards enforcement			Personal productivity based on function points
Total IS costs			Total estimated number of function points

Measures are either geared towards service excellence or cost efficiency, depending on the benchmarking service.

Network and Telecommunications

Although many participants have an interest in network and telecommunication benchmarks, they feel that the benchmarking market for telecommunications is immature. IS managers from FIRM17 were the only participants to hire a benchmarking service to assess this area. FIRM17 participants were generally pleased that the benchmarking service identified enough cost-saving tactics to cover the benchmark fee and noted that the market is maturing; several reputable benchmarking services have a growing database of network clients to compare cost and service of voice and data communications over wide and local area networks.

Applications Development and Support

Only one participant—FIRM2—hires a benchmarking service to assess applications development and support effectiveness. (For a description of FIRM2 see Lacity and Hirschheim, 1993.) The reticence to benchmark this area may be that of all benchmarking services, applications is the most difficult area in which to find a comparable base. Many benchmarking services use function points, which participants consider controversial at best. Dennis Farley, president of the development center, complains that the problem with application benchmarks is:

> "Getting bogged down in arcane statistics, such as measuring 'function points delivered,' may be a mistake anyway because it fails the 'so what test' of business managers." (Betts, 1992, p. 20)

IS Effectiveness/Customer Satisfaction

Two companies—FIRMs 21 and 19—employ a broad-based IS effectiveness/customer satisfaction survey. Although the benchmarking services claim to measure IS effectiveness on business variables such as rate of return on equity, the majority of the measures are based on users' perceptions of IS effectiveness. As an applications manager for FIRM21 notes, "Perceptions are 90% of the game when it comes to IS." Participants at FIRM21 believe the survey was valuable in understanding users' perceptions of IS. In some departments, IS thought they were performing well but users rated them poor. In other departments, IS thought they were performing poorly, but users rated them good.

Regardless of the type of benchmark used by participants, their main concern was selecting an appropriate benchmarking firm.

HOW CAN IS SELECT AN APPROPRIATE BENCHMARKING FIRM?

The most important criteria for selecting a benchmarking firm to help with an insourcing decision are:

1 Involve senior management in the selection process to ensure their acceptance of the benchmarking results;
2 Select benchmarking firms that measure what is important to management;
3 Select benchmarking firms that offer the stiffest competition possible;
4 Select benchmarking services that offer data gathering, data validation, normalization, and analysis processes in which you are comfortable.

Each of these criteria is explained below.

Involve Senior Executives in the Selection of the Benchmarking Firm

The best way to convince senior executives that benchmarks are objective is to involve them in the selection of the benchmarking service. At FIRM17, for example, the IS manager hired a benchmarking service without asking senior management's input. When the benchmarks indicated that IS costs were half of the average reference group, a subsidiary president claimed that IS costs were still too high. He hired his own consultant to assess IS costs. FIRM17's data center manager explains the process as follows:

> "The president hired [a consulting firm] and said, 'Hey guys, I'm in a pissing contest with the VP of IS, would you go and tell the guy I can get it cheaper outside?' Well they poked and prodded and examined and I couldn't talk to them because of the politics. So they got through and told the president, 'You guys are getting a good deal. You can't get it cheaper on the outside.' So this was an unbiased consultant. Well actually he was biased because the guy that was paying wanted to outsource."

The president was finally convinced by his own consultant's report and ceased to harass the IS manager. The IS manager still feels, however, that benchmarks—even benchmarks he solicits—truly help senior management to evaluate IS. Although benchmarks alone are not enough to sway senior management opinion, they help mount a case for IS:

> "I've learned a lot about marketing [to senior management]. I've learned to position us. I've used various benchmarking services and those tidbits effectively."

Thus, one way to convince senior executives of the validity of the benchmarking results is to involve them in the selection of a benchmarking firm.

Measure what is Important to Senior Executives

Senior executives may reject benchmarking results because the benchmarks do not measure what is important to them. Senior managers claim that benchmarks are too technical, fail to indicate whether IS uses the best architecture, or focus on the wrong IS values. An example of each complaint follows.

Benchmarks are Too Technical

A data center manager for FIRM17 claims his VP of manufacturing was unimpressed by the benchmarks because they focused on technical issues:

> "My new boss was disappointed because what the [benchmarking service] did, given an MVS data center, your costs are good. He doesn't care. He wants to know given you have a consumer products business of $2 billion, how are your costs? He was really disappointed with the benchmark because it was a narrow technical benchmark. He wants something that monitors for a company of your size in this business—is your inventory variance about right? Things like that."

Benchmarks do not Indicate whether IS has Adopted the Right Architecture

In another case, an IS manager at FIRM15 used a benchmarking service to assess the cost efficiency for his data center. To his surprise, his data center scored much poorer than anticipated, probably because the benchmarking service compared his IS shop to a best of breed. The benchmarking service identified specific remedies to reduce costs. After three years of working closely with the benchmarking firm, the IS manager reduced headcount by 37%. The third year, his IS shop placed among the best of breed. He proudly presented the benchmarking results to senior management. However, senior management dismissed the results. The IS manager explains:

> "After this last report, I walked out of the policy meeting and thought, 'Alright, we've done something real good.' Well after we left, some of the finance guys said, 'Yeah, that's fine and dandy, you look good against MVS shops, but how does that stack up against some other platform? How does that compare to an AS400 shop of the same size?' So they took a lot of self-esteem we accumulated on the report and blew it away."

Benchmarks Focus on the Wrong IS Values

The experiences of one IS manager at FIRM17 underscores the importance of selecting benchmarks that are important to senior management. The IS manager prided himself on excellent service. He bought extra equipment to reduce response time and purchased redundant systems to protect availability. To demonstrate his effectiveness, he hired a benchmarking service that also values service excellence. Not surprising, the benchmarks indicated an above-average service performance. Business unit leaders, however, were unimpressed by the benchmarks because their agenda for IS was cost containment, not service excellence. The IS manager was fired. The new IS manager, who listened to the business unit leaders, reduced costs by eliminating the hardware and software his predecessor installed to protect service. His users responded:

> "You cut my bill by a couple of million dollars. My response time is a little more erratic. If you made response time slower, could you save me a couple of million more?"

Ironically, a few years later the new IS manager hired the same benchmarking service his predecessor had used. He received a terrible report card. The data center manager explains:

> "[Benchmarking Service A] is 100% correct within their value set. So, what happens, they value response times, if a company aligns with their values, the benchmark is good. They look at us as we are not running a big modern CPU, their value set is different. My costs are about half of their average but they felt I was incompetent because response times are only average."

In this instance, the bad report card confirms that the IS manager responded to the senior management's main concern: costs.

To summarize, benchmarks should measure what is important to senior management—be it technical or business-oriented, architecture dependent or independent, or cost efficiency versus service excellence.

Select Benchmarking Firms that Offer the Stiffest Competition Possible

With whom an IS organization is compared obviously affects the outcome of the benchmark. As one benchmarking service provider noted:

> "I can make you appear as the best ski jumper, it's just a question of who I choose as a comparative base. I can always make you appear as the best ski jumper. If you tell me you know nothing about ski jumping, we just have to find a comparative base where people know even less."

Benchmarking services either compare a current client with the best of breed or with a larger pool from their client database. If IS managers are primarily concerned with a good report card, they will fare better against a larger reference group. Senior executives, however, are more impressed by favorable reports when a best of breed reference group is selected; falling in the fiftieth percentile of a huge, unknown client database is less impressive than scoring in the fiftieth percentile among the best of breed. Participants claim that benchmarking firms must compare clients with the stiffest competition possible—a "best of breed" comparison—or IS managers may falsely believe they can compete against an outsourcer.

An example from one of the cases will highlight the importance of selecting a best of breed reference group. When the previous IS manager at FIRM17 received a favorable report from one benchmarking service, he naively assumed that the benchmarks indicated that an outsourcer could not undercut his current costs. The data center manager explains:

> "[The benchmarking service] said, 'You guys are a pretty good data center. Your costs are pretty good.' So we said, 'Fine.' Well [one of the business unit managers] found an outsourcer who could do it cheaper."

The IS manager questioned how such a discrepancy could exist between his benchmarking results and the outsourcing bid. The data center manager responded that since they failed to benchmark against best of breed, their benchmarking results merely confirmed that they were adequate compared to the benchmarking service's entire database:

"The [benchmarking service] compares you to data centers of your size. I guarantee you that other data centers of your size are not the outsourcing competition. You need to benchmark against the toughest in town."

In addition to deciding whether to benchmark against a best of breed or a larger pool, IS managers must understand the criteria each benchmarking service uses to select a reference group. The criteria may be based on size of the IS shop, geographic region, or industry. The size of the IS shop is the most common selection criterion. The economies of scale associated with size greatly affect unit costs and efficiency measures. Most experts agree it is unfair to compare a small AS400 shop with an IBM 3090 shop, for example. Some clients prefer comparison to firms in the same geographic region because rents and salaries may be more comparable, although most benchmarking firms will normalize data for geographic differences. Some clients prefer comparison to other companies in the same industry. Airlines, for example, have much different computing environments than petroleum companies. Some benchmarking firms, however, have too few clients in their database from the same industry to make such comparisons. Benchmarking services may compensate by selecting other industries with similar on-line and batch processing requirements, such as using banks and airlines in the same reference group.

To highlight the importance of the reference group selection criteria, consider one IS manager's experience from FIRM18. He hired a benchmarking service to assess costs at each of his three data centers. Figure 5.1 contains a report which plots total data center costs against computing capacity for each data center (Site A, Site B, Site C). The

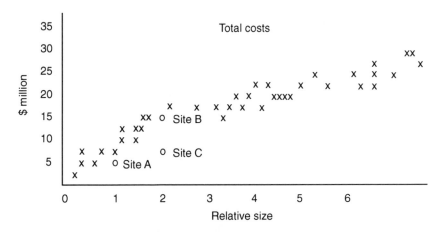

Figure 5.1

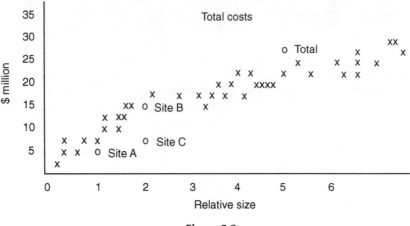

Figure 5.2

benchmarking report indicates a clean bill of health—all three data centers are average or below average compared to the reference group. The IS manager, however, did not consider the cost of running three separate data centers. If total costs are plotted against total capacity, the client's costs are above average (see Figure 5.2). In this case, a vendor convinced senior management that outsourcing could save money and senior management responded with an outsourcing evaluation. Thus, the benchmarks failed to convince senior management that IS was efficient because the reference group was other small data centers rather than one large data center. Fortunately for the IS manager he hired another benchmarking service to help him prepare an internal bid that eventually beat external bids.

Select Benchmarking Services that Offer Data Gathering, Data Validation, Normalization, and Reporting Processes in which You Are Comfortable

Each benchmarking firm has its own procedures for gathering data, validating data, normalizing data, and reporting data. Some of the issues that concerned participants are discussed below.

Data Gathering

The adage "garbage in, garbage out" certainly applies to benchmarking. The data gathered for benchmarks is either gathered manually or automatically. Manually collected data includes customer satisfaction surveys, headcount, salary, and types of equipment. Automatic data collection is typically limited to software monitors that gather information such as response time, tape mounts, and batch turnaround time. Manual data collection, in particular, provides opportunities for skewed data (a) through discriminate selection of survey respondents or (b) by having the IS personnel being evaluated provide the data. Examples of each are discussed below.

With a customer satisfaction benchmark, for example, the internal IS department often selects the pool of users to be surveyed. This pool can obviously be selected in such a way as to overlook notoriously unsatisfied users. After hearing that user confidence was very low, an IS manager at FIRM21 blamed the user sample. He asked the benchmarking service to recalculate the numbers, "If we took these four [users] out, what would confidence be?"

One assurance of data integrity is to request senior management or business unit leaders to select survey respondents. An applications manager at FIRM21 explains how this ensures data integrity:

> "Our first [Benchmarking Service A] study was an attempt to demonstrate to management that the DP operations area of the company was effective, as effective as any company out on the market. We came out of that looking pretty good. The problem with [Benchmarking Service A], I can fix the survey with my answers. The [Benchmarking Service B] one I couldn't fix, I had no control over what users said. With [Benchmarking Service A], the people being surveyed are the ones supplying the answers. I can manipulate the answers, I can control the answers through my responses. This survey is unique in that it depends on the users' perspective of IS, which is important."

The measurement period is also an important data gathering consideration. Benchmarking services either monitor operations for an average period or peak period. If they monitor average periods, the peaks and valleys are smoothed. The benchmarking results will reflect better service levels in terms of response time, availability and turnaround time, but benchmarking results may suggest that the client has excess capacity. Benchmarking services that monitor peak capacity counter that their measures provide a better test of service level measures and resource requirements. A president of a benchmarking service describes why he feels benchmarking data should be gathered during peak periods:

> "Customers are interested in what capacity they need on board to handle peaks. What is it that drives the capacity requirements up? It's typically not the average utilization. It's the peaks. For the New York Stock Exchange, they estimate 10 times as much load during a rally."

Data Validation

After the data is gathered, most benchmarking firms will validate the input data via a data validation seminar. This seminar ensures that clerical or political errors are identified and corrected before the data is normalized. The VP of a benchmarking service explains how validation seminars identify fallacious data:

> "Occasionally you do see things that are jaded and then it's found at the correction meeting because people see that and say, 'You don't have three people, you have five people.' And so those things come out."

Normalization Process

Once clients are satisfied that the input data is valid, data is normalized to attempt to ensure that IS shops are fairly compared to one another. Although no normalization process is perfect, IS managers feel that it is important to understand how a benchmarking service normalizes data. Each benchmarking service has its own normalization formula, typically based on items such as the cost of floor space or personnel per geographic region. Some benchmarking services share their algorithms with their clients, while others merely give a description of the normalization process.

One IS manager at FIRM18 claims that dissatisfaction with the normalization process will prevent him from benchmarking again.

> "They normalize for floor space. Someone in New York City versus someone in Oklahoma, I have a much lower cost of doing business. He's just normalized away all my benefits. I think I am doing a good job at managing technology costs—we decided to build the data center in Oklahoma and not New York. All of these things that we have successfully done, I think he's just averaged me into oblivion."

Report Design

Some managers reject benchmarks because the reports look suspicious to them. Participants shared reports that included percentages that summed to over 100% (FIRM3, see Lacity and Hirschheim, 1993), an average response far from the fiftieth percentile (FIRM21), and a report in which all the data points clustered around zero (FIRM18). These errors are obvious, but one benchmarking service used by FIRM21 also had a subtler problem with its reports: the scales kept changing. When scales are altered from report to report, interpretation of the results becomes difficult. An example illustrates this point.

Figures 5.3 and 5.4 contain two typical reports that a benchmarking service provides to a client. The reports are based on a survey that rates different aspects of user satisfaction on a seven-item Likert scale, with seven representing the highest level of satisfaction. The client's average response is plotted for each measure as well as the high, average, and low performers from the reference group. The client is advised to attend only to measures that fall below the average in the reference group. Thus, if the client meets or exceeds the fiftieth percentile, he or she is given a clean bill of health for that measure. In Figures 5.3 and 5.4, the client appears below average on both measures. The variability in the reference group in Figure 5.4, however, is significantly less than the variability in Figure 5.3. The benchmarking service claims Figure 5.4 indicates an area of weakness even though the variance is very small.

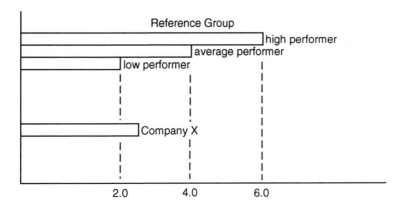

Figure 5.3

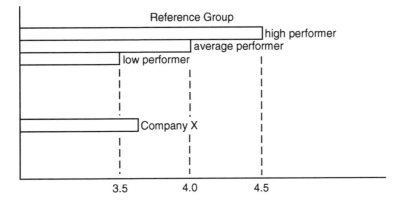

Figure 5.4

BENCHMARKING RECOMMENDATIONS

As identified by participants, benchmarking services can often facilitate outsourcing/insourcing decisions. Specific guidelines for selecting benchmarks and benchmarking services include the following.

Benchmark what is Important to Management

In some organizations, senior management and IS managers possess different views on the primary concern for IS. IS managers, for example, may incorrectly perceive the relative importance of service excellence versus cost containment. Benchmarking results may be discounted or ignored if IS managers hire benchmarking firms to validate performance on measures that are unimportant to senior management.

Have Senior Management Select the Benchmarking Service

Participants claim that senior managers may not attend to benchmarking results because the benchmarks are not viewed as objective. As Peter Drucker once noted—anyone over the age of 21 can find data to support their position. Senior managers think, "big deal, you hired a guy to prove you are good." To counteract these claims, IS managers should involve senior managers in the selection of the benchmarking service.

Select the Reference Group which Represents the Stiffest Competition Possible

Senior managers do not seem to care if performance is adequate against the multitudes represented in a client database. Who cares if you are average among the run of the mill? Senior managers are most impressed by benchmarks against the stiffest competition, such as best of breed within an industry.

Select the Reference Group Based on Criteria Important to Management

Benchmarking services can select reference groups based on size, geographic area, industry, or other criteria. Participants note that reference group selections should be based on senior management's preferences. For example, senior executives most concerned with salary levels may prefer comparisons with other local companies. Senior managers primarily concerned with direct competitors may wish comparisons with other companies within the same industry. Senior managers most concerned with overall efficiency may prefer comparisons to the best of breed operating similar sized shops.

Gather Data during a Peak Period

As a corollary to the toughest comparison using best of breed, participants note that senior managers are most impressed by measures taken at the busiest time. After all, who cares what response time and availability are at 2.00 a.m.! Measures taken during peak load are viewed as a fairer test of IS effectiveness.

Validate Data before Benchmark Calculations

The adage "garbage in, garbage out" applies to benchmarking. Participants claim senior managers have more confidence in the validity of the benchmarks if: (a) senior level people (those not threatened by the benchmarks) gather the data or at least select survey respondents, (b) the benchmarking service conducts a data validation meeting, and (c) the benchmarking service uses automated data collection software.

Repeat Benchmarks

Participants claim that senior executives place more validity in benchmark results if measures are repeated periodically. While senior executives favorably view positive benchmarks, they are more concerned that IS managers improve performance over time. As Xerox's guru of benchmarking, Robert Camp notes:

> "The fact is you can't rest on your laurels. You've got to be continuously looking for better ways to do things." (Linsenmeyer, 1991, p. 34)

Additionally, all normalization algorithms are limited, however, and so many IS managers feel that organizations should repeat benchmarks in subsequent years. Senior executives seem more impressed when IS improves over time rather than relying on a one-time snapshot of IS performance.

CONCLUSION

Although benchmarking is portrayed as being valuable for comparative purposes, for many participants in our study, its *real* value lay more in the perception it creates rather than as any serious mechanism for improvement. The exercise of undertaking benchmarking can help sway senior management's opinion that the IS organization is trying to be as efficient as possible. In a word, the IS organization is trying to be a good corporate citizen by comparing itself with others, hopefully learning new and better practices in the process.

With benchmarking, firms can feel good about themselves; feel as though they are "among the elite" in whatever functions they choose to benchmark. And that may be very positive and indeed desirable. The truth, however, is that benchmarking is often used to create an image of being among the "best of breed" when in fact it all depends on what metrics one chooses. If you know what result you want, it is almost always possible to choose a set of measures which can yield it. If one set of measures does not yield the desired results, just change the measures. Or, if the measures cannot be changed, then one simply "normalizes" the data to take into account "special endogenous factors." It is relatively easy to show how data can be manipulated to make a company a high performer by changing the scale (to lessen or increase dispersion), changing the reference point (size vs industry), changing the normalization process (square feet, analyst costs), and changing the reference group (compare top vs average). We like to term this creative use of benchmarking "mystical measures." It demonstrates the illusion of objectivity. No wonder then that benchmarking can be a powerful and carefully orchestrated vehicle for creating and/or managing of perceptions. It is, of course, possible to implement strategies to minimize bias, for example: demand normalization formulas to understand what is being normalized and why (so that the results of benchmarking are not "magic"); do not let IS collect the benchmarking data; know who is in the reference group, etc. Overall, a company should seriously consider the benchmarking recommendations offered in the previous section.

6
Summary of Lessons Learned

INTRODUCTION

This chapter addresses the question: What overall lessons can we learn from the insourcing cases? Based on participants' experiences, we have identified six lessons:

1 Conflicting stakeholders' expectations place IS managers in the precarious position of providing a Rolls Royce service at a Chevrolet price.
2 Senior management must empower IS to implement change.
3 Successful sourcing depends on comparing vendor bids against a newly submitted internal bid, not against current IS performance.
4 Cost efficiency largely depends on adoption of efficient management practices and to a lesser extent, economies of scale.
5 Internal IS departments actually possess superior cost advantages for some IS cost drivers.
6 Selective sourcing—which treats IS as a portfolio—is the key to rightsourcing.

These lessons corroborate the lessons generated from the outsourcing lessons, but provide more clarity and depth of understanding of the underlying issues.

LESSONS LEARNED

Lesson 1: Conflicting Stakeholders' Expectations Place IS Managers in the Precarious Position of Providing a Rolls Royce Service at a Chevrolet Price

From our outsourcing cases, we discovered that the outsourcing phenomenon appears to be a symptom of demonstrating the value of IS to senior management. We argued that senior management do not readily perceive value for their IS expenditures and subsequently wish to minimize the costs of IS. The insourcing studies confirm this finding, but provide a richer understanding of not only senior management's perceptions of IS, but also the perceptions of different stakeholders. In reality, many different stakeholders—senior managers, business unit managers, IS managers, IS staff, and end-users—possess different preferences, expectations, perceptions, and agendas for IS. An analysis of these stakeholders provides an understanding of why IS is set up to fail in many companies.

Based on our case studies, we have characterized the following stakeholder expectations and agendas for IS. In general, senior management perceives the entire IS function as a utility, and therefore sets the IS agenda to be cost minimization. In general, business units and end-users perceive that IS critically contributes to business operations, and therefore set the IS agenda to be service excellence. These two stakeholder groups set a conflicting agenda for IS because IS managers cannot provide a Rolls Royce service at a Chevrolet price.

This so-called "IS cost/service trade-off" is depicted in Table 6.1. It represents the different stakeholder's perceptions and expectations of IS as they relate to IS costs and service levels. In general, costs are directly proportional to service levels, i.e. the better the service, the higher the costs. This relationship is evident in virtually all IS activities. Consider, for example, software costs. Users' demands for service excellence suggest that packaged software be customized to their idiosyncratic needs, a practice that drives up IS development and maintenance costs. If IS managers try to contain costs by implementing packaged software as is, users complain their needs are not being met. An example in the area of hardware is response time. Users demand service excellence, defined as sub-second response time all the time. This drives up hardware costs because IS managers purchase excess capacity or other devices to deliver service excellence.

Because of the direct relationship between service and costs, IS can be realistically expected to perform in one of two boxes: IS can provide a premium service for a premium cost *or* a minimal service for a

Table 6.1 *IS cost/service trade-off*

	Minimal cost	Premium cost
Premium service	*Superstar* Senior management's and users' *expectations* of IS	*Differentiator* Realm of possible IS performance
Minimal service	*Commodity/ low cost producer* Realm of possible IS performance	*Black Hole* Senior management's and users' *perceptions* of IS

minimal price. If organizations perceive that a given IS function is a critical contributor, then IS can be expected to perform in the *Differentiator* quadrant. As a differentiator, IS can provide customized IS products and services to meet idiosyncratic business needs. If organizations perceive that a given IS function is merely a utility, IS can be expected to perform in the *Commodity* or *Low Cost Producer* quadrant. As a commodity, IS can be expected to deliver a standard service at a minimal cost. Unfortunately, the failure to align senior management's priorities for IS with users' priorities creates the precarious expectation of IS operating in the *Superstar* quadrant—a goal few IS departments can realistically achieve. IS managers attempted to respond to conflicting goals by compromising on cost and service. The result: neither stakeholder group was satisfied and began to perceive that IS performed in the *Black Hole* quadrant. The black hole analogy seems particularly appropriate as management simply sees IS as a bottomless cost pit.

We can use the IS cost/service matrix to diagnose and understand the IS dilemma in our insourcing cases. We have selected data center operations as the IS activity to evaluate, since this function was the primary focus of the insourcing cases.

FIRM15

Prior to insourcing, IS managers at FIRM15—an apparel manufacturer and retailer—operated two data centers, located on the same headquarters campus. The data centers were originally designed in this fashion to serve as disaster recovery sites for one another, but were an expensive design due to excessive replication. When increased competition from Italy, the Pacific rim, and South America forced senior management to slash overhead, they pressured IS managers to cut costs. IS managers perceived that consolidating the data centers would meet senior management's mandate to cut costs, but user groups resented IS managers' attempts, preferring that their perspective data centers remain servicing their idiosyncratic needs. Consequently, IS was perceived as a *Black Hole*.

FIRM16

Prior to insourcing, FIRM16—a public university—operated three separate data centers for three business units: hospital administration, the central campus, and university administration. When student enrollments dropped, the board of curators mandated that IS cut costs. One potential solution was data center consolidation, but business units resisted IS managers' plans, arguing that data centers were on different platforms and specifically designed to meet their idiosyncratic needs. Stakeholders subsequently perceived that IS was a *Black Hole*, senior management did not get their cost cuts and business units resented consolidation proposals that would reduce their service.

FIRM17

Prior to insourcing, FIRM17—a food manufacturer—operated one large data center that operated many different systems to meet idiosyncratic needs for particular departments. When a change in management called for cost cuts, IS managers attempted to meet the mandate by standardizing software. However, users resisted and resented the IS managers' attempts, arguing that their software provides distinctive capabilities and that standardization would hinder their operations. Once again, the resulting inconsistent agenda led to a general perception that IS operated in the *Black Hole* quadrant.

FIRM18

Prior to insourcing, FIRM18—a petroleum and chemicals company—operated three data centers. After several years of declining profit margins, senior management demanded that IS cut costs. IS managers foresaw that consolidation was the answer. Business units agreed in principle to consolidation, as long as "their" data center was chosen as the consolidation site. IS managers' attempts to persuade managers to close their data centers were met with resistance. Some business unit managers claimed local data centers were so vital to operations that they were willing to pay an extra $5 million a year to retain them. In the end, IS managers could not convince them, and perceptions of IS as a *Black Hole* resulted.

FIRM19

Prior to insourcing, FIRM19—a telecommunications company—operated one small data center. The operating costs were high due to an IS trade union that implemented inefficient work rules requiring an excessive headcount. IS managers had previously tried to negotiate better work rules, but the labor union resisted. Although users were generally happy with the service—because of the extra attention provided by the overmanned trade union—senior management perceived that IS was a *Black Hole*.

FIRM20

Prior to insourcing, FIRM20—an energy company—operated one large data center. Due to economic hardship, senior management mandated a reduction in IS costs. IS hoped to implement a set of policies to lower costs but business units balked at the proposed lower service levels. IS's failure to lower costs led to their being perceived as a *Black Hole* by senior management.

Common themes run through the insourcing cases. Prior to the outsourcing evaluation, senior management in all of our cases perceived data center operations to be a utility that should be cost-minimized. On the other hand, business managers and end-users perceived that their data centers provided critical support and wanted a differentiated service. Unlike senior managers, business unit managers and users assert that data centers are hardly homogeneous. Different companies use different hardware configurations, operating software, software utilities, facilities for cooling/lighting/fire prevention, levels of software automation, and disaster recovery strategies. All of these contribute to service levels in terms of response time, availability, and in particular, support. Users wanted their own dedicated support staff who understand what systems they run at what times with what particular problems.

As a consequence of the differing views of the nature of data center operations, stakeholders expected IS to perform in the *Superstar* quadrant. IS managers attempted to meet these inconsistent expectations by giving senior managers *some* cost savings and providing users *some* level of service. Such compromise strategies backfired. Inevitably, IS managers were unable to meet the conflicting expectations of providing a superior, differentiated service at a minimal cost. Consequently, IS was perceived by three stakeholders—senior management, business unit managers, and end-users as—operating *Black Holes*.

In our insourcing cases, senior managers eventually doubted that IS managers would meet their cost reduction mandates and decided that outsourcing was the solution. The outsourcing threat served to align all stakeholders to their cost minimization agenda. By creating this shared agenda, IS managers were able to compete with vendor bids by proposing to replicate their cost reduction tactics. Business unit managers and users realized that either their familiar IS managers or external vendors would implement cost reduction tactics. Most elected to support IS managers with their new insourcing bids that contained cost reduction schemes users had previously resisted. After insourcing, all six firms moved to the *Commodity* quadrant, providing a minimal acceptable service level for a reduced cost as depicted in Table 6.2.

This so-called IS cost/service trade-off is something of a double-edged sword. While companies desperately attempt to reduce IS costs, most IS executives prefer to believe that customer service is crucial. In spirit (if not necessarily in deeds) IS attempts to highlight the criticality of customer support. The recent emergence of the function "relationship management" within IS is a case in point. This function ostensibly creates an "account manager" role between IS and its business unit customers, and clearly demonstrates that customer service is valued. However, customer service does suffer if cost considerations become the guiding light. This is clearly documented in the cases. For example, FIRM17 increased response time, reduced its software portfolio, eliminated testing (which

Table 6.2   Mapping case studies to the IS cost/service trade-off

	Minimal cost	Premium cost
Premium service	*Superstar*	*Differentiator*
Minimal service	*Commodity/ low cost producer*	*Black Hole*
	After insourcing: FIRMS 15, 16, 17, 18, 19, 20	Before insourcing: FIRMS 15, 16, 17, 18, 19, 20

could lead to errors in installation); yet senior management put up with this reduced service because IS costs are 40% lower. Apparently, the people who make the decisions (senior management) are different from the recipients of the service (the users), feeling that the reduced service is OK. The same was true for FIRM18—they now provide a "Chevrolet" instead of a "Rolls Royce" level of service. The IS manager's job is to run the legacy systems into the ground. These insourced centers basically run like outsourcers—trying to meet some minimum service level while reducing costs as much as possible.

One of the benchmarking consultants we spoke to confirmed our suspicion about reduced service. He stated:

> "Too often IS provides a 'Rolls Royce' service when a 'Chevy' will do. This is particularly true in the help desk."

Of course this notion of service is highly perceptual. What to one is a "Rolls Royce", is but a "Chevy" to another. Furthermore, there is the issue of whether a Rolls Royce is justified in the first place. If the firm differentiates itself on the basis of service then such a high class of service, i.e. Rolls Royce, may be necessary. Taking the analogy further, a Chevy might be fine until the first time one gets into an accident. Then suddenly the Rolls Royce appears no longer a luxury, but a necessity. As usual, such decisions involve trade-offs. Reduced service (Chevy) may be acceptable in the short run but what about the long run? Is a firm potentially mortgaging away its future for short-run savings now? Such questions may not have simple answers but organizations must consider the long-run implications of their actions. It is indeed worrying if long-term gains are sacrificed for short-term cost savings.

There is something of a balancing act between customer service and cost reductions. In evaluating outsourcing, the balance swings in the direction of cost savings. Perhaps this should not be too surprising given that IS is perceived as overhead. As such, the corporation does anything it can to reduce costs. It either does not value or see the strategic significance of IS.

Perhaps the goal of senior management should be: "Cut costs by any means possible while trying to keep the level of customer support satisfactory." But since "satisfactory" is ambiguous at best (depends on who you talk to) a drop in quality should not be unexpected.

Lesson 2: Senior Management must Empower IS to Implement Change

As noted in the previous lesson, implementing cost savings measures requires IS to adopt policies which may not be readily agreed to by the business units in the organization. Internal politics often drives what can and cannot be implemented. For example, in a number of cases, there was a recognition that consolidating data centers would yield cost savings, however corporate politics precluded it from happening. Each business unit felt that "their" data center provided special services which could not be provided from a single, consolidated center. Their data centers understood the idiosyncrasies of their particular business requirements, were responsive to their needs, and were, fundamentally, more controllable by the business units. They owed their allegiance to the business units they supported rather than to the corporation as a whole. Hence the business units vehemently resisted any form of consolidation. In such an environment, it was often impossible for IS to push through consolidation; the business units had too much power. It was only when senior management empowered the IS department did IS actually have the authority, i.e. the political muscle, to implement consolidation.

The same occurs when IS wants to implement a standard platform of hardware and software. This often leads to user departments feeling that their particular needs are not being catered for. In FIRM20, for example, IS decided upon providing a standardized suite of applications. This made the regular upgrading of software easy—they simply downloaded the new versions from the server to all users' desktops via the network. This standardization was only possible after FIRM20 created a new CIO position and gave him the appropriate support from senior management. The point is made by the director of IS planning in FIRM20 who notes:

> ". . . he [the CIO] is very seriously talking about owning the software on the desktop and telling people what they can run and what they can't run . . . he's talking and nobody's greatly exercising; I'm sure a lot of people aren't very happy, but nobody's voicing any concern."

Apparently, the reason why the users are not "voicing [their] concerns" is because the CIO has been empowered by senior management to embark on strategies which will reduce IS costs, and the standard software platform is one key vehicle. And it is yielding results. The director of IS planning states:

> "So we're able electronically to deliver software to the desktop because it's a controlled standard environment. And the productivity gains from managing those otherwise diverse environments, the benefit to the business is just tremendous."

There are other examples in our case studies (see the examples in lesson 3 below) where IS knew of ways to reduce costs but simply could not convince the business units to agree to implement them. For example, the implementing of a full-cost chargeback scheme is one of the best mechanisms for getting the user departments to recognize the true costs of providing various services to them. Many organizations have chargeback schemes, but they are simply allocation schemes agreed to by some IS steering committee to apportion costs. And the way these costs are apportioned are often very unfair. The director of IS planning at FIRM20 cites the following example:

> "The engineering folks burned lots of cycles, didn't store much on disks, maybe kept some things on tape. Didn't necessarily print a whole lot, at least not proportioned to the cycles they burned. They . . . got one consolidated number and were getting hit with disproportionate bills. The customer folks were getting a free ride in a lot of cases, although they didn't think so."

Unfortunately, it is not an easy task to change the allocation scheme. Business units tend to resist because they feel with full-cost chargeback they will be charged for services that previously were absorbed by someone else (often another department or the corporation as a whole). With allocation schemes rather than a true chargeback scheme organizations run into the "restaurant check" syndrome. It refers to the behavior exhibited by groups of people who go together to a restaurant for a meal. Because it is common for groups to just "split the bill equally" among the people, it is in a person's best (perhaps "selfish" is a more appropriate word) interest to order the most expensive dish on the menu because its cost will be subsidized by those ordering less expensive dishes. Similarly in IS, it is in the interest of user departments to order the most expensive service possible because in an allocation scheme, these costs will be shared with the other business units. In such a world, everyone will order what could be thought of as a "Rolls Royce" service when a "Chevy" might just as easily do. IS costs rise because the business units can demand whatever they want knowing (or even not knowing) that the costs will be shared with others. Of course one can just imagine how such a scenario might play out. Business unit A requests a particular expensive type of service (e.g. reports produced in color), so business unit B—not wanting to be outdone—requests something equally exotic (e.g. multi-media interface to some corporate database). One can imagine how this might escalate. The implementation of a true chargeback scheme would stop such potentially frivolous requests as the user department requesting such services would have to pay the full amount of IS providing that service. But implementing such a chargeback scheme is problematic, and will only be possible if senior management empowers and supports IS to do so. To put it differently, IS needs a "big stick" to hammer resistance with in order to implement cost-saving policies. This big stick can only come from senior management.

Lesson 3: Successful Sourcing Depends on Comparing Vendor Bids against a Newly Submitted Internal Bid, *not* against Current IS Performance

As noted in the previous lesson, IS is often unable to implement the necessary cost reduction strategies until senior management empowers them to do so. The internal politics of an organization often precludes the IS department from successfully applying cost-saving strategies. Consider the following three cases where internal politics between IS and users prevented IS managers from implementing cost reduction tactics. Only after senior management threatened the organization with outsourcing, were IS managers able to overcome resistance. It afforded them the opportunity to implement cost reduction strategies. These cases illustrate how an outsourcing evaluation can mobilize the internal IS department to become more efficient.

FIRM17

Senior executives at FIRM17 felt that IS costs had become too expensive and decided to outsource its large corporate data center. The internal IS department had previously tried but failed to reduce costs by getting the business units to agree on a standard set of software. Despite IS's efforts, each business unit insisted on their own operating systems, utilities, report generators, statistical packages, spreadsheet packages, etc. The cost allocation system exacerbated the problem by spreading software costs across the entire company. Thus, if a business unit leader requested a software package, he or she knew that the cost would be spread over *all* the business units, regardless of use (the "restaurant check" syndrome again). After receiving two external vendor bids, the business leaders agreed to allow the internal IS department to submit a bid that eliminated redundant software. Through that measure, along with proposals to eliminate redundant employees and services, the IS department submitted the low cost bid. Within three years, the internal IS department cut costs by 45%.

FIRM18

Senior management at FIRM18 became concerned over the continually rising costs of IS. The internal IS department had repeatedly tried in the past to reduce costs by consolidating their three data centers, but business unit managers refused to allow the consolidation, feeling that the new consolidated center would not effectively cater to their needs. Only after senior management entered into an outsourcing evaluation did the business unit managers reluctantly allow the internal IS department to submit a bid which included data center consolidation. Three bids were received (two external plus the internal bid), and the internal bid won, as it was the lowest bidder. The internal IS department consolidated the data centers and reduced headcount by 51% resulting in a 43% cost reduction. The IS staff who were involved in the insourcing bid realized that headcount would be reduced but the attitude they had is cogently captured in the following quote:

> "It's not a question of like 30 people leaving the boat. It's a question of all 160 people leaving the boat. So when we said 30 here, and couple here, they said, 'Fine, that's what we need to do in order to save our own jobs. It's better than losing the whole data center.'"

FIRM19

Senior management at FIRM19 decided to outsource after reading about Kodak's success. They rightfully perceived that the internal IS department was not cost competitive due to a strong labor union which hung on to archaic and inefficient work practices, for example, by specifying narrow job descriptions resulting in excessive manpower. Although IS management had tried on numerous occasions to negotiate better terms, the labor union resisted. Only after senior management initiated an outsourcing evaluation did they acquiesce and agree to allow the internal IS department to include revised union rules in their internal bid. In effect, the union either had to succumb or risk losing everything. One of the union representatives expressed the following view: "When you are in a frying pan you get creative." The insourcing project wound up resulting in IS reducing headcount by 46%.

These examples suggest that while IS managers can theoretically implement cost reduction tactics, internal politics often prevent them from doing so. This is why senior executives must allow internal IS managers to submit internal bids in competition with external vendors. The outsourcing threat may overcome political obstacles and allow IS managers the freedom and power to propose drastic cost cuts. If senior executives merely compare external bids with current costs, they may allow the vendors to "pick the low lying fruit." That is, vendors may make drastic cost cuts but absorb most of the savings themselves, merely passing some benefit to customers in the form of modest price cuts.

Lesson 4: Cost Efficiency Largely Depends on Adoption of Efficient Management Practices and to a Lesser Extent, Economies of Scale

One lesson generated from the outsourcing studies is that internal IS departments may be able to achieve similar results without vendor assistance. We noted that vendor bids are often based on efficient management practices, such as data center consolidation, that allegedly, could be replicated by in-house IS. This would explain why many companies in our studies found that insourcing was a more cost efficient alternative—cost efficiency has more to do with these efficient practices than just economies of scale. Just because vendors are bigger, does not mean they are better.

This assertion is demonstrated through an analysis of data center operations in the six insourcing cases. In Table 6.3, we have mapped the adoption of efficient IS management practices against economies of scale. For economies of scale, we can characterize companies as either possessing or lacking the critical mass (size) associated with economies of scale. In the area of data processing, convincing evidence suggests that economies of scale are achieved at 150 MIPS. Three of our insourcing cases have achieved critical mass—as FIRM17 operates 180 MIPs, FIRM18 operates 200 MIPs, and FIRM20 operates 150 MIPs. Prior to insourcing, none of these data center operations was cost efficient due to inefficient managerial practices. After insourcing, the IS managers replicated vendor tactics for reducing costs and subsequently achieved significant savings: FIRM17 reduced costs by 45%, FIRM18 reduced costs by 43%, FIRM20 reduced headcount by 25%. These cases make intuitive sense: because the companies already possessed the size associated with economies of scale, they were able to achieve economic efficiency equivalent to external vendors.

What about small IS shops? Three of our insourcing cases were below the critical mass associated with economies of scale in data processing: FIRM15 operates 56 MIPs, FIRM16 operates 106 MIPs, and FIRM19 operates 32 MIPs. Due to their size, senior managers assumed that outsourcing vendors would be able to outbid the internal IS

Table 6.3 *IS cost efficiency: economies of scale and efficient IS practices*

	Sub-critical mass	Critical mass
Leading IS management practices	After insourcing: FIRMS: 15, 16, 19	After insourcing: FIRMS: 17, 18, 20
Lagging IS management practices	Before insourcing: FIRMS: 15, 16, 19	Before insourcing: FIRMS: 17, 18, 20

department; a vendor's size should lead to lower average costs by spreading costs over greater volumes. Yet all three of the internal IS departments still outbid external vendors by replicating their cost reduction strategies. After insourcing, all three achieved significant savings: FIRM15 reduced costs by 54%, FIRM16 reduced costs by 20%, and FIRM19 reduced headcount by 46%. These insourcing cases strongly support our assertion that cost efficiency depends more on best practice than economies of scale.

Lesson 5: Internal IS Departments Actually Possess Superior Cost Advantages for Some IS Cost Drivers

We note that although cost efficiency largely depends on efficient practices rather than size, economies of scale do a play a role. One lesson generated from the outsourcing study was that these economies of scale are often associated with a size of IS operations achieved by many medium- and large-sized companies. This preliminary finding was based primarily on an analysis of hardware and software costs which placed internal IS companies at equal advantage with vendors. The insourcing studies confirm these findings but extend the assertion: IS departments may actually possess *superior* cost advantages for some IS cost drivers. By decomposing the cost drivers of information technology, we can apply the theory of economies of scale to determine the relative advantage of insourcing and outsourcing (see Table 6.4). Based on our research, the major cost drivers are data center operating costs, hardware purchasing costs, software licensing costs, labor costs to acquire both business and technical expertise, shareholder costs (the need to generate a profit), research and development costs, marketing costs, opportunity costs, and transaction costs. As is discussed below, internal IS departments possess an inherent advantage on many of these cost drivers.

Data Center Operating Costs

In the area of data processing, economies of scale are achieved in the 150–200 MIP range, which is approximately equivalent to the size of a large mainframe. Thus, most large companies have the critical mass required to achieve economies of scale. In cases where companies operate multiple smaller data centers, economies of scale could be achieved through data center consolidation. Indeed, many outsourcing vendors generate bids for large companies based on the premise that they will consolidate the data centers once the contract is signed. From our cases, internal IS departments can accomplish consolidation through insourcing. Given the internal IS departments' inherent cost

Table 6.4   *Theoretical economies of scale*

Sources of IS costs	Internal IS departments	Outsourcing vendors
Data center operating costs	Comparable to a vendor for 150–200 MIP range	Comparable to large IS departments. Inherent advantage over small IS departments
Hardware purchase costs	Large companies: volume discounts comparable to a vendor	Volume discounts comparable to large IS departments. Inherent advantage over small companies
Software licensing costs	Comparable due to group licenses	Comparable
Cost of business expertise	Inherent advantage	
Cost of technical expertise		Inherent advantage
Cost to shareholders (the need to generate a profit)	Inherent advantage	
R&D costs		Inherent advantage
Marketing costs	Inherent advantage	
Opportunity costs		Inherent advantage
Transaction costs	Inherent advantage	

advantage for other cost drivers, insourcing is more cost efficient than outsourcing to achieve data center economies of scale.

We also note that smaller companies can achieve similar average costs to a vendor even though they operate data centers below the 150–200 MIP range. As documented in Lacity and Hirschheim (1993), small companies are often willing to lag one or two generations behind, allowing them to capitalize on the large savings of the used computer market. For example, one IS manager who operates a mid-sized machine describes why his average costs of computing are comparable to a large vendor's average costs:

> "I said as long as we stay on the trailing edge of technology—and I've been pushing this concept to senior management—we have an opportunity to capitalize on cheaper computing costs."

Theoretically, vendors could also duplicate these savings, but vendors sensibly position themselves as technology leaders rather than laggards.

Hardware Purchase Costs

The theory of economies of scale suggests that lower average production costs are partly achieved through volume discounts. Suppliers are willing to offer large customers volume discounts to secure the business. In the area of IS, most hardware suppliers do indeed offer significant discounts off published price lists to their larger clients. Thus, large companies typically purchase heavy iron for approximately the same costs as outsourcing vendors. For example, one consultant claims that mainframes that retail for $15 million dollars may be sold to large companies such as Exxon or EDS for as little as $11 million. Thus, large internal IS departments and outsourcing vendors possess comparable economies of scale for hardware purchases.

Smaller companies may indeed be at a disadvantage. FIRM19, for example, diligently tried to negotiate lower costs with their hardware suppliers. Due to their size, however, the suppliers were unwilling to offer the same volume discounts enjoyed by their larger customers. Thus, outsourcing vendors possess an inherent cost advantage for hardware purchases over smaller IS departments.

Software Licensing Costs

As discussed in Lacity and Hirschheim (1993), at one time vendors possessed an inherent cost advantage over internal IS departments because of site licenses. With site licenses, outsourcing vendors spread licensing fees over multiple customers, yielding lower average software costs than internal IS departments. As a backlash to lost revenues due to outsourcing, software houses have restructured their licensing practices. Instead of offering site licenses, software houses now offer group licenses in which the customer is charged based on the size of machine. According to one vendor account manager for a mining company we interviewed, this has greatly reduced the vendors' inherent cost advantage:

> "Computer Associates is thinking, 'Every time these deals are signed, the outsourcer can channel everything into one box, use one copy of the software. Therefore, we are going to lose.' So what the software vendors have done is gone to group pricing. And of course, the outsourcer operates a larger box than [the mining company], so it pays more fees . . . this has dire consequences for outsourcing deals."

Thus, internal IS departments typically possess a comparable cost advantage to vendors for software licenses.

Cost of Business Expertise

The cost of acquiring business expertise is a major cost driver, particularly in the areas of applications development and support. The critical skill required to deliver these functions is understanding how business requirements can be met through available technology. Most internal IS departments possess superior knowledge of their users' business requirements. As company employees, internal IS managers and systems analysts understand the idiosyncratic business requirements required to deliver a cost-effective service. For example, every company possesses significant quirks even in their allegedly "commodity" type applications such as payroll, inventory control, purchasing, order processing, etc. As any business person will attest to, it is the exceptions that potentially cripple an application. Internal IS staff have acquired significant understanding of these quirks and thus have an inherent advantage over vendors.

Technical Expertise Costs

The cost of acquiring technical expertise is also a major IS cost driver, particularly in the area of emerging technologies. The vendors are primarily the creators of new technologies, such as LANs, expert systems, and neural networks and therefore possess an inherent cost advantage over internal IS departments. We do not, however, suggest that all new technologies should be outsourced; rather, it is the combination of applying business requirements to emerging technologies that yields value to the firm. Technology in and of itself is of no value; it is merely a general purpose vehicle.

In cases where companies wish to develop applications involving new technologies, companies can access vendor expertise while still maintaining control over applications development. For example, rather than outsource the entire development of an application using a new technology to an outsourcing vendor, companies can maintain managerial control, use the internal IS staff to determine business requirements, and merely hire vendor resources to learn about the new technology. In this scenario, companies can exploit the inherent efficiencies of both internal IS departments and vendors.

Shareholder Costs

Shareholders purchase company stock in return for sharing in company profits. In the area of IS, outsourcing vendors must generate a profit for their shareholders whereas internal IS departments merely need to recover costs. Some participants claimed that this cost driver alone provides internal IS departments with a significant cost advantage. As one IS manager from a manufacturing company states:

> "[Outsourcing vendors] are not a small company by any stretch of the imagination . . . But those guys look for a gross margin of 50–60%. So can they do it cheaper?"

Although recent trends suggest 50–60% margins are now no longer reasonable, vendors still look for 15% margins. As is evident from this analysis, a vendor cannot undercut internal IS departments on most cost drivers. When participants were asked how vendors can operate without such an advantage, participants responded that vendors often underbid contracts in hopes of selling more lucrative excess services and products to their customers.

Research and Development Costs

IS research and development costs are incurred to fuel the development of new technologies. Few internal IS departments have the critical mass to justify large expenditures in R&D. Rather, vendors possess an inherent advantage because they can recover R&D costs by selling the new technology to many customers.

Also included in R&D costs are the costs of environmental scanning and retraining staff. Here too, a vendor possesses an inherent cost advantage. An outsourcing vendor can recover the costs of environmental scanning by selling selected technologies to multiple customers. In addition, an outsourcing vendor can efficiently train their staff, which may include as many as 50 000 people. Internal IS departments simply cannot reach the critical mass required to achieve economies of scale in these areas.

Marketing Costs

Marketing costs are incurred to attract IS customers. For internal IS departments, marketing costs are minimized because they have to a large extent a captive audience. Outsourcing vendors, however, incur considerable costs to attract customers and submit bids. Thus, internal IS departments possess an inherent advantage over vendors in the area of marketing.

Opportunity Costs

Opportunity costs are an important cost driver, but often ignored because they are not captured in accounting calculations. When management chooses to focus resources in one area, they lose the opportunity of applying those resources elsewhere. In the area of IS, some senior managers consider opportunity costs in their sourcing decisions. Willcocks and Fitzgerald (1994a) describe several companies that decided to outsource their legacy systems so that the internal IS department could focus on the development of more strategic applications. Even though these legacy systems could have been efficiently run and maintained in-house, the opportunity cost of not developing strategic applications was significantly high to warrant outsourcing.

Transaction Costs

Transaction costs may be the single most important cost driver. Transactions costs are the management costs associated with coordinating, monitoring, and controlling the delivery of products or services.

Transaction costs explain why many companies produce goods and services internally rather than acquire them on the market. Internal organizations minimize transaction costs because they presumably administer an efficient system of rewards and punishments that discourage employee opportunism. When goods or services are acquired through a vendor, the transaction costs increase because the vendor may behave opportunistically by being untrustworthy, dishonest, or purporting unfair representations. Thus, companies incur transaction costs to negotiate sound contracts, monitor vendor performance, solve vendor disputes, etc. Transaction cost economists also suggest that transaction costs increase when only a small number of suppliers exist in the market. With few competitors, a vendor may take advantage of their captive customer. Thus in general, economists argue that internal companies possess an inherent transaction cost advantage over external vendors.

In the area of IS, the transaction costs associated with outsourcing can be considerable. Companies accrue significant management costs creating RFPs, soliciting vendor bids, analyzing vendor bids, negotiating contracts (which may take six months), monitoring vendor performance, paying bills, and solving disputes. With large companies, outsourcing increases transaction costs due to the few number of vendors large enough to provide their IS services. Typically, only one or two vendors respond to bids solicited by *Fortune* 500 firms for comprehensive IS services. Some participants feared that if they outsourced, they would have no other sourcing alternatives in the short run if their vendors did not perform. The following quote from a CFO captures this fear:

"Once you sign with a vendor, you have no options other than onerous contract terms . . . what are you going to do? Fire them? Sue them? Stop buying services? There is nobody else, in a short period of time, who you can buy services from."

Thus, internal IS departments possess a significant transaction cost advantage over vendors.

From an analysis of the theoretical economies of scale, it becomes apparent that vendors only possess an inherent cost advantage for IS functions whose cost drivers are dominated by new technologies, R&D costs, and opportunity costs. Conversely, large internal IS departments possess equivalent or superior economies of scale to vendors for several major cost drivers: data center costs, hardware purchasing costs, software licensing costs, business expertise costs, marketing costs, and shareholder costs. When considering sourcing alternatives that are primarily driven by these cost drivers, managers should consider whether insourcing is the most efficient sourcing strategy.

The limitation of the analysis of the theoretical economies of scale is that it ignores the political aspects of organizational life. Just because an internal IS department can theoretically achieve efficiency, does not mean that the political environment is receptive to changes required to achieve efficiency. The following lesson explores how political obstacles can be overcome to empower the internal IS department to implement cost reduction tactics.

Lesson 6: Selective Sourcing—which Treats IS as a Portfolio is the Key to Rightsourcing

Taken as a whole, the previous lessons point to the conclusion that selective sourcing is the key to rightsourcing.

Total outsourcing proved a poor sourcing strategy because the entire IS function cannot be treated as one homogeneous utility. By outsourcing the entire IS function, senior executives realized that they lost control of core IS activities, such as strategic planning, scanning the environment for new technologies applicable to business needs, development of business-specific applications, and support of critical systems. Consequently, companies engaged in total outsourcing experienced significant difficulties a few years into the contract. After the initial honeymoon period, companies complained of a loss of alignment between IS strategy and business strategy, failed promises to access new technologies, and contractual costs which were significantly greater than current market prices. Consider the experiences of FIRM12.

Senior executives signed a seven-year, total outsourcing deal, perceiving the entire IS function as a commodity. They selected a particular vendor partly because vendor representatives promised access to industry-specific systems used by other chemicals customers. Because vendor representatives presented themselves as "partners," senior executives from the chemicals company neglected contract negotiations and hastily signed the vendor's generic contract. They failed to analyze the economics of the deal, question how the vendor would cut costs or whether an internal IS department could implement practices to reduce costs on their own—they merely assumed the vendor was more efficient because of its size. The first month into the contract, the vendor's excess charges for items missing in the contract exceeded the fixed monthly price. As time went on, promises of access to additional software vaporized, and instead the chemical company paid the vendor to build new systems. When these systems were late and overpriced, users purchased cheaper PC-based solutions, funded through discretionary moneys. Rather than continue to "partnership" with the outsourcing vendor, senior executives paid a stiff penalty fee to terminate the contract, purchased hardware and software, and hired a new IS staff of 40 people. Despite the undisclosed expenditure, which the IS director characterized as "embarrassing," senior management believes IS costs will be lower in the long run.

Although total outsourcing "war stories"—which are by no means atypical—rightfully discourage total outsourcing, they do not suggest that total insourcing is necessarily the answer. By ignoring the external services market altogether, senior executives had unwittingly created an environment of complacency and erected political barriers for continuous improvement. Consider the experiences of FIRM1.

An IS manager from FIRM1—a chemicals company—initiated an outsourcing evaluation when he realized users were buying PC-based solutions without consulting him. Although his superiors were not cognizant of the situation, he felt his contribution to the company would come into question. He delegated the evaluation process to his subordinates who would potentially lose their jobs if IS was outsourced. They created an RFP and invited external bids from several small outsourcing vendors. Of the three vendors that submitted bids, only one indicated a moderate saving of 7%. The IS manager believed that the outsourcing evaluation confirmed that current IS costs were not unreasonable, so he continued to manage IS in the same manner. Senior executives, however, questioned the validity of the evaluation and remained unconvinced of the value they received from IS expenditures. Six months after the evaluation, the IS manager was fired and replaced with a manager with an accounting background.

With the failures of treating IS as a either a utility to be totally outsourced or a differentiator to be totally insourced, a more selective sourcing strategy appears warranted. Such a strategy treats IS as a portfolio of activities. While some well-defined, isolated and mature IS activities can be safely handed to a vendor, other IS activities require senior management's attention, protection, and nurturing to ensure current and future business success. Consider the case of Sun Micro-systems. They signed a three-year, $27 million deal with CSC to handle all of Sun's mainframe operations while the in-house IS staff rewrites its mainframe-based manufacturing and financial applications to run on a client/server platform (*I/S Analyzer*, 1993). Sun's use of selective sourcing is suggestive of how this can be an effective sourcing strategy. But while selective sourcing offers much promise, the greater choice of options increases the complexity of the sourcing decision (see below).

Our conclusion that selective sourcing is the key to rightsourcing is also supported by experiences in British companies. Willcocks and Fitzgerald (1994a) report on 63 selective sourcing decisions from 20 companies of which 43 were "successful," 13 "relatively successful," and 7 "failures" based on criteria relating to the objectives sought. However, even among the "successful" cases, their research corroborates many of our findings. Their participants widely recognized that the major determinants of success could have been handled better. In particular:

- A better identification of which IS activities to keep in-house and which to outsource was needed.
- A more detailed financial and quantitative evaluation of the in-house and vendor bids was required. Many participants in their study commented on the "hidden costs" that materialized during contract performance.
- The requirements specification needed to be defined more clearly. Contracts needed to be tighter and more comprehensive than first thought, and vendor performance monitored more closely and regularly.
- Active management of the vendor and contract was required, and many organizations underestimated the degree of managerial effort and time this entailed, especially in the first 12–18 months of any contract.

CONCLUSION

The five lessons from the insourcing cases supplement and extend our findings from the outsourcing cases. These lessons flushed out many of the false assumptions of IS sourcing and reveal the problems with "all-or-nothing" approaches. Based on successful and unsuccessful sourcing decisions in both camps, we recognize the need for a more reasoned and selective approach to IS sourcing. But while these lessons answer some questions, they naturally generate others:

- We found that stakeholders possess different perceptions and agendas for IS, but how can organizations achieve alignment?
- We found that IS must be treated as a portfolio, but how can organizations decide whether a given IS activity is a "commodity" or "differentiator"?
- We found that some commodities can be outsourced, but how can organizations evaluate the economics of in-house provision versus vendor offerings?
- Finally, once organizations made a sourcing decision, how do they implement it to ensure success?

Based on the successes and failures, we present a detailed methodology to address these issues in the next chapter.

PART 2

Evaluating the Various IS
Sourcing Options

7
Information Systems Sourcing Methodology

INTRODUCTION

This chapter presents a sourcing methodology based on the lessons learned from the outsourcing and insourcing case studies. Rather than treat sourcing decisions as simple make-or-buy decisions, the methodology addresses a myriad of political and rational issues. We assume a stakeholder approach in which senior executives, business unit managers, and IS managers work together to evaluate the portfolio of IS activities. Together, stakeholders assess current IS performance by flushing out differing expectations and perceptions. Once current performance is assessed, stakeholders create a shared agenda for the portfolio of IS activities and investigate sourcing alternatives. While some IS activities require internal management's attention, protection, and nurturing to ensure current and future business performance, others can be potentially handed over to vendors. Once outsourcing candidates are identified, stakeholders can make sourcing decisions by comparing in-house provision of these activities with vendor offerings. Whether insourcing or outsourcing is selected, continued management of IS activities ensures that sourcing expectations are realized.

The methodology comprises six phases. We highlight the purpose and lessons learned from each phase:

1 *Stakeholder assessment.*
   Purpose: Understand why stakeholders possess different perceptions and expectations of IS performance.

(a) senior management's view: cut costs
(b) business units' and end-users' view: service excellence
(c) IS managers' view: caught in the middle
(d) understanding stakeholder perspectives: the cost/service trade-off
Lesson: Conflicting stakeholders' expectations place IS managers in the precarious position of providing a Rolls Royce service at a Chevrolet price.

2 *Create a shared agenda for IS.*
Purpose: Create a shared agenda by evaluating the business contribution for the portfolio of IS activities.
(a) align IS strategy with business strategy
(b) classify IS activities as "differentiators" or "commodities"
Lesson: Stakeholders must ignore generalizations about alleged IS commodities and differentiators and not let superfluous accounting mask IS's contribution.

3 *Select outsourcing candidates from IS portfolio.*
Purpose: Identify outsourcing candidates among the IS commodities by examining the economic efficiency.
(a) efficient IS management practices
(b) economies of scale
Lesson: Cost efficiency largely depends on adoption of efficient management practices and to a lesser extent, economies of scale.

4 *Compare in-house provision with vendor offerings.*
Purpose: Conduct an official outsourcing evaluation for the outsourcing candidates.
(a) Inform IS staff of the evaluation
(b) create teams
(c) create an RFP
(d) create evaluation criteria
(e) invite internal and external bids
(f) assess validity of submitted bids
Lesson: Successful sourcing depends on comparing vendor bids against a newly submitted internal bid, *not* against current IS performance.

5 *Negotiate contract with external vendor.*
Purpose: If an external bid is selected, stakeholders must attend to 15 rules of contract negotiations.
Lesson: Value talk of "partnership" is no substitute for a sound contract.

6 *Post-decision management.*
Purpose: Whether internal or external bids are selected, continued management of IS activities is vital to ensure success.

(a) insourcing: providing continued support for internal IS managers

(b) outsourcing: creating the role of the contract manager

Lessons: For insourcing, senior managers must support IS managers against user backlash and commit to IS investments to reduce costs. For outsourcing, contract managers must learn four new skills: manage contract, manage demand, manage profit and loss (P&L), and balance risks and costs of monitoring.

STAKEHOLDER ASSESSMENT

The need to align IS strategies with overall business strategies is heralded as the cornerstone of IS management and the basis for sound sourcing decisions. In our experience, however, alignment is often difficult because different stakeholders perceive IS differently and subsequently set different agendas for IS performance. Therefore, the first step in selective sourcing is for stakeholders to understand each other—why do perceptions and expectations differ? Once a common understanding is reached, stakeholders can negotiate a common agenda for IS performance.

In our cases, we found that senior executives, business unit managers, IS managers, and end-users often hold different perceptions and hence different expectations for the performance of IS. These different perceptions were noted in the last chapter in our discussion of the cost/service trade-off. We continue the discussion here, elaborating on the resulting dilemma faced by IS management.

In general, senior executives tend to view the entire IS function as a commodity rather than a strategic asset or core competency. Senior executives actually compared IS to "utilities," "electricity," "heating," and "cafeterias." With metaphors connoting IS as a commodity, senior executives mandated that IS be run more cost efficiently. Usually couched in a larger business context of a general downsizing and restructuring, senior management told IS managers to trim the budgetary fat along with other support functions. On the other hand, business unit managers tended to take a more territorial approach. They often viewed their own IS activities as critical to business success, but dismissed other units' IS activities as commodities. For example, when IS managers propose to consolidate data centers, business unit managers often agree in principle, but only agree if *their* data center is selected as the consolidation site. Like business unit managers, end-users tended to view IS as a critical contributor to daily business processes. As such, users demanded differentiated services, such as custom-tailored applications, a devoted staff of analysts and programmers to respond to daily needs, and locally run data centers to immediately submit runs (and reruns). IS managers were caught somewhere in the middle, trying to juggle the conflicting IS priorities set by senior management and the business units. We further explore the different perceptions and expectations set by stakeholders.

Senior Management's View of IS: Minimize Costs

In many participating companies, senior executives were frustrated with IS performance. At one time, IS managers may have captured senior management's attention with promises of IS for competitive advantage, an idea largely propagated by the trade press in the 1980s. Most senior executives perceive that IS failed to deliver—systems continued to be late, over budget, and lacked the promised functionality. The nagging question continues to haunt them: where is the value from these IS expenditures? The corporate manager of planning and administration from FIRM18 typifies the frustration of many senior executives with the questionable value of IS:

> "All they [senior management] see is this amount of money that they have to write a check for every year. Year after year after year. Where is the benefit? IS says, 'Well, we process data faster than we did last year.' They say, 'So what?' IS says, 'Well, we can close the ledger faster.' And they say, 'So what? Where have you increased revenue? All you do is increase costs, year after year after year and I am sick of it. All I get are these esoteric benefits and a bunch of baloney on how much technology has advanced. Show me where you put one more dollar on the income statement.'"

Because of the questionable value of IS, many senior executives view IS as a commodity they must endure, as a necessary cost to be minimized. As such, they continually pressured their IS managers to operate at a minimal cost. Quotes from the other participating companies capture senior management's perception of IS.

FIRM15

The director of IS administration at FIRM15 describes senior management's complaints about the cost of IS:

> "They are always telling us our processing for payroll is too damn expensive. Then when you say, 'Well have you looked outside?' 'Oh yes, we beat the heck out of them.' So our costs are too high but they can't get it any cheaper."

FIRM16

At FIRM16, the board of curators at the university is comprised of attorneys who view IS as a necessary university cost. The CIO at FIRM16 describes the board's view of IS: "The board could care less about IS. They treated it like they treated the heat or electricity."

FIRM17

The data center manager at FIRM17 describes his senior management's perceptions of IS: "There was a feeling that this was a rat hole to pour money down."

FIRM19

The IS manager at FIRM19 describes the president's view of IS:

> "One of the questions I asked was, 'How do you view IS, Mr President, particularly in the operational center, as an asset to your corporation? Of potential value?' For the most part, business people don't see it that way. They see it as cost."

The data center manager at FIRM19 confirmed this perception:

> "As a line item in the budget, IS expenses were going up. We were constantly being challenged. We had a new business unit president who came in from the deregulated side of our business who really challenged us and pushed for an environment to really look at the cost of IS."

FIRM20

The director for IS planning felt that IS was perceived by management as simply an overhead, where costs are highly visible but the benefits, less so. A rallying cry of management was: ". . . get rid of that overhead."

In summary, senior management in all the participating companies viewed IS as a commodity and/or overhead. As such, they expected IS should be run at a minimal cost and perceived that IS cost too much. Senior management sent the mandate to IS managers: *cut IS costs*.

Business Unit Managers' and Users' View of IS: Service Excellence

Unlike senior management, business unit managers and users did not view IS as a commodity; IS is not a sack of cement, but must be custom-tailored. Thus, users demanded that IS services be customized to meet their processing requirements. Throughout the cases, participants describe users' expectations for excellent, customized service. In general, users demanded customized software to meet idiosyncratic business needs, dedicated analysts and programmers, excess IS resources "in case they are needed," sub-second response time all the time, 24-hour help, information centers, training, etc.

For example, FIRM18 users demanded their own local data centers and did not want to consolidate to save money at the corporate level. One business unit leader declared, "If it cost $5 million more dollars to have this in my business unit and be able to control it and make it responsive to my needs it's worth $5 million dollars to me."

At FIRM17, the data center manager explains that users were generally pleased with IS:

> "These people never complained about service or price. They were big users, in many ways, they were a perfect customer. They had only a couple things a week they cared about. And we had it hardwired, execute those two things routinely with no trouble. The rest of the week, they didn't care what we did to them. They were the perfect customer."

No wonder why FIRM17 users were satisfied—each business unit had custom-tailored software. Even when standard packages were appropriate, different business units chose different packages for word processing, electronic mail, fourth-generation languages, and spreadsheets. From the business unit perspective, it made more business sense to use packages with which users were familiar rather than incur the inconvenience and expense of learning another package.

In part, users' demands for customized services were encouraged and legitimated through general allocation chargeback systems. With general allocation chargeback systems, the entire IS budget is spread to users through some superfluous accounting rules enacted at year end. On a daily basis, users demand the best IS services and products to meet their local idiosyncratic needs with little financial impact. It is not surprising that users' expectations for IS were service excellence, given the fact that their demands only inadvertently resulted in higher costs. The chargeback systems also explains why senior management was so obsessed with increasing IS costs because they were the ultimate recipients of the year-end IS bill.

IS Manager's View: Caught in the Middle

With chargeback systems that juxtaposed senior management's cost reduction mandates with users' pleas for customized service, IS managers were left to juggle increasing user demands from autonomous business units. Because chargeback systems and other organizational processes failed to curb user demand, IS was placed in a logical paradox: provide a Rolls Royce service at a Chevrolet cost.

Senior management's mandate suggests that IS implement cost reduction strategies that would result in lower service levels for users. IS managers attempted to compromise local needs for the higher goal of reducing the company's IS costs—IS managers attempted to consolidate data centers, implement software standards which would require all users in the company to share one software package, and provide "just in time" rather than "just in case" resources. All of their efforts were resisted by users. At FIRM17, for example, the IS manager tried to pool requests across user divisions by suggesting that a certain software product could be used by two different business units. The users refused to agree on a package. At FIRM18, the IS manager tried to consolidate three large data centers into one. Each division agreed in principle as long as their data center was selected for the site of consolidation. In all, IS managers' proposals for cost reductions were viewed as intrusions: users accused the IS department of not understanding their business needs. IS managers were also viewed as failures by senior management since they failed to reduce costs. The discrepancy between senior management's and users' expectations resulted in everybody being unhappy with IS.

Understanding Stakeholder Perceptions: the Cost/Service Trade-off

In the previous chapter, we mapped different stakeholders' perceptions and expectations of IS by plotting IS costs and service levels (see Table 6.1). This matrix depicts the IS cost/service trade-off—that costs are directly proportional to service levels (the better the service, the higher the costs). This matrix can be used to help understand different expectations and perceptions of IS held by different stakeholders.

We noted that IS can be realistically expected to perform in one of two boxes: IS can provide a premium service for a premium cost *or* a minimal service for a minimal price. If organizations perceive that a given IS function is a critical contributor, then IS can be expected to perform in the *Differentiator* quadrant. As a differentiator, IS can provide customized products and services to meet idiosyncratic business needs. IS is a potential source of competitive advantage. If organizations perceive that a given IS function is merely a utility, IS is expected to perform in the *Commodity* quadrant. As a commodity, IS can be expected to deliver a standard service at a minimal cost. It affords no competitive advantage to the company.

But as noted above, there exists a misalignment of stakeholder expectations. Senior management's priorities for IS are for it to deliver service at minimal cost while users expectations are for premium service. This results in the rather dubious expectation of IS operating in the *Superstar* quadrant. IS managers typically respond to these conflicting goals by compromising on both cost and service. But such compromises often fail, resulting in neither stakeholder group being satisfied. They wind up perceiving IS as performing in the *Black Hole* quadrant. The black hole analogy seems particularly appropriate as management simply sees IS as a bottomless cost pit. So what can IS do? Create a shared vision. This is explored next.

CREATING A SHARED AGENDA FOR IS

Different stakeholders' perceptions and expectations of IS performance create *inconsistent* agendas for IS, prevent IS strategy alignment with corporate strategy, and offer IS virtually no hope for even marginal success, let alone stardom. Unfortunately, our cases suggest that IS is not only excluded from the strategic planning process, senior management may not even communicate business strategies to IS. One participant from FIRM15 describes the problem:

> "[Senior executives have] very poor communication across the business lines into the ranks. I'm a director. I should be able to recite what the directions are for this coming year. I don't know what they are. I asked. Senior managers are all Harvard MBA types—very bright, articulate people when they get in front of the stockholders and analysts, but poor communicators when it comes to dealing within FIRM15."

Aligning IS Strategy with Business Strategy

Ideally, senior executives, users, and IS managers work together to set IS priorities by not only aligning IS strategies with corporate strategies, but by including IS in the *formulation* of corporate strategies. Proponents of IS argue that because IS is an enabler of business transformation, it should be an aggressive participant in corporate strategic planning. Unfortunately, most IS managers lack the prestige or credibility to participate in corporate planning.

The next best scenario is for IS to participate in high level meetings in which senior management and business unit leaders agree on an IS strategy that fits into the corporate strategy. Together, the stakeholders agree on the commodity/differentiator strategy for different IS functions, treating IS as a portfolio. Perhaps senior managers can convince users that data centers are a commodity and that consolidation is the appropriate strategy for this function. Perhaps users can convince senior management that certain applications must be customized to meet critical business needs and that differentiation is the appropriate strategy for this function. The important thing is to agree on is an IS priority list that makes business sense.

Classify IS Activities as "Differentiators" or "Commodities"

We have identified two critical success factors for classifying different activities into "commodities" and "differentiators." First, stakeholders must ignore conventional arguments and generalizations. Second, stakeholders must not let the accounting structure mask IS's business value.

Generalizations about which IS activities are "commodities" or "differentiators" are often fallacious. For example, conventional wisdom has it that payroll, accounting systems, and data center operations are "commodity" IS functions, while on-line reservation systems are "differentiators." For some companies, alleged IS commodities actually serve to critically differentiate them from competitors. For example, in one security guard firm, payroll is a strategic application because on-time payment attracts a better quality of staff, leading to superior customer service and more market share.

Generalizations about IS "commodities" and "differentiators" cannot even be made within industries. For example, senior executives from one hospital may view accounting systems as differentiators because the integrated, on-line patient records system swiftly moves patients through the notorious "paperwork" process for admissions and check-out. Such systems may serve to increase patient satisfaction and boost the hospital's reputation. In another hospital—perhaps operating in the same city—the accounting systems may be merely useful, but necessary "commodities." Thus, each company must analyze the delineation of IS activities into "commodities" and "differentiators" for their specific organization.

Second, many companies do not operate highly visible competitive systems, so senior executives may mistakenly classify all IS activities as commodities. In many cases, the business contribution of IS may be masked by accounting for IS as an overhead, which serves to highlight only the costs of IS. In FIRM5, a petroleum company, the CEO continually asked his CIO why IS costs were rising when other departments had managed to cut costs. The CIO explained that other departments primarily reduced costs through IS—transportation costs were cut when IS automated 16 truck terminals and market costs were reduced when IS implemented a new credit card system. By abandoning the view of IS as a cost to be minimized, this CEO realized IS's business contribution and he subsequently rejected an outsourcing vendor's invitation to bid.

Once IS activities have been classified as "differentiators" or "commodities," stakeholders can set performance objectives. Typically, the performance objective for "differentiators" is service excellence, be it customization for a new strategic application, or 24-hour support for current critical systems. Typically, the performance objective for IS "commodities" is cost minimization. After priorities are established, differing sourcing alternatives can be explored.

SELECTING OUTSOURCING CANDIDATES

In most organizations, IS activities classified as "differentiators" will not be considered for outsourcing. Because of their vital contribution to the business, most companies prefer to insource IS "differentiators." By insourcing, management can ensure that the differentiated activity outperforms the key competitors by providing service excellence, can deploy resources immediately if the activity falters, and can protect their ideas, expertise, and ability to adapt the IS activity to changes in business direction. Although "differentiators" should be managed internally, some organizations may boost their in-house talent by bringing in specialists from an expert vendor. However, these "outsiders" work alongside in-house people under the company's own management.

In contrast, IS activities classified as "commodities" may make viable outsourcing candidates if the market can provide cheaper costs than in-house IS while still maintaining an acceptable service level. Gauging the costs of insourcing versus outsourcing is by no means an easy task, but we have noted *cost efficiency largely depends on adoption of efficient management practices and to a lesser extent, economies of scale.* This assertion was demonstrated through an analysis of data center operations in the six insourcing cases in the previous chapter.

Efficient IS Management Practices

In Table 7.1, we have mapped different levels of IS cost performance against the adoption of efficient IS management practices. The point of this matrix is to highlight that efficient management practices—regardless of the size of the IS shop—contributes greatly to IS cost efficiency. This relationship has been well documented by benchmark-

Table 7.1   IS cost/performance on commodity services

	Low performance (excessive cost)	High performance (minimal cost)
Leading IS management practices	*Rising Stars?*	*Best of Breed* in operating IS commodities
Lagging IS management practices	*Black Holes*	*Falling Stars?*

ing firms. Benchmarking firms measure IS cost efficiency—such as cost per MIP, cost per function point, cost per line-of-code, personnel costs—and measure IS management practices, such as data center consolidation, employee empowerment, and software standardization. By plotting these measures, benchmarking firms have established that most IS departments operate in one of two quadrants.

Most IS departments fall into the *Best of Breed* or *Black Hole* categories, establishing a clear linkage between adoption of efficient managerial practices and IS cost performance. There are anomalies. *Rising Stars* are companies that have implemented best practices but have not yet seen an impact on cost performance. Benchmarkers theorize that rising stars will soon realize cost savings once investments have been recouped and the organization has adjusted to the changes. A less optimistic possibility is that political obstacles, such as user resistance, may prevent IS practices from being effective. *Falling Stars* are companies that have low IS costs despite failure to adapt best practice. Benchmarkers argue the performance of *Falling Stars* will eventually slip if they fail to implement best practices. From our case studies, we believe that another possibility to explain *Falling Stars* is that these companies have such a cost-conscious culture that their "rambo" techniques are not considered sound IS practices. For example, in FIRM18, even senior IS managers were found working overnight to lay cable, saving the cost of a contractor. In FIRM8, the director of IS purchases outdated equipment—his ancient (but working) mainframe only costs $4000 a month to lease.

Our insourcing cases serve to corroborate the relationship between adoption of efficient managerial practices and IS cost performance. Prior to insourcing, FIRMs 15, 16, 17, 18, 19, and 20 operated in the *Black Hole* quadrant. After insourcing, all companies moved to the *Best of Breed* quadrant through the adoption of efficient managerial practices.

When gauging where to place certain IS activities in the IS cost/performance matrix, some stakeholders elicit the services of benchmarking firms. In Chapter 5, we detailed the important issues in selecting a benchmarking company, but stress here the need to select a service that will not only diagnose current IS performance, but help to identify best practices to reduce costs. In our insourcing cases, FIRMs 15 and 17 found a benchmarking service instrumental in transforming *Black Holes* into *Best of Breed*.

Economies of Scale

Although we argue that IS cost efficiency is based more on managerial practices than inherent economic efficiencies, there are undeniable economies of scale in some aspects of IS, but they often occur at a level achievable by many medium-sized and certainly large-sized firms. As we have noted before, in the area of data processing, convincing evidence states that economies of scale are achieved at 150 MIPS, the size equivalent to one large mainframe. In the area of software development, *dis*economies of scale can occur very soon, as small development teams are markedly more productive and successful than larger ones. We have addressed the issue of size by highlighting the relative cost advantages of insourcing and outsourcing in Table 7.2. The idea here is to evaluate the cost drivers for the IS activity deemed as an outsourcing candidate. In many cases, stakeholders may find that the internal IS function actually possesses the cost advantage. (See our discussion in the previous chapter.)

In general, our research suggests that vendors are inherently more efficient at providing technical expertise because they can spread

Table 7.2 *Economies of scale: cost advantages of insourcing and outsourcing*

Costs	Small IS department	Large IS department	Outsourcing vendor
Technical expertise			Advantage
Opportunity cost			Advantage
Business expertise	Advantage	Advantage	
Transaction costs	Advantage	Advantage	
Shareholder costs	Advantage	Advantage	
Marketing costs	Advantage	Advantage	
Data center costs		Advantage	Advantage
Hardware costs		Advantage	Advantage
Software costs		Advantage	Advantage

recruitment, training, and R&D costs over more headcount. Vendors also serve to minimize a customer's opportunity costs by providing commodity IS services while internal IS departments focus on more strategic IS issues. In general, internal IS departments are inherently more efficient at providing business expertise, minimizing transaction costs (cost to coordinate, monitor, and manage an IS function), minimizing shareholder costs (internal IS departments do not need to generate a profit), and minimizing marketing costs (internal IS departments do not have to advertise or solicit customers). In addition, large IS departments have comparable economies of scale as vendors in the area of data processing costs, hardware purchase costs, and software licensing costs.

The analysis of cost drivers merely provide rules of thumb, as exceptions can be found among our cases. For example, FIRM16 has low software costs despite its small size because they are a beta-test site. Other organizations will rightfully reject this practice, because they perceive testing a vendor's software as a distraction. In a previously cited example, FIRM8 uses outdated hardware, a practice other companies may find undesirable.

By attending to both economic issues—adoption of efficient IS practices and economies of scale—stakeholders can make a preliminary assessment of the economic validity of outsourcing a given IS commodity. For example, if IS managers have already achieved cost efficiency for a given IS commodity, outsourcing may offer little economic advantage. Indeed, outsourcing may actually increase costs because transaction costs can be significant. On the other hand, the major cost driver may be opportunity costs—stakeholders may decide they would rather focus internal resources on IS differentiators and outsource this IS commodity anyway. See, for example, the case of Sun Microsystems which we referred to in Chapter 6.

In another scenario, IS managers may operate in the *Black Hole* quadrant, due to a failure to adopt efficient IS practices. Stakeholders must assess why IS managers have not adopted best practices. As our cases highlight, user resistance—even outright sabotage—may be preventing IS managers from reducing costs. In other companies, a lack of in-house expertise or lack of economies of scale may be the cause, suggesting that outsourcing may be a viable alternative.

Once stakeholders are agreed, in principle, on the possibility of outsourcing, they must face one more reality check: the cost of an outsourcing evaluation, which can be substantial. These costs include senior management's time in attending to an outsourcing evaluation and the costs to prepare an RFP, invite internal and external bids, and evaluate proposals. If a vendor bid is selected, negotiating costs can be substantial, as outside experts—often costing $300 an hour—will be needed to develop a sound contract. After outsourcing, contract managers will be needed to monitor vendor performance and serve as intermediaries. Thus, stakeholders must be convinced of the potential economic benefit before embarking on a formal outsourcing evaluation.

In summary, outsourcing candidates are typically restricted to IS commodities that vendors can potentially provide more efficiently than in-house IS. Although the underlying economics of IS commodities can be perplexing, we have found that cost efficiency largely depends on adoption of efficient management practices and to a lesser extent, economies of scale. By thinking through these economic factors, stakeholders will be in a better position to identify outsourcing candidates.

COMPARING IN-HOUSE PROVISION WITH VENDOR OFFERINGS

Once stakeholders have identified outsourcing candidates, they may begin to compare vendor offerings against in-house provision. This step entails informing the IS staff, creating an RFP, creating teams, inviting *both* external and internal bids, and evaluating the validity and value of all bids.

Informing the IS Staff

As soon as stakeholders decide to evaluate outsourcing, senior management must address human resource issues head-on. IS staff will naturally panic and question their future. Some members of the IS staff—typically the most talented and marketable—may decide to leave rather than await the outsourcing outcome. Others will stay, but may become demotivated, assuming that management does not value their contribution. Some senior executives or IS managers may be tempted to hide the evaluation from employees, arguing that it is in their employees' best interests to inform them *after* the completion of the evaluation. This strategy typically fails because employees almost always find out anyway. In one chemical company, employees read about the evaluation in the trade press, creating a near mutiny.

A better practice is to treat employees as adults. Senior management may place the outsourcing evaluation in a larger business context, such as the need to reduce costs. Senior management must also explain that they realize that IS costs may be high, in part due, to previous resistance to cost reduction tactics, conflicting agendas for IS, etc. But hopefully much of this has been sorted out by aligning IS strategy with business strategy. IS employees play a vital role in this strategy by proposing ideas to cut costs to an internal bid team. While senior managers cannot guarantee job security, they can guarantee the evaluation process will be fair and that many IS employees will have opportunities either in the newly insourced environment or with an outsourcing vendor. To ensure that the best and most vital talent remains on-board, some IS employees may be offered incentive packages. For example, FIRM17 offered $2000 bonuses every three months to retain key IS employees.

Informing the IS staff of the evaluation process can alternatively act as a galvanizing force, where the staff develop a sense of team spirit and comradery as they work together to develop an internal bid. It can be the catalyst for creativity as they seek new ways of providing IS service in a cost-effective manner. This was the case in FIRMs 18 and 19.

Creating Teams

Although we witnessed a variety of approaches to evaluation, one model that consistently proved effective was creating at least three internal teams: an evaluation team, an RFP team, and an internal bid team.

The evaluation team is typically headed by a senior executive and contains representatives from affected business units and the senior IS manager. This team will develop bid analysis criteria, ensure fair treatment of bidding parties, analyze bids against the criteria, and make the sourcing decision.

The RFP team is typically headed by an IS manager who will not be affected by the outcome of the decision—perhaps an IS manager from another business unit, but one who has enough technical understanding to create a detailed proposal. He may solicit members of the IS staff to help prepare the proposal. To ensure their motivation and performance, special financial incentives may be offered to participating IS employees.

An internal bid team will comprise a number of IS managers and employees, but typically no members of this team may participate on the evaluation or RFP teams. To ensure a fair play, internal bid teams should be removed from the organization—in FIRM18 from their local offices to a remote site in a different city (they termed it their "bunker")—and treated with the same formality as vendors. Most team members prefer isolation rather than having to face their anxious colleagues every day. To prevent favoritism of the in-house bid, all bidders should be treated the same, such as requiring that all questions be submitted in writing and responses are distributed to all bidding parties.

Creating an RFP

By definition, IS commodities are standard IS applications that are well-defined and understood. As such, RFPs should contain details about the services required, but *not* costs. Costs should never be included because they temper bids, providing vendors with a number to back into. Some companies also believe that headcount should not be included in an RFP for the same reason.

Typical RFPs are very technical and may be completely incomprehensible to a lay person. Thus, the need for a technically literate IS manager to man the RFP team. For example, an RFP for a data center typically included the following:

1   Services:
   (a)   number of MIPs
   (b)   megabytes of RAM
   (c)   gigabytes of DASD
   (d)   gigabytes of tape
   (e)   number of tape mounts per month
   (f)   bits-per-second on various circuits.
2   Service levels:
   (a)   on-line availability and downtime
   (b)   batch turnaround time based on priority class
   (c)   response time for various systems.
3   Hardware configuration: number, make, and model of devices like printers, plotters, modems, and control units.
4   Software: list of every software used such as operating software, schedulers, utilities, security packages.
5   Disaster recovery:
   (a)   list of critical systems
   (b)   annual testing.

The RFP contains mandatory requirements that all bidders must meet, but may also invite bidders to propose alternatives to handle personnel, physical location of the data center, the conversion process, etc. Both mandatory and any auxiliary proposals will need to be evaluated based on the decision criteria developed by the evaluation team.

Creating Evaluation Criteria

Because the outsourcing evaluation is restricted to commodity IS activities, the major evaluation criterion will obviously be price. Typically, bidders are required to estimate a fixed price for the mandatory requirements, but may suggest unit prices for increases in volumes. For example, bidders may state the cost of additional MIPs. In some participating companies, the evaluation team tried to convert technical prices into business terms more comprehensible to users. For example, FIRM9, a mining company, developed a "mine equivalent," based on the number of mines, number of people in each mine, the shifts worked, the tonnage removed, and the quality of the tonnage. They related these business volumes to the number of transactions run through the general ledger system. In the end, they developed an estimate of the IS costs associated with supporting all their mines. They envisioned that potential vendors would adjust prices to reflect any mine openings or closings. In other industries, IS prices may be based on number of insurance policies, number of bank accounts, number of oil wells, etc.

As far as auxiliary issues are concerned, the evaluation team may develop a host of criteria for such issues as personnel, disposition of current IS assets, disaster recovery, conversion processes, access to supplemental technologies and talent, contract administration, and termination. Although criteria will vary by company, typical questions may include the following.

Personnel Issues. What does the bidder propose to do with the current IS staff—will the vendor hire them? If so, will they work on this account? Will their salaries and benefits be comparable?

Disposition of Current IS Assets. Will the bidder purchase the company's IS assets? Will they pay book value or market value? Will they pay cash for such assets or adjust prices to reflect the value of the assets?

Disaster Recovery. Does the bidder have an alternative facility in case of a disaster? In how many hours/days can the bidder recover from a disaster? Is there a proven track record of this?

Security and Confidentiality. Will data and systems be secure? How? Is there any chance that competitors could get access to any of the company's systems? Are telecommunications lines encrypted? Will analysts and programmers working for my competitors leak information?

Conversion Process. Will the bidder run the processing at the current facility or move processing to another site? How long will the conversion take?

Access to New Technologies and Technical Talent. Will the bidder provide access to new technologies or applications? Which ones and at what price? How will switches to new technologies reduce volumes and prices on the current contracted technology? What technical expertise will be injected to supplement current talent? At what price?

Contract Administration. Who will manage the account? What procedures will users follow to submit requests or complaints? How quickly will their needs be serviced? What details will the monthly bill contain? What will performance reports look like? What procedure will be used to settle disputes?

Termination. What if either party goes out of business? What if either party is acquired by a third party? What if either party wishes to terminate the contract early? If both parties successfully complete the contract, how will the vendor facilitate the transfer of service back-in or potentially to another vendor?

In some companies, the decision criteria were formally weighted. For example, FIRM19 weighted price as 30%, personnel issues as 10%, service levels beyond mandatory levels at 10%, and distributed the remaining percentage over other criteria such as disaster recovery, security and confidentiality, etc. In other companies, a more qualitative assessment was made for auxiliary items extending beyond the fixed price for mandatory service levels.

Inviting Internal and External Bids

The hallmark of successful companies we studied is that they do not simply compare vendor bids against current IS offerings, but against a newly submitted bid prepared by internal IS managers. As previously discussed, many IS managers possess a plethora of ideas to reduce costs, but internal user resistance or even outright user sabotage may have hindered their efforts in the past. We have noted that the problem stems from stakeholders within organizations who have different performance expectations for IS. Senior executives—who typically write the check for IS every year—often set cost minimization as the performance expectation for IS. Business units and users—who actually consume computer resources—often demand service excellence as their primary performance expectation. These expectations are in conflict because service excellence drives up IS costs. Senior management's threat of outsourcing often serves to align IS performance expectations, typically to the cost minimization agenda. IS managers are then free to prepare bids which include cost reduction tactics practiced by vendors. These practices include chargeback systems to curtail user demand, employee empowerment to reduce supervision costs, consolidation of data centers to one physical site, standardization of software, automation of data center operations, and archiving of inactive data. (See Chapter 4 for details on cost reduction tactics.) Users understand that if their internal IS managers—who are at least familiar to them—do not implement these practices, vendor employees certainly will.

After inviting both internal and external bids, companies usually schedule a series of bidders' meetings where bidding parties can ask questions about the RFP. In these meetings, the internal bid team is treated with the same formality as external bidders. Participants caution that these meetings can get very heated. At FIRM19, for example, bidders often asked loaded questions to highlight weaknesses of other bidders. After the official meetings, bidders should be required to submit additional questions in writing. Both questions and answers are periodically distributed to all bidders, to prevent information asymmetry.

Assessing the Validity of Bids

Once bids are in, the evaluation team sets to work on the difficult task of not only comparing bids, but assessing the validity of proposals: can bidders actually deliver on these promises? Prudent managers question *where* and *how* the vendor proposes to earn a profit while still meeting the bid. In the most desirous scenario, the winner clearly outbid others based on a number of valid reasons—superior management practices, inherent economies of scale, or superior technical expertise. But in many cases, the winning bid may be based on "voodoo" economics—customers are offered long-term, fixed prices which are attractive in year one but will be out of step with price/performance improvements a few years into the contract. If external bids win, the evaluation team must ascertain whether the vendor may be trying to buy a market share in a fiercely competitive market. Once the contract is signed, the vendor may recoup losses by charging large excess fees for any change, realizing that customers are captive. Bids may contain hidden costs, particularly external bids. For example, FIRM6 failed to question a software transfer fee license clause which ended up costing half a million dollars.

In rare cases, some companies may actually *seek* a purely economic package based on financial manipulations rather than inherent best practices or efficiency. Two of our case studies—FIRM10, a transportation company and FIRM14, an aerospace company—used outsourcing to escape financial peril. The CFO from the transportation company signed a 10-year outsourcing contract when his company went bankrupt. Senior executives from the aerospace company signed a 10-year contract after several years of negative profits. These arrangements bought in multi-million cash infusions when the vendor purchased IS assets, transferred 2000 employees in one case and 1600 employees in the other to a more stable vendor, and postponed fixed fees until the later portion of the contract.

Regardless of the impetus for outsourcing, senior executives must be convinced of the validity of internal and external bids before making a final decision. In some participating companies, the evaluation team invited the top candidates to present their bids in a daylong meeting. During these meetings, the evaluation team asked poignant questions on where and how the bidder proposed to meet their bid.

CONTRACT NEGOTIATIONS WITH EXTERNAL VENDORS

If an external vendor is awarded the bid, the company enters into contract negotiations. This step is vital because companies can only ensure that outsourcing expectations are realized by signing an airtight contract. *The contract is the only mechanism that establishes a balance of power in the outsourcing relationship.* Every person spoken to in the outsourcing research who decided to outsource stated that the contract is the *key* to a successful outsourcing relationship. In our study, the companies most dissatisfied with outsourcing all signed contracts that dramatically favored the vendor. These contracts merely stipulated that the vendor would provide the same level of service that the company received prior to outsourcing. However, the service levels in the base year were poorly documented, so customers were subjected to costly excess fees for services they presumed were included. In contrast, participants most pleased with their outsourcing arrangements, found that rigorous contracts reduce the threat of opportunism. When service levels, cost structures, and penalties for non-performance are specified in the contract, the vendor becomes legally obligated to accommodate.

Table 7.3 *Lessons in contract negotiations*

1   Avoid vague "partnership" talk
2   Discard the vendor's standard contract
3   Do not sign incomplete contracts
4   Hire outsourcing experts
5   Measure everything during the baseline period
6   Develop service level measures
7   Develop service level reports
8   Specify escalation procedures
9   Include penalties for non-performance
10 Include incentives for superior performance
11 Determine growth
12 Adjust charges to changes in business volume
13 Select your account manager
14 Include a termination clause
15 Beware of "change of character" clauses

The following lessons provide advice on how customers should negotiate contracts with outsourcing vendors. Although the lessons seem to favor the customer over the vendor, the true motive is to establish a balance of power that benefits both parties. Since the initial position favors the vendor (they are typically the experts at negotiation and have experience in outsourcing, unlike the customer), the customer needs to leverage his position by attending to the major lessons presented in Table 7.3.

Avoid Vague "Partnership" Talk

Some participants were wooed by vendors to sign flimsy contracts under the spirit and trust of a "strategic partnership." This contracting model proved a poor option to manage the vendor because outsourcing vendors and customers lack shared goals. Vendor account managers are often rewarded for maximizing profits, primarily by charging customers additional fees for services extending beyond the contract or by reducing the vendor's internal costs which subsequently reduced service levels. In reality, these "strategic partnerships" quickly deteriorated into adversarial relationships as customers realized every dollar out of their pocket goes into the vendor's pocket.

Discard the Vendor's Standard Contract

Vendors will likely parade their standard contract in front of their perspective customers. The VP and director of IS for FIRM6 who outsourced, notes that this contract should be immediately discarded. She, as well as other participants, feels that the key to successful outsourcing arrangements is building a site-specific contract:

> "One thing for sure: you cannot use the vendor's contract. It is too one-sided. I mean I tell people—the vendor gave us a generic contract, but we didn't use it. The problem is that all deals are so different."

The vendor's standard contract typically obligates the vendor to perform the same level of service that the company's internal IS department provides during a baseline period. These contracts do not, however, set performance standards or include penalty clauses if the vendor fails to meet requirements.

The payment schedules in these standard contracts may also favor the vendor. For example, an outsourcing vendor for FIRM9 wanted them to sign their standard contract. This contract required the metals company to pay the bill on the first day of the month, prior to service delivery. The IS consultant who assisted the metals company with their contract negotiations, explains the impact of the vendor's proposed payment schedule:

> "[the outsourcing vendor] wanted it day one net 15. We got it to in arrears net 45. There was a difference in a 10-year contract, there was a difference of $8 million. So [the outsourcing vendor], they play those games."

Do Not Sign Incomplete Contracts

Since both parties are often anxious for the relationship to begin, the temptation to close negotiations swiftly is strong. The outsourcing vendor, in particular, may try to convince their customers to sign the contract before items are clearly specified. They assure their customers, "we'll take care of the details later." But since the vendor is not legally bound to alter the contract a posteriori, they may never agree to supplement the original contract.

At FIRM7, for example, the CEO signed an incomplete outsourcing contract in January of 1989. The vendor promised to define services, service level measures, and service level reports within the first six months. Four years later, these items still remained incomplete, primarily because of the discrepancies over the contents of the baseline bundle. Managers at the company argue that certain services were understood to be covered in the contract. The vendor argues that if they were not already in the contract, then those services are subject to excess fees. This major problem could have been avoided if the commencement date was postponed in order to complete the contract.

Hire Outsourcing Experts

During negotiations, the vendor uses a host of technical and legal experts to represent their interests. These experts thoroughly understand the way to measure information services and how to protect their interests. In order to counterbalance the vendor's advantage, the customer should hire experts to represent their interests. Participants in our study noted that experts are a critical success factor in negotiating an equitable contract. Although participants admit that outsourcing experts are expensive, they believe experts will help prevent excessive above-baseline charges.

Two types of outsourcing experts are recommended—a technical expert and a legal expert. A technical expert is particularly helpful when measuring baseline services. They not only create technical measures of the customer's information resources, they are able to convert these measures to the technical idiosyncrasies of the vendor's environment. In simpler terms, technical experts convert the customer's apples to the vendor's oranges—a crucial skill that many customers do not possess. In addition, customers may feel wary about using their in-house technical staff to assist in baseline measures since many of these people may be affected by the outsourcing contract.

A legal expert familiar with outsourcing contracts is also recommended. These legal experts, who typically work in conjunction with the customer's internal legal department, ensure that the customer's wishes are adequately documented in the contract. Together, the legal expert and internal lawyer can pose a formidable legal team.

As far as timing is concerned, customers will typically wish to hire a legal expert at the final stages of negotiation. A technical expert, however, is typically needed much sooner, particularly during the measurement of baseline services.

Measure *Everything* during the Baseline Period

During contract negotiations, the customer's current information services are documented during the baseline period. The baseline period becomes the yardstick that determines what services the vendor is obligated to provide to the customer. The outsourcing vendor will charge a fixed fee for delivering this bundle of services, but will charge an excess fee for services above and beyond the baseline. Therefore, customers must measure every service during the baseline period to ensure that these services will be included under the fixed fee obligation.

Assuming the outsourcing arrangement encompasses the entire IS department, customers should measure data processing, telecommunications, applications development, applications support, and residual services. Residual services include any services that are not captured in the other categories such as user consultation, training, report distribution, and office moves. Each of these areas is briefly discussed below.

Data Processing and Telecommunication Services

Of all the IS service areas, participants felt that data processing and telecommunications were the easiest to measure. Most participants used the system's monitoring facilities (SMF) to capture resource usage during the baseline period. In IBM environments, for example, SMF data was typically used to assess baseline data processing activity. Monitoring facilities track the number of jobs submitted, the resources used for each job (tape mounts, data storage, computer minutes), turnaround time for jobs, on-line response time, and system availability. Similar reports are generated by network management systems for telecommunications.

During the baseline period, participants felt confident that their monitoring systems adequately captured their current level of processing. Resource requirements, however, vary based on the machine. Thus, a company's systems may perform significantly differently on a vendor's machine. Care must be taken to convert the company's baseline activity to a comparable load on the vendor's machine. Vendors will typically develop a conversion model based on a sample set of test transactions run on their test machine. One technical expert we spoke to advises customers to discard the vendor's conversion model since a vendor's test environment may vary significantly from their operating environment. The customer runs the risk of being charged excess fees if the vendor underestimates the resources required to run the customer's systems. To avoid this risk, the customer may stipulate in the contract that the conversion model be updated after the customer's systems are run at the vendor site.

Applications Development and Support

These service areas are difficult to measure since the activities are labor intensive. Participants in the study typically decided to use headcount as the baseline measure. Thus, if 200 analysts and programmers currently work in applications, the customer becomes entitled to 200 full-time equivalents (FTEs). Two hundred FTEs typically equate to 8000 hours' worth of work a week (200 people times a 40-hour work week).

Participants, however, cited four problems with this measure. First, the vendor may eliminate people and make the remaining staff work excessive hours. The IS manager at FIRM12 explains the problem when the vendor reduced staff:

> "They (the remaining staff) pick up the slack so I still get my 1000 hours so contractually I couldn't do anything about it. The programmers, so they have to pick up more hours, they are tired, sick. They make mistakes."

Second, several participants complained that the quality of the analysts and programmers diminished. Vendors siphoned their best employees from the account to attract other customers. Third, non-productive hours are included in the FTE hours such as vendor group meetings and analyst training. Fourth, the FTE does not provide a measure of productivity, merely hours worked. Since the vendor charges for hours that exceed the FTE, customers fear that they have no way to detect if vendors exaggerate project estimates. These service problems, however, cannot be blamed on the vendor. They are free to hire, fire, and assign staff any way they see fit. If the customer wants control over headcounts, hours worked, project estimates, and staff quality, perhaps they should not outsource applications development and support.

Residual Services

In full blown outsourcing arrangements, companies often neglect to measure many services because: (a) they are not reflected in current IS budgets; (b) they are not currently monitored or measured; and/or (c) customers assume they fall within other service areas. For example, many times users ask in-house analysts to help them set up their printers, verify spreadsheets, recommend products, etc. The analysts usually respond without documenting or charging users for these favors. However, if the customer does not document and measure these services, the vendor will not include them in the baseline.

Residual services include such items as disaster recovery testing, environmental scanning for new hardware and software, microcomputer support (purchase decisions, installation, training, repair), office relocation services such as rewiring and node changes, storage management to balance cost and performance trade-offs, teleconferencing support, etc. As evidenced by these examples, many residual services are difficult to measure. How do you measure intangible items such as advice, courteous service, and environmental scanning? In most cases, these services can only be measured during the baseline period by maintaining service logs. Since outsourcing decisions often cause a degradation in morale, management may fear that IS employees might ignore or sabotage the measurement effort. Therefore, some companies assigned their users to maintain the service logs during the base period.

The consequences of not measuring services were readily apparent in our study. Participants that neglected this phase all suffered serious service problems and excess charges because they failed to measure all information services during the baseline period. Some participants assumed that their RFPs documented their service needs, but RFPs are only high level descriptions of service requirements. Baseline measures must be monotonously detailed.

The length of the baseline period is also an important consideration. Since service volumes typically fluctuate with the tax season, seasonal business oscillations, end-of-year processing, etc., a baseline period of six months is recommended. Typically, measures are calculated once a month for each service. For example, during March the customer may use X hours of a computer resource. During April, volumes may decrease or increase. At the end of the baseline period, six observations exist for each service. The customer and vendor must then establish an algorithm to determine the baseline number. Vendors often suggest averaging monthly measures, but this results in the customer exceeding baseline services 50% of the time. Perhaps a more equitable solution is to create a volume variance for each service level. The customer will not be charged an excess fee as long as volumes remain within specified ranges.

Develop Service Level Measures

Some may question why service level measures need to be developed since the baseline period allegedly covered this issue. The answer is simple: the customer or vendor may wish to add, combine, improve, or delete measures. Thus, baseline measures merely provide a yardstick for what the vendor's obligations will be during the arrangement. For every service that the vendor is expected to provide, a service level measure should unequivocally express the level of required service.

During this phase of contract negotiations, participants warn that vendors may try to manipulate measures in their favor. At a diversified services company, for example, the vendor attempted to dilute measures in two ways. First, they tried to dodge accounting for 100% of services. Second, the vendor tried to manipulate the laws of probability in their favor. Both these issues are discussed below.

Specify 100% Service Accountability

Measures typically require vendors to deliver a certain amount of work in a certain period of time. For example, vendors may agree to process 90% of all service requests within three days. The customer, however, may never know what happens to the remaining 10% of the service. This 10% may be serviced very late or never at all. Despite the fact that 10% of the work may never be accounted for, vendors technically meet their service level requirements.

The best way to avoid services from falling through the proverbial cracks is to specify 100% service accountability. For example, if the vendor agree to process 90% of all service requests in three days, then make an additional requirement that specifies the remaining 10% must be completed within five days. The customer should require that exceptions be fully documented and reported.

Know the Basic Laws of Probability

Vendors may also dilute measures by exploiting some simple laws of probability. Returning to the outsourcing experiences of FIRM7, the vendor finally agreed to deliver 95% of a particular service within the agreed upon time frame. The company agreed to the measure, as long as the service was delivered correctly. The vendor countered with a proposal to implement two measures. The first measure specified that 95% of the service is completed by the target date. The second measure specified that 95% of the service will be accurate. By proposing two measures, the vendor attempted to dilute the service level since the probability of the service being delivered on time *and* accurate is only 90%.

✕ Develop Service Level Reports

During outsourcing negotiations, companies may spend a significant amount of time developing measures, then fail to require the vendor to report on these measures. Vendors may tell their customers that their standard reports address their measures, but several participants found this assertion untrue.

One participant from FIRM7, for example, complained that the vendor's standard reports only indicate the volume of service performed. For instance, the vendor's security request report indicated "100 security requests were implemented this month." This report does not specify how many security requests were submitted or the average turnaround time for the requests. According to the contract, the vendor was meeting service levels. Users, however, complain that requests took an excessive time to process:

> "We have, at one time, in excess of 17 working days to get somebody through security. We have a big problem with that."

Users find it unacceptable to wait over two weeks before receiving a logon identification or access to a needed dataset.

Service level reports should document the service level agreed upon, the service performance for the current time period, exception reporting for missed measures, and a trend analysis of the performance from previous reporting periods. Customers are often charged for the creation of these reports. The investment is well worth it—how can service level measures be monitored without service level reports?

Specify Escalation Procedures

Customers realize that IS is oftentimes a volatile business—there are bound to be occasional events that prevent the vendor from meeting a service level measure. In some instances, the customer may even be at fault. Thus, in addition to the service level reports, the customer and vendor must agree upon problem escalation procedures.

Typically, the vendor will request that fault (customer or vendor) be determined for each missed measure. This protects the vendor's interests—since they are contractually bound to meet measures, they should not be punished for customer errors. Perhaps a bipartisan committee will determine blame for missed measures. Granted, this task is repulsive to most; as professionals we want to fix problems, not fix blame. However, the reality is that dollars may be exchanged as a result of non-performance.

Services may be divided into critical versus non-critical categories to prevent micromanagement. For non-critical measures, such as analyst training hours, perhaps the vendor may miss this measure once or twice a year. For critical services, such as on-line availability, the customer may require immediate reporting, problem resolution within a specified period of time, and perhaps even a cash penalty.

Include Cash Penalties for Non-performance

In cases of severe service degradation, the customer may insist on cash compensation. At FIRM6, for example, there are penalty charges for failure to meet end-user response time, system availability, and batch delivery deadlines for critical systems. Customers may also wish to escalate cash penalty amounts with frequency. For example, the first occurrence may result in a penalty of $25 000. Another occurrence for the same service within a specified time period may cost the vendor $50 000, and so on.

Participants that specified cash penalties in their contracts hope that they will never need to enact the penalty clause. The CFO at FIRM10 notes that penalty clauses do not fully compensate the customer. Rather, the purpose of penalty clauses is to ensure that the vendor's senior management will attend to service level problems:

> "You don't get total reimbursement for your lost profit and your lost cash. But you do have a penalty that is significant to [the outsourcing vendor] and gets their attention. Our penalty is in the $100 000 range up to $1 million. So it's not enough to compensate us for the downtime, but it will certainly get their attention. It will get somebody fired. You know it will get to the top layers within [the outsourcing vendor]."

Include Incentives for Superior Performance

Although cash penalties for non-performance are a useful vehicle for getting the vendor's attention to problematic areas, it is simply the "stick" component of the well-known "carrot–stick" approach. But what about the "carrot"? The customer should similarly offer incentives to the vendor for superior performance. If the service levels are exceeded, the vendor should be compensated in some appropriate fashion for this achievement. Again, some type of cash payment could be specified.

Determine Growth Rates

Most outsourcing contracts include a growth rate where the customer gets a certain amount of growth for free. The reasoning is that the cost of a unit of processing decreases every year, so the customer deserves to share the benefits of price/performance improvements. The problem, however, is that the vendor understands growth rates much better than the senior executives with which they typically negotiate. The customer is warned that the vendor may underestimate growth so that they may charge excess fees in the future.

The following example illustrates the problem. The vendor may convince the customer that their growth rate is 5–6% per year, based on IS budget increases. The vendor then offers to provide a 6% increase in resource requirements (MIPS, storage, tapes) free of charge. To a customer unfamiliar with the intricacies of IS, this deal seems appealing. However, in actuality, the resource requirements may be growing at 10–20% since the IS department is able exploit price/performance improvements discussed before. During the outsourcing arrangement, the customer will either pay extra for resource growth above 6% or they will curtail growth.

Adjust Charges to Changes in Business

Customers should also include a clause for severe volume fluctuations caused by acquisitions, mergers, or sale of business units. In cases of a sale of a business unit, the customer may specify a major reduction in the fixed fee expense. The vendor, however, may insist on several months' notice to allow ample time to redirect resources. The customer may also want the vendor to promptly accommodate mergers or acquisitions. The vendor may insist, again, on advance notice. In addition, the vendor may insist on charging the customer a transition fee for the volume adjustment.

Select Your Account Manager

At FIRM11, the controller insisted on one truly unique feature: he specified the name of the account manager in the contract. The controller had so much faith in this particular individual, one of the vendor's account managers, that he required him to manage the arrangement. This account manager is indeed a special character; as a previous outsourcing customer, he was once the vendor's most vocal critic, often complaining about services and fees. The vendor finally hired him "to shut him up." The controller feels that the account manager's background as a former outsourcing customer will prevent the threat of opportunism. His choice was wise; after one and one half years with the vendor, the mining company has never contested the vendor's bills or service. Although the contract seems weak in other areas (lack of service measures, penalty clauses), the controller's utter trust in the account manager compensates for any legal loopholes.

Include a Termination Clause

Most lawyers will insist that a termination clause be included in the contract. This clause protects both parties, since the desire to terminate by one party will severely affect the other. Either party may need to terminate because of bankruptcy or sale of the company. In addition, the customer may wish to terminate because of failure to provide services. Most contracts require either party to notify the other within a specified time period, such as three months. Failure to give adequate notice may result in a severe penalty charge.

The customer, however, will typically require more than three months to find an alternative to meet their information needs. Negotiation with another vendor may require six months;

rebuilding an internal IS department may require a year or more. In addition, the customer needs the vendor's assistance to transfer systems to an alternative site. Therefore, vendor assistance should be specified as a requirement for termination—regardless of the initiating party.

Watch out for "Change of Character" Clauses

Another weakness of several outsourcing contracts is the "change of character" clause. This provision states that the customer will be charged for any changes in functionality. This clause has triggered several disputes. At FIRM7, for example, the vendor wanted to charge for changing their word processing software. The vendor argues that this represents a change of character since the new product was not supported during the baseline period. The customer argues that this is not a change of character since the function—word processing—has not changed, only the software.

Personal computers are another point of contention. Their contract says that the vendor will service all personal computers for a fixed price. However, the number of computers has doubled since 1989, and many PCs are now connected to LANs. The vendor claims that LAN technology is a "change in character," whereas the customer claims it is only a difference in technology. In addition, the outsourcing vendor wants to charge a particular dollar amount for each additional PC supported. The customer contends that "volumes do not equal costs." In other words, doubling the number of PCs does not require double the cost to support them.

These 15 negotiating guidelines provide the foundation of a sound outsourcing relationship. But this is merely the beginning, and vendor relations must be managed during the entire duration of the contract.

MANAGING THE DECISION

Whether an internal or external bid is selected, continued management of IS activities is vital to ensure success. Although most companies that selected an external vendor's bid attended to the process of managing, coordinating, and monitoring vendor performance, many companies that selected the internal bid failed to provide internal IS managers with continued support. We address both of these issues in this section, beginning with managing insourcing.

Insourcing: Provide Continued Support for Internal IS Managers

To ensure that internal IS managers can implement their cost reduction tactics outlined in the internal bid, senior managers must perform two tasks:

1 Support IS managers against user-backlash;
2 Commit to investments to reduce costs.

After an internal bid is awarded, senior management must continue to support IS by clearly communicating IS's priorities to lower level users, squelching user resistance, and absorbing user backlash. In particular, senior management must be prepared for user complaints about reduced service levels as drastic cuts in IS costs will almost always be accompanied by reduced service levels. As one senior executive noted, "They bitched about IS before, they bitch now, but at least it is costing me a lot less." Two other examples from the cases highlight the need for senior management support and intervention. The experiences of FIRMs 17 and 18 demonstrate the support IS managers need from their senior management.

The controller from FIRM17 fully supported the IS department when users complained about service degradation. The data center manager relays a conservation with the controller: "My response time is a little more erratic [as a result of insourcing] . . . if you made the response time slower, could you save me a couple more million dollars?" Whenever users complained about service levels, senior management congratulated IS.

The seven CFOs from FIRM18 work together to curtail user demand and complaints. In order to achieve the 40% cost savings, each business unit committed to a particular workload on the CPU. If the daily consumption report indicates that actual usage exceeds projected usage, the CFOs immediately investigate. The IS manager explains that "the users lived in fear of their CFO. He wanted to know who it was who put him over. That helped us a lot because we were no longer the bad guy." Senior management supports IS to such a degree that if IS costs rise due to user demand, it is the business unit that will incur senior management's wrath, not IS. The IS manager concludes:

"So the unwritten rule is, if one division uses more than what was budgeted and causes the data center to upgrade, the person who is going to talk to executive management is the line of business that caused the data center to go over."

Thus, top management support is a requisite for enabling IS to implement changes proposed in their internal bid.

Senior management must perform one last step to ensure the success of insourcing: they must commit to investments required to reduce costs. In other words, it takes money to save money. In two of our cases, senior management failed to invest in the resources required to reduce costs. For example, at FIRM19, the IS managers released several staff members in anticipation of automation software. Because these employees had opportunities elsewhere, the IS manager felt that ethically he should encourage them to leave prior to automation. Once the staff was gone, however, senior management failed to release the funding for the automation software. Participants complained that senior management perceived that they were operating fine without the software. Unfortunately, the remaining staff has been working overtime for a year in anticipation of the software. Morale is extremely low as a data center manager explains:

> "My staff [thinks of management] 'you bought off on redeploying people, why aren't you buying off on the product I told I needed to justify that? . . . You are awfully quick in taking away my peers and leaving me with long hours. When it comes to the products that will make my job easier you tell me you can't do it.' "

At FIRM15, a similar situation occurred. The IS manager consolidated two data centers. Previously, the data centers functioned as disaster recovery sites for one another. After the consolidation, the IS manager asked senior management to release funds for a disaster recovery service:

> "We told [senior management] we were going to go to a hot site. It was a three-year process. We made all these changes. [Senior management] picked on this $120 000 blip in our spending for the hot site. They said, 'We can't afford that.' I said, 'Wait a second folks. It's too late to back out now.' "

Eventually the IS manager secured funding by appealing to the internal auditors.

In hindsight, participating IS managers claimed that they would have waited for management to release funds prior to implementing the cost reduction tactic. Otherwise, IS managers may be powerless in securing funding after the fact.

Outsourcing: Creating the Role of the Contract Manager

Although a detailed contract is the most critical factor in ensuring successful outsourcing relationships, transforming the contract from a piece of paper into the hearts and minds of stakeholders from both the customer and vendor organizations requires a strong contract manager. Senior executives must select a contract manager who can serve as primary intermediary between users and the vendor, work closely with the vendor account manager to prioritize requests and handle disputes, monitor vendor performance, and question and review monthly bills and excess fees. In many companies, senior executives select the senior IS manager to fill this role. For example, in FIRM7, the previous VP of IS was named contract manager. Although he adjusted well to his new role, research by Willcocks and Fitzgerald (1994a) suggests that many IS managers have difficulty with the transition. In particular, contract managers must learn to:

- manage contracts, not people
- manage demand, not supply
- manage profit and loss margins
- balance costs/risks of vendor monitoring

Manage Contracts not People

Prior to outsourcing, IS directors spend a large portion of their time managing people's careers, assignments, training, and performance. After outsourcing, personnel management is now in the vendor's domain. In some organizations, either the IS director or some users may have difficulty "letting go." For example, the vendor account manager at FIRM7 describes user complaints:

> "The guy running the business, he says, 'Wait a minute. You can't take Mary Jo away from me, she's been with me 17 years.' Well now is that being fair to Mary Jo? So we get a lot of criticism from customers about how we are always turning people over. And yet that is one of our strengths."

The account manager makes a valid point: senior management at FIRM7 partly selected the vendor because they would provide better career opportunities for their transitioned employees, but are annoyed when those opportunities mean transferring people off the account.

Manage Demand not Supply

Contract managers are in charge of specifying and clarifying service requirements, not getting involved in hardware and software procurement. This can be another difficult transition—as many contract managers want to specify the makes, models, and versions of hardware and software, but this again is now the vendor's domain. The contract manager may request, for example, additional MIPs, but the vendor may choose which of their computers will fulfil the request.

Manage Profit and Loss Margins

Although many IS directors had previous experience with managing IS costs, the role becomes even more important with outsourcing. Prior to outsourcing, chargeback systems may have been general allocation systems in which a given user's request—for, say, screen modifications—would not be reflected in the year-end bill. With outsourcing, any demand for service above the baseline may be subject to excess fees. The contract manager must work with users and their managers to determine the business value of such requests, prioritize these against other requests, and work with vendors to price and deliver such requests.

Balance Costs/Risks of Vendor Monitoring

Contract managers, in conjunction with senior management, must decide how closely to monitor vendor performance. On the one hand, tight monitoring reduces risks but increases transaction costs. On the other hand, loose monitoring reduces transaction costs but increases risk. Willcocks and Fitzgerald discuss the trade-off:

> "Tight monitoring is associated with high costs, because there are a lot of specialists checking all aspects of the service provision at regular stages in the process. In terms of risk it is relatively low because the tight monitoring will pick up any problems and hopefully make sure they are rectified at an early stage, before too much damage is done to the business. The loose, end-result monitoring is lower cost, with fewer people involved, but is potentially higher risk because if things go wrong they will not be picked up until the end-results are seen by users, or the business in general, or even more damaging, by end customers." (Willcocks and Fitzgerald, 1994a, p. 18)

As time progresses, stakeholders from both the customer and vendor organizations adapt. The contract may play less of a role, delegated to reference document, as contract managers and vendor account managers learn to work with one another. But the contract is always there if needed. The director of IS at FIRM8 concludes:

> "A lot of people at [the outsourcing vendor] were uncomfortable with this [contract]. In fact their VP said, 'Can't we put this thing in the drawer?' I said, 'Yeah, but this is still the operating agreement.'"

CONCLUSION

In this chapter, we have presented a sourcing methodology that stresses both "rational" and "political" issues. From our experiences, companies may go through the motions of a rational process—identifying outsourcing candidates, creating RFPs, inviting external bids, evaluating bids, and making a selection—but the whole process can be sabotaged if political issues are ignored. For example, if people whose careers will be significantly affected by the outcome are in charge, they may conduct a cursory evaluation that merely appears rational. We saw this in the case of FIRMs 1, 5, and 8. From outward appearances, the evaluations seemed on the "up-and-up," but closer scrutiny revealed that numbers were manipulated to reflect the decision-makers' preferences. Consequently, no change in IS performance resulted.

From the beginning, we have recognized that organizations are comprised of diverse individuals with their own preferences, expectations, perceptions, and agendas for IS. We believe these "political issues" must be confronted and managed to make sound sourcing decisions. Much of this depends on senior management's ability to corral different stakeholders—business unit managers, IS managers, IS staff members, and end-users. Senior managers must work with stakeholders to define a shared agenda for IS, to evaluate the business contribution of the IS portfolio, and to identify potential outsourcing candidates. If a decision is made to formally evaluate outsourcing, senior management must further enlist the support of IS, but manage the potential sabotage. We have recommended that such management comprises: allowing the internal IS staff to submit a counter bid, enlisting a senior IS manager who will not be affected by the outcome to lead the RFP team, and to offer bonuses to select IS staff members to prevent them from jumping ship. After the decision, senior management must squelch user backlash, support IS managers in the instance of insourcing, or manage vendor performance in the instance of outsourcing. These political issues cannot be swept under the proverbial carpet, reenforcing our previous assertion that the management of IS cannot be outsourced. In the next chapter, we offer our thoughts on the future direction of IS sourcing.

8
Beyond the Bandwagon

INTRODUCTION

In this last chapter we would like to offer some concluding thoughts about two important issues associated with IS sourcing. The first revolves around the issue of whether IS is different from other organizational functions which are outsourced. There appears to be a growing number of proponents arguing for the outsourcing of all organizational functions which are non-core. And if IS is not a core competency of the business, it should be outsourced to allow the company to focus on its core business. We believe that such a belief is misguided and will explain our rationale for conceiving of IS as different from other outsourcing candidates. Our second issue relates to the future of IS sourcing. We think the future will involve a move away from pure outsourcing and insourcing strategies, focussing instead on new creative relationships. These will be performance-based arrangements involving the sharing of risks and rewards.

INFORMATION SYSTEMS *IS* DIFFERENT

Senior executives often argue that the outsourcing of IS is no different from the outsourcing of other non-core business functions, such as legal, administrative, and custodial services. This appears to be the direct result of companies abandoning diversification strategies to focus on whatever it is they believe to be their core competencies. Senior executives now presume that the most important sustainable competitive advantage is strategic focus by concentrating on what an organization does better than all others. Everything else should be outsourced. Since most senior executives appear to view the entire IS function as a non-core activity, and concomitantly, that third party vendors possess economies of scale and technical expertise to provide IS services more efficiently than internal IS departments (since for these vendors IS *is* their core competency), it makes sense to outsource it.

Based on our research, however, we conclude that IS is not like other organizational resources which have been successfully outsourced in the past. In particular, there are six characteristics associated with IS which make it different from other outsourcing candidates. These distinctive features, which were developed in Lacity, Willcocks, and Feeny (1994) and Lacity and Willcocks (1994) are:

1 Information technology evolves rapidly.
2 The underlying economics of information technology (IT) changes rapidly.
3 The penetration of IS to all business functions is ubiquitous.
4 The switching costs to alternative ITs and IS suppliers is high.
5 Customers' inexperience with IS outsourcing.
6 IS management practices rather than economies of scale lead to economic efficiency.

Information Technology Evolves Rapidly

Because IT evolves so rapidly, predicting beyond a three-year horizon is highly speculative at best. Hence, IS outsourcing decisions—particularly decisions which may result in long-term contracts—are always accompanied by a high degree of uncertainty. Although participants initially perceived that outsourcing vendors would reduce the uncertainty associated with rapid IT evolution, many discovered that outsourcing actually locks them into older technologies; it can act as an inhibitor to the adoption of new technology. Indeed, it is precisely because of the dizzying pace of IT change that outsourcing contracts typically only make unspecific or vague reference to future technologies.

Participants from a number of the companies involved in our studies considered outsourcing with the expressed intention of having access to new vendor technologies. Senior managers, in particular, found keeping up with the rapid evolution of IT an overwhelming task. They reasoned that by outsourcing IS, the vendors would help them keep abreast of new IT advancements. In reality, participants found that vendors are motivated to maintain the same level of technology rather than implement advancements. For example, FIRM7 signed a 10-year outsourcing contract in 1988. At that time, the majority of their systems were running on mainframe technology. With the advent of client/

server technology, FIRM7 participants wanted to migrate to the smaller platform but found their outsourcing contract erected significant obstacles. In the end, business unit leaders used discretionary funds to adopt client/server technologies while still paying on the 10-year contract for the increasingly obsolescent mainframe.

Other companies experienced the same fate as FIRM7. The manager of data processing from FIRM12 complains that his vendor was motivated to simply run the technology "into the ground":

> "I think you find with outsourcing that any innovation in technology comes from your own people. Requirements from users on your staff. But basically the [outsourcing vendor] just cranks it. And so we were operating old software. Some of it was written in the 1960s. All batch."

The purchasing manager from FIRM11 argues that access to new technologies can be very costly:

> "None of it is cheap. I guess there is a perception that once you have an outsourcer hooked in that you have a conduit to all this expertise, but you pay."

Because of the uncertainty associated with rapid IT evolution, participants felt (in hindsight) that contracts over three years in duration lock customers into older technologies, and should typically be avoided.

The Underlying Economics of IT Changes Rapidly

Although price/performance improvements occur in every industry, there can be few industries where the underlying economics shift as fast as they do in IS. A mainframe MIP that cost $1 million in 1965 costs less than $30 000 today. Today's computing resources will cost 20–30% less next year (Benjamin and Blunt, 1992). The rapid change in the underlying economics causes extreme uncertainty and thus makes it difficult for decision makers to evaluate costs of outsourcing bids. While a 10% discount on IS for the next 10 years may be appealing to a senior executive today, by next year he may be paying the vendor above market prices for computer resources. Fundamentally, the problem appears to be that there is no simple basis for gauging the economics of IS activity.

The Penetration of IS to all Business Functions is Ubiquitous

Many senior executives we interviewed treated the IS outsourcing decision in much the same way they treated other outsourcing decisions. For example, one senior executive questioned why he should treat outsourcing IS any differently from advertising. The answer is that unlike advertisement—and unlike many other products and services—IS cannot be easily isolated from other organizational functions. IS penetrates every business function in the value chain as well as all support activities (Porter and Millar, 1985).

Fundamentally, IS is not a homogeneous function, but comprises a wide variety of IS applications. Some IS applications uniquely enable business operations and management processes, such as American Airlines' Sabre system which allows travel agents to book directly into American's computerized reservation system. Other IS activities, such as accounting systems, may appear less critical, but closer scrutiny often reveals the value of such systems lies in the cross-functional integration of business processes—in many organizations, IS integrates product design, material purchases, manufacturing processes, sales, and customer service.

The ubiquitous nature of IS penetration makes outsourcing difficult because idiosyncratic knowledge of an organization is required for most IS activities. When participants tried to isolate IS activities for outsourcing, they often discovered that changes to the outsourced function affects other areas of the business. The vendors typically lacked the specialized knowledge to cope with organizational inter- faces outside the boundaries of the IS outsourcing contract. For ex- ample, one company outsourced the development of factory automation. Not long into the contract, participants realized that the new system had profound implications for the existing systems in almost every department in the business. Although the vendor had specialized technical knowledge on factory software, they lacked the specialized business knowledge to cope with interfaces. As a conse- quence, the system took four years to develop instead of two. In an- other case, a US petroleum company outsourced the development of its downstream accounting functions—refining and marketing, only to discover that the system hindered upstream accounting functions in exploration and production.

Even IS activities described by participants as "commodities," such as data center operations, payroll, and PC support, require specific adaptation—and thus specialized knowledge—of a particular organ- ization. For example, participants often used the notion of "com- modity" when they referred to their data centers. In actuality, data centers are hardly homogeneous. Different companies use different hardware configurations, operating software, software utilities, facil- ities for cooling/lighting and fire prevention, levels of software auto- mation, disaster recovery strategies, and provide different service levels. Specialized knowledge of a given organization's production schedule is also a critical skill—knowing what users run what systems at what times with what particular problems can make the difference between a successful and unsuccessful data center.

The Switching Costs to Alternative ITs and IS Suppliers is High

For the economic benefits of market forces to be accrued, ample competition is necessary in order to dissuade vendor opportunism. In the area of IS, high switching costs make the circumstances of a small number of suppliers the norm rather than the exception. Once participants sign with an outsourcing vendor, the threat of opportunism is extremely likely because the switching costs to another vendor or to an in-house IS function are extremely expensive. As the CFO from FIRM10 notes:

> "Once you sign with a vendor, you have no options other than onerous contract terms, so when you get into a situation it's a lose/lose for both parties. What are you going to do? Sue them? Fire them? Stop buying services? There is nobody else, in a short period of time, who you can buy services from."

Although some participants terminated relationships with outsourcing vendors, this was done at great expense. For example, participants from FIRMs12 and 13 paid a stiff penalty to terminate the contract early. They made investments in hardware and software, built new data centers, and hired a new IS staff. These extreme cases demonstrate that IS outsourcing almost always involves only a small number of suppliers.

Customers' Inexperience with IS Outsourcing

Participants were at a significant disadvantage when negotiating contracts with outsourcing vendors. While vendors sign large contracts relatively often, participants typically had no experience with negotiating large IS outsourcing contracts, even though they may have had significant experience with outsourcing other functions. Because of the customers' inexperience with outsourcing there is a likelihood that the vendor will take advantage of their ignorance. Due to information asymmetry, the vendors were able to negotiate deals which strongly favored their position. Several examples illustrate this point. Participants from FIRM7 did not question the vendor's "change of character clause." This clause stipulates that any changes in functionality are subject to excess fees. When FIRM7 changed from one word processing package to another, the vendor charged them a stiff excess fee, referring to the change of character clause. At FIRM6, the vendor had a clause that stated that FIRM6 would pay any fees associated with transferring software licensing agreements. Participants were more than shocked when their major software provider charged them $500 000 to transfer their software licenses to the outsourcing vendor.

IS Management Practices rather than Economies of Scale Lead to Economic Efficiency

Based on the experience of our participants, economic efficiency has more to do with IS practices than inherent economies of scale. Although there are indeed economies of scale in some aspects of IS, they occur at a size achievable by many medium-sized and most large-sized companies. For example, small development teams are markedly more productive and successful than larger ones. In the area of data center operations, economies of scale are achieved at the 150–200 MIPs level. Because many companies operate IS functions large enough to achieve economies of scale, vendor outsourcing bids reflect more on management practices than inherent economies of scale. For example, vendors may cut costs through chargeback mechanisms which motivate business users to manage demand, by consolidating data centers from multiple sites to one site, empower employees to reduce supervision costs, automating data center operations, archiving of inactive data, or by standardizing hardware and software platforms. Of course, IS managers can duplicate these cost reduction tactics if empowered by senior executives to overcome user resistance. For example, IS costs at FIRM15 were high because users refused to let IS managers consolidate their data centers. Once senior management threatened users by inviting outsourcing bids, users acquiesed and agreed to let IS consolidate rather than have a vendor do it for them. IS costs subsequently dropped by 54%.

In sum, it is our belief that because IS is distinctive, senior management must treat IS sourcing decisions differently, from say mailrooms or legal departments.

THE FUTURE OF IS SOURCING

After completing two comprehensive studies on both outsourcing and insourcing, we try to assess the likely future of economically efficient and politically feasible sourcing decisions. In general, we conclude that total outsourcing or total insourcing are generally poor sourcing strategies. Instead, selective sourcing enables companies to exploit the inherent cost efficiencies of both internal IS departments and external vendors. Several trends in the outsourcing market will facilitate selective sourcing. We summarize each of these observations below.

Total outsourcing is a poor IS strategy for most companies because it fails to capitalize on the inherent cost advantages of internal IS departments. In general, large IS departments possess the economies of scale to achieve cost efficiency; outsourcing this only transfers the potential savings to a vendor. This observation is particularly relevant in the area of data center operations. In the area of applications development, business expertise is the critical skill required to deliver value to the firm. By outsourcing all development, companies rightfully exploit a vendor's technical expertise, but lose their inherent advantage on defining business requirements to exploit new technologies. In the area of applications support, business expertise of the particular idiosyncratic exceptions required to support even "commodity" applications may be more efficiently delivered with the in-house function.

Total outsourcing is also a poor strategy because companies get locked into a certain vendor. It is very difficult to find alternative sourcing options in the short run if the outsourcing arrangement fails. Companies that have terminated total outsourcing arrangements incurred an incredible expense to rebuild data centers and restaff internal IS departments. Even if total outsourcing relationships work well for the first couple of years, changes in technology, such as the move from mainframes to LANs, can generate significant excess fees. Most participants felt that long-term contracts restrict their ability to exploit new technologies because the contract centers on delivering the same services and technologies defined in the baseline year. Moreover, it restricts a company's flexibility to move quickly to exploit a new business opportunity.

Total insourcing is a poor strategy for most companies because it fails to capitalize on a vendors' inherent cost advantages and creates a political environment of complacency. In general, outsourcing vendors possess an inherent cost advantage on providing technical expertise. By pursuing a policy of total insourcing, companies may incur greater expense on developing new technologies that are more effectively acquired through the market.

Total insourcing is also a poor strategy because it creates a political climate which promotes complacency. Like any monopoly situation, lack of competition is not conducive to responsive changes in consumer demand. When senior management demands that IS cut costs, users can often stonewall cost cutting measures. Through the threat of competition with an outsourcing vendor, internal IS departments are empowered to implement tactics which enable them to compete with vendor bids.

Selective sourcing, which capitalizes on the inherent advantage of both internal IS departments' and external vendors' inherent cost advantages, is recommended. When selecting among sourcing alternatives for given IS strategies, companies should determine the major cost drivers of that function to determine the inherent advantage of insourcing or out- sourcing. Oftentimes, a combination of both outsourcing and insour- cing will allow companies to exploit the inherent advantages of both. Consider the following examples.

For many companies, the two major cost drivers for new systems development are business and technical expertise. To exploit the inher- ent advantages of the internal IS department, business requirements can be determined in-house. To exploit the inherent advantages of vendors, perhaps coding and conversion can be outsourced to a vendor. Rather than totally insource or totally outsource applications development, companies can efficiently access both sets of skills through selective sourcing. This is what is being done today in a num- ber of companies who use offshore "software factories" for program- ming and maintenance.

In the area of applications support, two major cost drivers for most companies are again business and technical expertise. Business exper- tise is needed to understand exceptions, quirks in the accounting cycle, requirements for business enhancements, etc. Technical expertise is needed to fix errors, improve performance, and upgrade technology. Again a selective sourcing strategy may be preferred. However, an- other major cost consideration may be opportunity costs. If in-house analysts and programmers focus their efforts on maintenance of legacy systems, they cannot be used for the development of new applications on new platforms. Thus, general rules for insourcing or outsourcing cannot simply be determined. Rather, companies must assess the cost drivers for their particular IS environment.

Several Trends in the Outsourcing Market will Facilitate Selective Sourcing in the Future

According to Millar (1994), there are a number of changes in market trends that are fueling the growth of interest in outsourcing which will have important consequences for the likely growth of selective sourc- ing. First, he notes that business benefit and value rather than cost containment are driving outsourcing. This is a change from the pre-1990s rationale for outsourcing which focussed almost exclusively on cost issues. Second, outsourcing has become widely accepted as a viable business arrangement, not simply for IS and not simply for large companies but for virtually any function, at any sized organization. It is also a worldwide trend. Third, the market has seen a dramatic growth in the number of third party providers offering services in a variety of areas. Competition has become intense and will become even more so, leading to shrinking vendor margins. Making profits in the IS outsourcing market has necessitated new and creative arrangements. The future of IS outsourcing will thus require innovative, customized relationships involving the joint sharing of risks and rewards. Future arrangements will likely be performance-based, where the client's payment to the vendor is based on the vendor's actual delivery of the benefits articulated in the contract.

In general we agree with Millar, but see three dominant trends in the outsourcing market: (1) an increased number of vendors and vendor offerings, (2) shorter contracts, and (3) tighter contracts. These trends are in response to more intelligent customers who demand more equity in their outsourcing relationships. But like Millar, we believe there is no doubt that the future will see the dramatic growth of arrangements which force vendor and client to share risks and rewards (although the development of such balanced deals will continue to be thorny).

Growing Number of Vendor Options Facilitate Selective Sourcing

At the time of the original case studies in 1991, a few large outsourcing vendors dominated the market. With a small number of available vendors, the transaction costs associated with outsourcing were considerable. The increase in the number of outsourcing vendors decreases the transaction costs associated with outsourcing because the threat of vendor opportunism decreases when the customers have sourcing alternatives.

Recently, vendors find that they can no longer require customers to include all their IS functions in negotiations before they are willing to bid. In the past, for example, an outsourcing vendor may have refused to submit a bid to operate data centers unless applications development and support were included. In recent times, other vendors anxious to secure a niche are willing to submit bids to meet customer requirements without insisting that the entire IS department be placed on the auction block.

As a result of the increased competition, established vendors and new entrants are offering more market-focussed products and services that facilitate selective sourcing. For example, many vendors now serve as brokers to the Asian programming market. Many customers are discovering that once business requirements are determined in-house, they can efficiently and effectively outsource the coding and testing phases to these brokers. Companies can thus exploit the inherent cost advantages of using foreign programmers without sacrificing their cost advantage derived from business expertise.

Shorter Contracts to Promote Flexibility

Due to the increased competition, vendors no longer have the muscle to insist on 10-year contracts. As a result, we are seeing companies sign shorter-term contracts of 2–5 years in duration. This allows a company to sign contracts while their service requirements are relatively stable. For example, several companies have outsourced mainframes for their expected remaining life of 3–5 years. During the contract period, the internal staff is migrating to smaller platforms. By the time the outsourcing contract expires, companies will be in a position to replace their legacy systems.

Tighter Contracts Ensure Successful Outsourcing Relationships

Due to more accumulated experience with outsourcing, companies are also signing tighter contracts. Until recently, many companies naively signed loose contracts believing that vendors were strategic partners. As evidenced by a growing number of examples, a tight contract that specifies service levels, definitive measures, penalties for non-performance, and termination clauses is a critical factor to successful outsourcing. Companies now spend more time negotiating contracts and hire specialist lawyers to ensure that their outsourcing expectations are realized.

CONCLUSION

In the 1980s, we propagated the metaphor that IS was a strategic weapon to be secretly harnessed by internal IS departments. Now, in the 1990s, we propagate the metaphor that IS is a utility best provided by an outsourcing vendor. Which metaphor is correct? Neither—the key to rightsourcing is neither total outsourcing nor total insourcing, but rather an intelligent combination of both. With selective insourcing, internal IS departments are empowered to replicate a set of cost reduction strategies usually implemented by outsourcing vendors. With selective outsourcing, only IS activities which pass business, economic, political, resource, and technical validity tests are out-sourced. Moreover, an organization should only consider outsourcing "commodity" services. Even outsourced activities, however, must be properly managed with sound contracts and service level reviews to ensure that outsourcing expectations are realized.

In summary, the two research projects on outsourcing and insourc-ing have led to the overall conclusion that selective sourcing is indeed the key to "rightsizing." This is consistent with the finding of Willcocks and Fitzgerald (1994b). Although easily stated, selective sourcing adds another burden on IS managers. Rather than merely juggling senior management's and users' demands for IS, IS managers will need to coordinate the IS supply side which will likely encompass multiple vendors.

References

Ambrosio, J., "Outsourcing at Southland: Best of Times, Worst of Times," *Computerworld*, Vol. 25, No. 12, March 25, 1991.

Anthes, G., "Perot wins 10-year Outsourcing Deal," *Computerworld*, Vol. 25, No. 14, April 8, 1991, p. 96.

Applegate, L., "Eastman Kodak Co: Managing Information Systems through Strategic Alliances," Harvard Business School Case 9–192-030, 1992.

Applegate, L. and Elam, J., "New Information Systems Leaders: A Changing Role in a Changing World," *MIS Quarterly*, Vol. 16, No. 4, December 1992, pp. 469–489.

Benjamin, R. and Blunt, J., "Critical IT Issues: The Next Ten Years", *Sloan Management Review*, Summer 1992, pp. 7–19.

Betts, M., "Benchmarking helps IS Improve Competitiveness," *Computerworld*, Vol. 26, No. 48, November 30, 1992, pp. 1, 20.

Feeny, D., Edwards, B., and Simpson, K., "Understanding the CEO/CIO Relationship," *MIS Quarterly*, Vol. 16, No. 4, December 1992, pp. 435–447.

Fitzgerald, G. and Willcocks, L., *Information Technology Outsourcing Practice: A U.K. Survey*, Business Intelligence, London, 1993.

Gardner, E., "Going On-line with Outsiders," *Modern Healthcare*, July 15, 1991, pp. 35–47.

Gillin, P., "EDS Rides Outsourcing to Riches," *Computerworld*, Vol. 24, No. 42, October 15, 1990, pp. 113, 117.

Hamilton, R., "Kendall Outsources IS Chief," *Computerworld*, Vol. 23, No. 46, November 13, 1989, pp. 1, 4.

Hovey, V., Presentation to the University of Houston's Information Systems Research Center, January 22, 1991.

Huber, R., "How Continental Bank Outsourced its 'Crown Jewels,'" *Harvard Business Review*, January–February 1993, pp. 121–129.

Huff, S., "Outsourcing of Information Services," *Business Quarterly*, Vol. 55, No. 4, Spring, 1991, pp. 62–65.

I/S Analzyer, "New Wrinkles in Outsourcing," Vol. 31, No. 9, 1993, pp. 1–18.

Kass, E. and Caldwell, B., "Outsource Ins, Outs," *Information Week*, Issue 260, March 5, 1990, p. 14.

Kass, P., "The Dollars and Sense of Outsourcing," *Information Week*, Issue 259, February 26, 1990, pp. 26–31.

Lacity, M. and Hirschheim, R., *Information Systems Outsourcing: Myths, Metaphors and Realities*, John Wiley, Chichester, 1993.

Lacity, M., Hirschheim, R. and Willcocks, L., "Realizing Outsourcing Expectations: From Incredibile Expectations to Credible Outcomes," *Journal of Information Systems Management*, Fall 1994, pp. 7–18.

Lacity, M. and Willcocks, L., "Information Systems Outsourcing: A Transaction Cost Interpretation of Empirical Evidence," OXIIM working paper, Templeton College, Oxford University, Oxford, 1994.

Lacity, M., Willcocks, L., and Feeny, D., "Information Systems Outsourcing: A Decision-making Framework," OXIIM working paper, Templeton College, Oxford University, Oxford, 1994.

Linsenmeyer, A., "Fad or Fundamental: A Chat with Bob Camp of Xerox, the Man who Wrote the Book on Benchmarking," *FW*, Vol. 160, No. 19, September 17, 1991, pp. 34–35.

Loh, L. and Venkatraman, N., "Determinants of Information Technology Outsourcing: A Cross-Sectional Analysis," *Journal of Management Information Systems*, Summer, 1992a, Vol. 9, No. 1, pp. 7–24.

Loh, L. and Venkatraman, N., "Diffusion of Information Technology Outsourcing: Influence Sources and the Kodak Effect," *Information Systems Research*, Vol. 3, No. 4, December 1992b, pp. 334–358.

Loh, L. and Venkatraman, N., *Stock Market Reaction to Information Technology Outsourcing: An Event Study*, Cambridge, Massachusetts: MIT Sloan School of Management, Working Paper No. 3499–92BPS, November 1992c.

McManus, J. (ed.), "Fortune 500: Largest U.S. Manufacturing Companies," *Fortune*, Vol. 123, No. 8, April 22, 1991a, pp. 279–336.

McManus, J. (ed.), "Fortune 500: Largest U.S. Service Companies," *Fortune*, Vol. 123, No. 11, June 3, 1991b, pp. 254–286.

McMullen, J., "New Allies: IS and Service Suppliers," *Datamation*, Vol. 36, No. 5, March 1, 1990, pp. 42–51.

Mason, T., *Perot*, Dow Jones-Irwin, Homewood, Illinois, 1990.

Millar, V., "Outsourcing Trends," paper presented at the *Outsourcing, Cosourcing and Insourcing Conference*, University of California, Berkeley, November 4, 1994.

Porter, M. and Millar, V., "How Information Gives You Competitive Advantage," *Harvard Business Review*, July–August 1985, pp. 149–160.

Quinn, J., Doorley, T., and Paquette, P., "Technology in Services: Rethinking Strategic Focus," *Sloan Management Review*, Vol. 31, No. 2, Winter 1990, pp. 79–87.

Radding, A., "The Ride is no Bargain if You Can't Steer," *Computerworld*, Vol. 24, No. 2, January 8, 1990, pp. 67, 70–72.

Rochester, J. and Douglas, D. (eds), "Taking an Objective Look at Outsourcing," *I/S Analyzer*, Vol. 28, No. 8, September 1990, pp. 1–16.

Rothfeder, J. and Coy, P., "Outsourcing: More Companies are Letting George Do it," *Business Week*, No. 3181, October 8, 1990, p. 148.

Stephens, C., Ledbetter, W., Mitra, A., and Ford, F. Nelson, "Executive or Functional Manager? The Nature of the CIO's Job," *MIS Quarterly*, Vol. 16, No. 4, December 1992, pp. 449–467.

Sullivan-Trainor, M., "Study: Users Key to System Development," *Computerworld*, Vol. 27, No. 17, April 26, 1993, p. 72.

Ward, B., "Hiring Out: Outsourcing is the New Buzzword in the Management of Information Systems," *Sky Magazine*, Vol. 20, No. 8, August 1991, pp. 37–45.

Wibbelsman, D. and Maiero, T., "Cosourcing", paper presented at the *Outsourcing, Cosourcing and Insourcing Conference*, University of California, Berkeley, November 4, 1994.

Willcocks, L. and Fitzgerald, G., *A Business Guide to IT Outsourcing*, Business Intelligence, London, 1994(a).

Willcocks, L. and Fitzgerald, G., "IS Outsourcing and the Changing Shape of the Information Systems Function: Recent Research Findings," Research and Discussion Paper RDP94/4, Oxford Institute of Information Management, Templeton College, Oxford University, Oxford, 1994(b).

Index

Index compiled by Michael Heary

Index compiled by Michael Heary